INSURGENT ERA

INSURGENT ERA

New Patterns
of Political, Economic,
and Social Revolution

by   Richard H. Sanger

POTOMAC BOOKS, INC.
PUBLISHERS
WASHINGTON, D. C.

Other books by Richard H. Sanger
The Arabian Peninsula
Where the Jordan Flows

Copyright © 1967
by Richard H. Sanger
Revised Edition, 1970

Cover design and photographic layout
by Julia Cuniberti

All rights in this book are reserved.
No part of the book may be used or reproduced
in any manner whatsoever without written
permission except in the case of brief quotations
embodied in critical articles and reviews. For
further information, address: Potomac Books, Inc.,
Publishers, 1518 K Street, N.W., Washington, D. C. 20005

Printed in the United States of America

Library of Congress Catalogue Card Number 70-136479
ISBN 0-87107-007-3

To my children,
Patience, Dick, and Anne Cary,
who learned about insurgency firsthand.

CONTENTS

INTRODUCTION   1
    Chapter   I: The Life Cycle of a Revolt   9

SOCIETAL REVOLUTIONS   27
    Chapter   II: Russia and China: Different Paths to Communist Victory   29
    Chapter   III: Egypt: The Army Brings Social Change   43
    Chapter   IV: Cuba: A Revolution Betrayed   57

INDEPENDENCE REBELLIONS   75
    Chapter   V: Indochina: The Communists Dominate a Violent Rebellion   77
    Chapter   VI: India: Gandhi's Non-Violent Victory   91

COLD WAR CONFLICTS   105
    Chapter   VII: The Congo: Africa Defeats the Communists   107
    Chapter VIII: The Philippines: How Magsaysay Stopped the Huks   127
    Chapter   IX: Vietnam 1954-1967: The Road to Limited War   141

WHAT LIES AHEAD   171
Appendix   173
    Political Violence 1945-1966   175
    A Word of Thanks and a Partial List of Sources   215
    Glossary   219
Index   223

Maps: China, 32; The Congo, 106; Cuba, 58; Egypt, 44; India, 90; Indochina, 76; The Philippines, 126; Russia, 28; Vietnam, 142. Photographic section follows page 104.

INTRODUCTION

WE are living in the period of greatest political, economic, and social change in the history of mankind. In our generation, thinking people everywhere—in Cuba, the Congo, Egypt, India, Vietnam, the Philippines, China—have discovered change is possible; no man need settle for a dirt floor merely because his father did. People have learned that change can be brought about by an active minority and that the leaders need not be prominent or wealthy.

The realization has also spread that less than a quarter of mankind can bring about basic changes through the ballot. For the rest of the world such goals must be achieved by violence, often aided by friendly or pseudo-friendly supporters from outside the country.

If revolt is based on widespread grievance, the revolutionary party is well organized, and the uprising properly carried out, statistics indicate that there is better than an even chance of its success.

It is not surprising, therefore, that since World War II there has been a revolution, rebellion, insurrection, coup, or uprising somewhere in the world approximately every month. Leaving aside about a dozen military operations such as the Korean War, military intervention in the Suez, the Indo-Pakistani clashes, and the battles in Vietnam, there have been at least 300 insurgencies of one sort or another during the past 258 months.

We Americans have become so complacent about news of violence in distant places that we fail to see the uprisings in their true perspective. Today's revolutions do not begin with a formal declaration of war in the traditional pattern. But thousands of people have been killed in them, tens of thousands have been wounded, property damage runs into millions of dollars and overall loss in productivity into the hundreds of millions. This may not be war in the accepted sense of the word, but it is certainly not peace. Rather it is a worldwide assault in depth on the historical institutions of society, an assault which in most cases assumes a violent form. We are in the midst of an unprecedented readjustment of man's relations with man and for the control and distribution of the goods and services which are being produced. It is a period which future historians may well call the "Insurgent Era".

* * * * * * * * * * * *

What we are seeing is a new aspect of an old phenomenon. The old phenomenon is the fact that of every one thousand persons there have always been one or two willing to risk imprisonment, exile, or death to bring about political change. Almost without exception their goal was not to alter the pattern of a state, but rather to take it over. Julius Caesar did not want basically to change Roman society; he merely wanted to run Rome—no doubt because he thought he could do it better than most. True, these revolts sometimes involved gaining independence from a central government, but this as a rule was a by-product; the real purpose was personal power for the new leader. Latin American revolts are frequently of this nature.

In recent times, however, we are seeing more and more of a new phenomenon: uprisings to bring about basic social change.

Leaders may seek to shift the base of power from a landed aristocracy to a new middle class in the cities. They may wish to strengthen the role of labor and the farmer. They may plan to shift the means of production from private to public ownership. They may want to realign the foreign relations of their nation, possibly within the context of the Cold War. Or they may be outright Communists. The important aspect is that in so many cases the goal is not primarily personal power but political, economic, or social change. That this should be happening almost every month and on a worldwide basis is unique in history and is perhaps the most important single aspect of the current international scene.

* * * * * * * * * * *

It may be said that there have been seven waves of revolts in the past three hundred years.

1. The first and perhaps the most fundamental had four parts: a) The British Revolution of 1648-88, which to a considerable extent put an end to the concept of the divine right of kings and produced the first modern constitution and a bill of rights. b) Peter the Great's "westernization" of Russia after 1698. c) The American Revolution of 1776-83, technically a rebellion for independence and not a revolution, which is still the classic anti-colonial revolt. d) The French Revolution of 1789-99, the prototype of an anti-royalist, anti-aristocratic insurgency. Although many of its original ideas were soon rejected in France, it went a long way towards ending the idea that power and promotion must come from birth alone.

The 19th century saw three more waves of social readjustment:

2. One of these was a series of economic-social revolts, in a way the growing pains of early capitalism, which occurred in various parts of Europe in 1825, 1830, 1848 and 1871. They were largely unsuccessful, but they showed that the steam of unrest was building up under the otherwise placid surface of 19th century Europe.

Actually they were part of a sweeping transformation which included greatly increased industrialization at home and the acquisition by a small number of European states of vast colonial empires overseas. These colonies produced raw materials; new industries, largely in Europe, processed them; increased trade distributed the products; and new patterns of society evolved. They were patterns which in general strengthened the new middle class and for a long time kept the workers at a low standard of living.

The colonies became "economic necessities", and the colonial powers in most cases became determined to hold them at all costs. This in turn led to bitterness from those in the colonies who saw that their wealth and labor were being used in large part for the economic and political benefit of people in the metropole. The fact that vast numbers of people in the colonies were also benefiting from this arrangement was usually lost from sight under the stress of local emotions.

3. During the 19th century a wave of independence rebellions occurred in Central and South America in which many of the colonies broke loose from European control. The newly-created independent states were run by dictators or by aristocratic, land-owning elites of European origin and often of European education. The lot of the peasants—most of whom were Indians or Negroes—was unaffected. But the process of change had at least begun.

4. In the 19th century there also occurred in the Middle East and in Asia a series of basic, and sometimes violent, societal changes or attempts at change stimulated by contact with westerners and the "new thoughts" growing out of the Industrial Revolution and the "Democratic" Revolutions in France and America. Such upheavals tended to be either "change from above", as occurred in Egypt under Mohammed Ali or in Japan after the visit of Commodore Perry, or they were efforts to correct grievances and social maladjustments such as the Indian mutiny or the Chinese Taiping Rebellion.

5. Then came a fifth wave of revolutions largely European and in general tied to events connected with World War I. These included two German revolutions, an Austro-Hungarian revolution, an Italian Revolution, a Turkish Revolution, and the momentous two-stage Russian Revolution.

6. The years between the two World Wars saw a series of Fascist revolts which were partly an effort to check the strength of Communism and partly a desire to deal with the problems of the Industrial Revolution, but which foundered on economic misconceptions and racist dogmas. During that period also occurred the Spanish Civil War, with its terror, guerrillas and outside intervention—a preview of many revolts to come.

7. In the past twenty years we have been living in the seventh wave of unrest, the most widespread and prolonged which the world has ever known.

In addition to furthering a handful of anti-communist rebellions in eastern Europe, the forces of change have burst the banks of the western world and are sweeping over the underdeveloped areas and the former colonial areas, most of which lie in the southern part of the globe. Many of the same factors, including travel, broader education, widespread communication, and the introduction of new inventions, which affected the European-American world so deeply in the preceding centuries, are now at work in these distant parts of the world.

Since World War I, but largely since World War II, the elites in the developing lands have realized what the leaders of the European nations had previously discovered: that all men are equal. They have come to understand that modernization is possible no matter how secure the traditional pattern may seem. They have seen that such change can be brought about by small groups in a population, sometimes five percent or less. Since Lenin took all of Russia with less than 150,000 real supporters, the Communists have been its great exponents. Mao's success in China gave the concept further proof.

It is also clear that the average man in a society can be a powerful factor. Obscure lawyers, middle-level officers, student and labor leaders are those who are making most of today's revolutions. And an examination of insurgencies since World War II (*see Appendix*) indicates that revolution is a good gamble, for more than half of them have been successful.

The concept that a few men can remake the pattern of society was heady wine in Philadelphia in 1776 or in Paris in 1789. Its appeal today is overwhelming in the underdeveloped nations of the world where more than half the people are impoverished, badly-educated and sometimes governed by people of different races, religions, and civilizations from their own. For the first time in history man everywhere has discovered that this need no longer be his situation. He has come to realize that if he organizes properly and acts boldly he can not only change his rulers but even the organization of the society in which he lives, his position in that society, and his share of the wealth which it produces.

* * * * * * * * * * * *

We should indeed be thankful to the founding fathers for the way they organized our government. Those who lived through 1931 and 1932 will never forget the terrible conditions prevailing in this country. Some 13 million unemployed, many of them hardworking college or high school graduates, walked the streets trying to sell apples. Half the factories were shut and most of the rest were working short hours. Farm land was selling for a few dollars an acre, yet everywhere there was an overabundance of food and goods which the unemployed could not buy. At the top of the economic pyramid a small percent of the population was still receiving a disproportionately large share of the national income, often in the form of unearned income. It was a revolutionary situation, and in most parts of the world it would have produced a bloody upheaval. Instead we had an orderly national election. But peaceful revolutions are a political luxury few men today can enjoy.

The breakup of European colonialism since World War II has been a factor for instability. Hundreds of millions of people who for generations have been governed by Europeans now find themselves in a position to govern themselves. In only a few colonies, such as India, was the groundwork for successful self-government well laid. There are many persons in the interior of the Congo whose grandfathers had never seen a wheel, let alone a ballot box. In a nation with a population of some 15 million, fewer than two dozen Congolese had received a college education at the time of independence.

Still another reason why so many of today's political movements end in violence is the fact that change in itself is deeply upsetting. Some twenty years ago many people believed that modernization produced both progress and stability. It followed then that all such countries needed were good ports, a road or railroad to the interior, some schools and hospitals, and simple industries like textile mills and bicycle plants. We now know that modernization created new wealth, but that almost without exception the wealth went to the people who were already the richest or most powerful elements in the country.

Meanwhile, it was usually the middle class elements who absorbed new ideas at home or through travel and study abroad. When they returned they found the gap between the haves and the have-nots had widened, while their own chances for advancement were small. In country after country the result has been revolution.

It is a fact that the thinking behind most of these revolts came from the western-oriented idea of the rights of men that produced the British, French, and American revolutions. Indeed, our own Declaration of Independence is a revolutionary document whose very possession can lead to arrest in many nations of the world today.

The newly-educated but economically-thwarted middle class leaders of so many new countries in most cases look to the West for ideas about progress but frequently end up turning to Russia or China for the tactics of action. These discontented elites find that we favor change and constructive progress, but it is progress brought about by peaceful and democratic means. This is a splendid pattern to advocate and to hold as a goal. But if the mechanism for bringing it about does not exist within a country, rising leaders are quite likely to turn impatiently to other and more violent ways of obtaining their ends. The Communists are making the most of this dilemma.

A statement of Soviet Chairman Nikita Khrushchev was published in Moscow on January 6, 1961:

> Now a word about national liberation wars. Can such wars occur in the future? They can. . . Can conditions be created in which people will lose their patience and rise in arms? They can. What is the attitude of the Marxists toward such uprisings? A most positive one. . . The Communists fully support such just wars and march in the front rank with the peoples waging liberation struggles.

In concentrating on internal political violence such as "wars of national liberation", rather than on atomic wars, Khrushchev showed himself a skillful analyst of world politics. He chose to ride the tide of history and to fight with familiar weapons which were tailor-made for his needs and which, almost without exception, his enemies in the west did not possess. These are the local communist parties.

Sovereign states do not like interference in their internal political affairs, and throughout history the quickest way for an ambassador to be declared *persona non grata* is to be found meddling in the politics of the state to which he is accredited, particularly if that meddling involves opposition to the government in power. The communist parties, however, or the front organizations under whose banners they so often masquerade, have several personalities. On the surface they appear to be organizations of local and patriotic citizens. Usually their philosophy, finances, and direction come from Moscow, Peking, or Havana. This means that the Communists can have their cake and eat it, too. They can interfere as much or as little as they wish in the internal affairs of other nations along lines most advantageous to world communism. At the same time the leaders of world communism can piously protest that they are not involved.

The United States government has been aware that the Communists were turning more toward revolution rather than open warfare since the subversions following World War II. But it was not until the winter of 1961 that the full significance of this new communist tactic was appreciated in Washington. After his meeting with Khrushchev, in June of that year, President Kennedy made these sobering remarks:

> I went to Vienna to meet the leader of the Soviet Union. For two days we met in sober, intensive conversation. . . [We talked of many things] but most of all he predicted the triumph of communism in the new and less developed countries. He was certain that the tide was moving his way, that the revolution of rising people would eventually be a communist revolution, and that the so-called wars of liberation supported by the Kremlin would replace the old methods of direct aggression and invasion.

In the 1940's and early 50's, the great danger was from communist armies marching across free borders, which we saw in Korea . . . . now we face a new and different threat. We no longer have a nuclear monopoly. Their missiles, they believe, will hold off our missiles, and their troops can match our troops should we intervene in the so-called wars of liberation. Thus, the local conflicts they support can turn in their favor through guerrillas, or insurgents, or subversion. . . .

It is clear that the struggle in this area of the new and poorer nations will be a continuing crisis of this decade.

This, then, is the heart of the problem. Throughout the developing lands people want change and they want it quickly. When their leaders turn to the west we encourage progressive moves through "peaceful democratic processes", which means through the ballot. If this succeeds, all is well. If it does not, the thwarted leadership of a local party may well carry out "a war of national liberation" or a "people's revolt".

We cannot stop the worldwide processes of political, economic, and social change, and we would not wish to do so if we could. But unless we can guide them into peaceful and democratic channels, and prevent their capture by the Communists, Khrushchev's prediction regarding the developing areas may well come true.

CHAPTER I

THE LIFE CYCLE OF A REVOLT

IN the recent wave of *societal revolutions, independence rebellions,* and *cold war conflicts* we find a considerable degree of uniformity in the steps through which they are apt to pass. To be sure, all such steps do not occur in all uprisings, and their timing, duration, and order may vary considerably. But there is a enough similarity, particularly in the cold war conflicts, to justify reviewing the probable life cycle of a typical revolt.

Almost without exception a revolt starts with a grievance. The grievance may have been in existence for years and "old hands" may tend to dismiss it as unimportant. It is not unimportant if it is coupled with a gap in communication between the persons running the state and the discontented elements. Such a gap may exist between the capital city and the people of the countryside, between management and labor, between the power elite and the students, or between elements of different races. The gap is particularly dangerous if it exists between the rulers of the state and middle elements in the armed forces.

Such a gap is most likely to cause trouble if the country in question does not hold elections or if such elections as it does hold are known to be fraudulent. This means that there is no political safety valve, no mechanism for a peaceful solution of the grievance.

The Leader

Into this situation, which may have lasted for years without a serious explosion, there comes at last a popular leader. He may be rich or poor; he may be young or old; he may be moved by a sense of justice and lofty ideals. He may be out for personal gain; he may be a tool of a foreign power; or he may be an open or disguised communist. Undoubtedly he will be dynamic, ambitious, and a persuasive orator. In the list of revolutionary leaders from Hitler through Castro to Lumumba and Sukarno, almost every one has had great charismatic quality. Gandhi was not an orator but nevertheless could communicate ideas and emotions with great effectiveness.

If one has to pick a candidate for leadership early in a revolt, the best bet is to choose a soldier turned politician. The list of such men is long and includes among others Nasser, Ayub, Batista, Kassim, Ataturk, and Peron. All these leaders concluded that change was needed in their countries, that it could not be accomplished through the ballot, and that since they controlled some or all of the military power it was up to them to use it.

The next best bet is a politician turned soldier. These include such leaders as Castro, Holden Roberto, and Mao Tse-tung, who, after failing to bring about reform through political means, became guerrilla leaders.

If a revolution is to succeed, in addition to the overall leader there must be other types of persons assisting the movement:

1. Politicians whose following gives strength to that of the leader.
2. Fund-raisers or financiers who provide the movement with needed cash.
3. Able political organizers. Hitler could spellbind but he could not organize, and he had to rely on others to build his political machine. Lumumba could spellbind but he had no really effective professional organizers with him. His party disintegrated at his death and became a factor responsible for part of the troubles in the Congo ever since.
4. Idea men—the Thomas Jefferson, the Thomas Paine, the Trotsky, the Che Guevara. These are the thinkers who take the local grievance, put it into a national or world context, and make it a cause for which men will die. Few top leaders have this ability, but without it a revolution is unlikely to have widespread appeal.

The Popular Cause

The movement becomes important when, through the clear thinking of the idea men, the grievance or discontent crystalizes into a popular cause. The list of such causes is long and varied, but again leaving out personal revolts they fall into five main categories:

1. *Nationalism, anti-colonialism, and the desire for independence.* Essentially these revolts are patterned on the American Revolution (rebellion) and have been frequent during the twenty years since the end of World War II—the period of voluntary or forceful breakup of the great European empires. Gandhi's Indian movement introduced a new technique for independence rebellions.

2. *Political injustice,* tyranny, corruption, inefficiency, and the breakdown of law and order. Nasser's Egyptian revolution grew from several of these factors.

3. *Economic maladjustment.* In recent times more and more people have refused to tolerate traditional differences between rich and poor, unfair land distribution, unfair taxation, large scale unemployment, and runaway in-

flation. They become particularly intolerable when the elite benefits openly and shows little interest in improving the lot of the masses. Another factor which aggravates these grievances is foreign ownership of large parts of the country's wealth, to the obvious detriment of the local inhabitants.

4. *Military imbalance*, although most likely to produce army or personal revolt, may in some cases contribute to societal, independence, or cold war conflicts. This is likely to be the case if the younger and better trained military officers feel they are being held down by older, stupid, or reactionary politicians and generals, who have the interest of neither the army nor the country at heart. The revolution staged by the Egyptian army in 1952 was in part an example of such an uprising. As a rough rule of thumb, in an undeveloped country, a revolt led by generals will be conservative, supporting the *status quo*. Majors and lieutenant colonels in revolt tend to be progressive, acting for the new middle class. And a sergeant's and corporal's revolt may well be extremist or communist, with someone other than the sergeant doing the thinking.

5. *The stresses of modernization.* Discontent in this field may spring from the too rapid breakdown of traditional society, either feudal or tribal; too rapid movement into the cities, producing unemployment and insecurity in contrast to stable and protected conditions in the villages. A population explosion due to low death rate coupled with a high birth rate, and limited literacy for large groups of the population, often gives a rising tide of expectations which cannot be met. The classic example of a tribe which cracked under the stresses of modernization is the Kikuyu of Kenya who developed the evil Mau Mau as a primitive solution. Even if political upheaval does not go to this extreme, a feeling may develop that things should be much better. The idea spreads that the people running the state are not fit to do so, and if they cannot be put out through the ballot it must be done by violence.

Indices of Revolt

The masses are slow to anger. They can be kept quiet for months with words, and for years by "crumbs of progress". However, if they begin to feel that their grievances are just, and that nothing is being done to correct them, they will eventually take the law into their own hands.

There are several indices of coming revolt. One of the easiest to spot is a change in attitude among the aristocrats or chiefs, landed gentry, leaders of business and finance, much of the clergy, and the senior military and government officials. These people normally run a country. The student of revolutions should watch for evidence of a weakening in their will to govern, a change sometimes referred to as "the disintegration of the elite". These symptoms have been noted before nearly every important revolution including the French, the

Russian, and the Algerian. As such persons lose faith in the way their associates are running the country they become critical of its top leaders. Some will resign from government posts, others will ask for reassignment, while still others go into retirement or take long trips abroad. A few will actually side with the insurgents.

The careful observer should also watch for signs of growing bitterness, impatience, and opposition among the intellectuals, professional people, and the leaders of labor, farmers, and students. Normally they stay close to "the Establishment" and are merely interested in limited reforms and democratic change.

However, before every important revolution there have been signs of "the desertion of the intellectuals". This means that they have given up hope that the "power elite" can meet the problems with which it is faced. The intellectuals are apt to talk much more freely than the government leaders and to show their disillusionment and anger more readily. Some will fall back on escapism, but many are ready to join the party of revolt. This occurred in Russia, in Egypt, and in Cuba, to cite but three examples. If there is evidence that both the power elite and the intellectuals are losing faith in a regime, there is good reason to expect a political upheaval of some sort.

There are other indices of trouble.

Is the country prone to revolt? Revolution is habit forming, and if a country has been the scene of several recent revolts it may well mean that more are to come.

Note also if there is a breakdown in law and order. Can the government collect taxes? Can it protect village headmen and police chiefs? Can it keep its school teachers teaching and its outspoken supporters including party members and journalists free from harm? Is it possible to move about safely at night? Can side roads be used without a military convoy? Is there a growing use of personal bodyguards? If a government official feels that he must travel about the country, or even attend parties in the capital under the eye of an armed man, it is clear that he feels the political situation is degenerating.

Further indices include the depletion of the stock of gunshops. Every capital has one or more centers for the open sale of shotguns, hunting rifles, and the like. If such a store suddenly runs out of these items it may mean that the government is buying them up, that the party of revolt is arming itself, or that average citizens feel the need of having weapons in their home—all of which are clearly signs of unrest.

It may be useful also to look at the windows and showcases of stores selling jewelry, oriental rugs, and other items of special value. In Arab Jerusalem in the late 1950's there was a jeweler who had a particularly valuable necklace. As long as it was in his window one could be sure that the town was quiet, but if he suspected rioting or trouble of any sort it disappeared into a safe hole under the floor of his house. So good was his intelligence that people referred to it as "the political necklace".

In the economic field, shortages of sugar, cigarettes, and other items not produced locally may indicate that insiders expect trouble and are hoarding. The return to their villages of an unusual number of servants or lesser tradespeople may well have political implications, since such persons tend to feel safer in the communities where they were born and brought up than in the big cities where political violence so often starts. Still another sign comes when prominent people keep their children home from school. If a cabinet member does not want his children on the streets it is clear he is expecting trouble.

Support for the Party of Revolt

Once the popular cause has been identified and the atmosphere appears favorable, the leader and his organizers will begin to build a party of revolt. There are three main ways:

The first is through a personal following. The leader collects his friends, relatives, and followers and in turn asks them to bring in their friends. The most successful example of this technique was the case of the Prophet Mohammed, who started Islam with his wives, slaves, and friends.

Secondly, there is the soapbox approach of speaking on street corners to attract malcontents. This method turns up a certain number of supporters, but it attracts extremists and police informers who can later do the movement great harm.

The third and professional way of gaining support, and the one most frequently used today by the Communists, is that of capturing existing organizations. Take the case of a country in which there are 4,000 students with most of them organized into an association which is run by a twelve-man executive committee. If the party of revolt can win eight or more of the twelve seats on the committee, it probably has put most of the other 4,000 on its side. This technique, of course, can be used only with organized groups—not only students but workers, farmers, journalists, teachers, and political splinter groups. The Communists give special priority to these elements, and if a particular association does not exist among them, they arrange to have one formed in order that it may be captured and later used.

A sufficient number of card-carrying supporters or dependable members of a party of revolt can be very small, three to five percent of the active population. In January of 1964 the little East African island of Zanzibar with a population of about 350,000 was taken over by extreme nationalists and leftist elements, which comprised at the start about one percent of the population.

Penetration of the Government and Front Organizations

If the movement of revolt is communist, it will probably hide its communist goals behind the slogans of a "front" organization, which works openly for one goal and secretly for another. Thus, the open goal advertised in speeches, slogans, and at meetings may be "overtime for government workers", while the secret goal is a general strike and chaos which will bring down the government so it can be replaced by one further to the left.

Communists often tip their hands through the use of unrelated slogans and placards. If the leaders are chanting "free lunches for school children and get the Americans out of Vietnam", it is most likely to be a front.

The Communists are sometimes surprisingly naive in the letterheads they use for their front organizations. If the names of the same men and women appear on the mastheads of a series of fronts working in unrelated fields, a careful check should be made on their political backgrounds.

High on any list for penetration by extremists will be the police and security forces. An unusual example occurred in a small pro-western country when the Communists penetrated the section of the security forces which kept the police files. It was discovered that hundreds of dossiers had been rewritten, giving clean political and police records to communists and their supporters. False and damaging items also had been placed in the files of a large number of men and women who were known for their anti-communist stands.

The movement of revolt may seek to penetrate other parts of the civil government by making converts, by planting members, by bribery, or by intimidation. A communist headquarters will have extensive lists of possible "soft targets", particularly persons known to have a weakness for gambling or sexual records which make them subject to pressure. Because of the views of society on the subject, homosexuals are often subjects for blackmail or bribery. Junior officials or girl secretaries serving their first tours of duty abroad are also rated as easy targets. If penetration of the civil government is successful, the operations of a party of revolt become much easier, since permits for demonstrations can be obtained, leaflets and newspapers distributed, halls for meetings rented, radio time secured, and contacts worked out with key officials.

Top priority is given to penetrating the armed forces. This is done on the theory that at the least it may prevent, or give warning of, an anti-communist coup, while at the best it may make possible a communist military take-over.

By this stage in an incipient revolution the government has naturally become aware of the movement of revolt and has also begun to penetrate it. This may take the form of making converts or of bribing or intimidating members. The government countermove, however, is most apt to center around the placing of police informers inside the party. Such persons, who must be carefully trained for their roles, are expected to "lie low" and follow the lead of the party for months or years. In many cases they are forbidden to make contact with

THE LIFE CYCLE OF A REVOLT   15

government security officers until told to do so. Sometimes such informers work their way into high position in a party of revolt and end up with a role in directing its operations. There is always pressure on the part of politicians within a government to persuade the security forces to surface their agents at the first sign of trouble, but the longer this can be delayed, up to a point, the greater will be the value of the information produced.

Outside Help

A personal revolt can be carried out by amateurs and without too much organization beyond agreement among friends, preferably in the officers' club of the capital city. However, an independence rebellion or a revolution to overthrow a regime requires technical skill and much organization.

As such a movement progresses it can be expected to seek outside help in various forms, including money, professional organizers, terrorists, demolition experts, and third degree technicians. All this requires a good deal of travel in and out of a country, and the Communists will frequently seek to penetrate the ranks of frontier police and guards in order to make illegal movement easier.

Another tip-off may come from trips by persons who would normally not travel. One well-planned revolt in the Near East was checked not long ago when it was discovered that a poor carpenter, who was usually without enough money to feed his family properly, had made three trips in as many weeks to a neighboring capital. When he came back from a fourth excursion he was carrying the equivalent of eighty thousand dollars and was followed by a lumber truck whose load consisted largely of Czechoslovakian machine guns.

Publicity

A coup or personal revolt must be accomplished by an inside group. An insurrection, rebellion, or revolution is a product which has to be sold to a considerable number of people. This does not require that they all have to become party members. Its simply means that they must be basically sympathetic or at least not opposed to the goals of the revolt. To bring it about there must be publicity, and much of the activity of a revolutionary group centers around bringing the cause to the attention of as many people as possible.

The first step towards publicity may be the setting up of "study groups". These are used particularly in countries where the Communist party is illegal, and they have proved effective in such different situations as mainland China, the Philippines, Greece, Cuba, and the Congo.

Next, radio stations outside the borders of the country under attack may begin broadcasts featuring the grievance, the evil actions of the government in power, and the merits of certain leaders of the revolt. Radio Cairo played this role effectively in the Algerian rebellion. Then, if possible, one or more clandestine radio stations may be set up inside the country, preferably mobile units which can give detailed information of local interest and can then be moved to avoid capture.

This may be followed by the distribution of handbills, possibly given out to persons walking in the streets or else pasted up on walls. The movement will also develop its own newspaper either through establishing one for the purpose, or frequently by taking over some small struggling daily. Most newspapers in developing countries are not very successful financially, and there is a good deal to the old maxim that "you don't need to own a newspaper, you just rent one." A few years ago in a small "neutral" capital, it was known that a certain newspaper could be rented for a day, a week, or a month. The editor was glad for "a reasonable consideration" to permit other people to write his headlines, his lead paragraphs, his editorials, and, as a special service, he would rewrite the speeches of prominent world leaders to make them most useful to the group putting up the money.

The Delegation Phase

If all has gone well so far the party of revolt is now ready to start direct action. The usual first step is the use of "delegations". Small groups call on key officials, such as the Prime Minister, War Minister, or other important public figures. The purpose is to get publicity by asking for help from anyone who could conceivably act to end a grievance. The leaders of the party of revolt expect few results from their delegations beyond publicity. In fact, in most cases the Communists would be unhappy if the delegations were so persuasive that action was taken and the grievance ended. On the contrary, the idea is to show the government leader as intransigent, lacking in understanding, and if possible, even brutal.

Many persons tend to dismiss delegations as unimportant and even boring efforts by cranks or splinter groups. Actually, however, the delegation phase may offer the first "cut-off point" for bringing an incipient revolt to a peaceful conclusion. On the one hand, the petition may be of an extreme anti-government or anti-western nature, or may involve some communist goal in another part of the world, thus making action on it unwise or impossible. On the other hand, the grievance may be justified and the petitioners may be seeking such reasonable goals as a reduction of unemployment, land reform, lower rates on farm loans, or better schools and hospitals. If this is the case, the government of the country involved would do well to listen to the delegations carefully, possibly setting up a committee to look into the problem. For if the grievance is real and a solution is possible, the local government may be able to put an end to the injustice, thus pulling the teeth of the revolt. The earlier in the revolutionary cycle that this can be done, the more likely it is that the insurgency can be stopped short of bloodshed. Thus, the surfacing of grievances in the delegation phase may be one of the best cut-off points in the life span of a revolt.

Demonstrations and Passive Resistance

The chances are, however, that little or nothing will come from the delegations, and that the leaders of the revolt will then intensify their drive for publicity and membership through the use of "quiet demonstrations". This usually involves parades of the faithful along a central route in the city, carrying placards, shouting slogans, singing songs, and ending up at some prearranged target such as a monument to a national hero, or the residence of the President. There prepared speeches are made, songs sung, and occasionally prayers held, after which the demonstration will break up and return quietly to headquarters, often by a series of different routes for the sake of better publicity. A variant of this is "the cross-country march", a technique first publicized by Gandhi when he was trying to focus world attention on the inequity of the British Salt Act in India.

Such demonstrations may be repeated day after day, with the marchers going to different targets until everyone in the city is aware of them and their goals. Demonstrations offer another possible cut-off point if the government in power chooses to act. Leaders of the demonstrations can be invited to a meeting, and it is possible that progress can be made toward the solution of the problem. It can be assumed, however, that if communists are involved they will not want this to happen and can be expected to pose impossible requests or to increase their demands day by day so that the negotiations will break off.

If nothing specific comes from such demonstrations or marches, the party of revolt may "shout a little louder". This essentially means attracting the attention of the populace through actions which upset the normal flow of life. These may take the form of nuisance demonstrations, organized sit-downs, or even stall-downs, if there are enough automobiles available to stall. These outdoor actions will probably be accompanied by demonstrations inside factories, universities, and office buildings.

All of these actions are aimed at disconcerting the lives of as many people as possible and stimulating sympathy and publicity, both in and out of the country, for the demonstrators. This "nuisance phase" of passive resistance is aimed in part at image building or image assassination. Thus newspaper photographs of police clubbing demonstrators will gain further sympathy for the party of revolt while the government is cast in an objectionable light.

Another effective technique is publicized fasting. Although this has been used since earliest time, the technique was developed into an art by Gandhi who pushed "non-violence" to its highest point of effectiveness. It is interesting to note how widely Gandhi's methods are now copied, as for example in some phases of the Negro movement for civil rights now going on in the United States.

It should be brought out, however, that passive resistance can succeed only in a democracy which takes into account human rights and due process of law. Thus, non-violence may be highly successful under the British raj in India, or in the United States, but non-violent or passive tactics are a waste of time in a dictatorship which simply sends in the tanks, shoots down some of the demonstrators, and ships the rest off to a concentration camp or a distant "Siberia".

The ultimate in emotional passive resistance occurs when a demonstrator chooses to burn himself to death in public. Even in a world accustomed to violence and cruelty, the impact of a political burning is tremendous, as we have seen recently in Vietnam. This technique has rarely been used in western countries, but should it be adopted its impact would be even greater.

The broad culmination of passive resistance is the general strike. If properly used this can paralyze the economy of a nation. It is the final form of peaceful participation in a cause and in putting pressure on the government for remedial action. It can of course be used effectively only if virtually all of labor is on the side of the revolt and if a considerable proportion of the rest of the population is willing to go along with the great inconvenience which it causes. If it does not bring about negotiation between the government and the party of revolt in its first few days it is apt to peter out, or else the government may use troops to provide transportation, oversee the distribution of food, and protect strike breakers. The general strike is most effective as a weapon in a small and highly industrialized European nation.

These phases of passive resistance mark another possible cut-off point at which a government can negotiate with the leaders of the revolt regarding legitimate grievances and thus prevent the further development of insurgency without losing too much "face".

Use of Elections

If the steps taken so far indicate solid and growing support for the movement and nothing has been done to meet its demands, the leader and his aides may next try to end their grievance through the ballot. If they do succeed in winning an election, the grievance will be taken care of and at least one phase of the revolt is over. Under these circumstances an election offers an automatic cut-off point for the ending of an insurgency. If the government leaders are smart, they may "permit" a few reform candidates to be elected to the country's parliament, and possibly put one in the cabinet itself. This closes the gap between the government and the people who are aggrieved and should permit ending an honest insurgency in an orderly way.

What is more likely, however, is that the party of revolt will be badly beaten at the polls. If this happens there will be widespread talk, possibly true, of fraudulent elections, trickery of the politicians, and brutality of the police. This probably marks the end of the peaceful steps of an insurgency. As a result, bitterness and disappointment will spread. Perhaps the revolt will collapse at this point, but what is more likely, however, is that the moderates and idealists will be pushed aside and that extremists, activists, and communists will take their place by dominating factions or splinter groups.

With the Communists moving in either openly or through the greater role played by members of front organizations, the whole character of the revolt now begins to change. It will, for instance, become more international and developments such as riots or mass meetings, which in the past received little notice, will be featured in the press and radio of Moscow and Peking. Also, new types of petitioners will appear at the United Nations to plead the cause.

Because morale among the members of the movement is low at this time, the Communists sometimes encourage the members of the inner circle to go around the city and pick out the house in which they want to live after the revolution. Less important members are urged to go about the city and select the automobile which they would like to drive when the great day comes. As a result the hard core no longer think of the revolution in terms of broad social goals, but they see themselves in a particular house, or driving in a special car. With these concrete objectives in mind, they are apt to work much harder.

Utilization of Mobs

In addition to changing the image of the movement throughout the world and bolstering the morale of its members at home, a Communist take-over will lead to violent marches or attacks aimed at sensitive and well-guarded targets. Clashes with the police will thus be deliberately provoked and mobs will be organized and used.

To most Americans, a mob is a mass of people milling around in the streets and city squares, often doing damage but without central direction and guidance. To the Communists, a mob is an organized device for obtaining certain objectives, and with this in mind it is usually broken into three elements:

    1. *The Minutemen.* These are groups of students, workers, or bureaucrats who have their own organizations and their own grievances, but they can be drawn into the streets quickly by the Communists, often for reasons unconnected with the main issue of the revolt. It takes time to organize an ordinary demonstration, but if something happens making it important that the crowds show "spontaneous support or sympathy", groups such as the "minutemen" can be put into the streets in less than an hour.

    2. *The Street Fillers.* The second part of the mob are aimless persons, whom the Communists try to round up in substantial numbers behind the

minutemen. These will include loafers, unemployed people with marginal jobs, and, if available, the inhabitants of nearby refugee camps. The leaders of these "street fillers" are on the regular payroll of the party of revolt and are usually in a position to pass on a little money to those whom they can turn out on such an occasion. Once the center of the city is beginning to fill up, most small business men will close their shops, pull down their steel shutters, and come out to see what is happening, thus further increasing the size of the crowd.

3. *The Actions.* All of these elements will accomplish little other than destruction unless they have guidance, and the Communists provide such guidance through action groups. These are squads of from fifteen to forty disciplined men and women, usually hard-core Communists who will obey orders, take risks, and spearhead attacks. Among them also are a certain number of younger party members who are anxious to rise in the party by proving their bravery. Each "action" has its own leader who often rides on the shoulders of some stalwart supporter. It has banners and slogans, its own messengers, probably young boys or girls who can slip through a crowd unobserved, and contains several orators who come with prepared speeches, and who often make use of hypnotic chants.

By these "actions" an aimless mob can be changed quite quickly into an instrument of attack. When the crowd is properly worked up, one or more of the "actions" will lead an attack against the "first target of the day", perhaps the Ministry of Labor or of Foreign Affairs, the Central Bank, or the national radio station.

Once a person is used to watching mobs from the vantage point of a hill or high building, the participation of "actions" can be quickly spotted. Their appearance makes it clear that one is not dealing with a spontaneous flareup, but with professionals who are using the mobs for their own ends.

The Communists utilize mobs in two ways. One is a carefully planned demonstration on a given day in which all the above elements are concerted, but which is made to look like a "spontaneous demonstration of the people's will". The other is a well-organized movement of revolt with "minutemen", "street fillers", and "actions" ready on a standby basis.

As a corollary to the use of mobs, the Communists frequently use the psychological weapon which they refer to as "the scum". During quiet periods they seek out and recruit criminals and others of the lowest elements in society. They are put on the communist payroll and are told that the time will come when most of the security forces in the city will be busy downtown trying to deal with mob action. The criminals will then find it easy to move about in the better sections of the city, committing whatever crimes they choose to commit.

Under the circumstances there is a good chance that they will not be caught, but if they are arrested the Communists promise to give them bail and legal aid. Thus a period of mob violence is frequently accompanied by a startling increase in violent crime in other parts of the city, leading to a general feeling that "the government has lost control of the situation". The importance of such a maneuver must not be overemphasized, but it shows how far and in how much detail the Communists are ready to go to undermine confidence in a government which they wish to bring down.

Curfew and Martial Law

With such wide breakdowns of order the government will at some point impose a curfew. The timing within a revolt varies widely, but it can be expected and the Communists count on it. Curfews run from the extreme of keeping everyone indoors all the time to the more normal restrictions of "off the streets from dusk to dawn".

Unfortunately a period of mob action and street fighting does not usually offer a reasonable cut-off point for the ending of an insurgency. On the contrary, efforts to start negotiations by a government in power at such a time are generally interpreted as signs of weakness. Thus, concessions made during a riot are likely to be followed by greater demands and still more violence, leading to a hopeless spiral.

Rather than negotiate at this time, governments are apt to declare martial law and use their troops to break up the rioting. This may lead to virtual civil war. Once it becomes clear that the soldiers are ready to shoot down the rioters the mob action probably will end. In some Near Eastern countries troops blacken their faces under these conditions so that they cannot be identified and tracked down later by relatives of rioters they may shoot.

Although, through the effective use of troops, the Communists or other organizers of the uprising may suffer a temporary defeat, they often feel that the development has played into their hands. Now they have clear proof that the government will not hesitate to shoot down students, workers, or farmers in order to keep itself in power. This proves that their charges are true and may well lead to a considerable increase in their popular support.

The Coup

Once an insurgency has progressed this far, the country and particularly the capital city are likely to be in great disorder; one side or the other may feel that the only answer is a military coup. If the party of revolt has penetrated the military and thus has supporters among the officers of the right regiments, particularly in the garrison of the capital city, it may try to stage a quick military take-over. If it succeeds, the movement has of course won, and the leaders can set about putting their platform into effect.

On the other hand, if rioting and bloodshed have lasted a long time, (a rough rule of thumb based on observation is that a riot which continues for five days is not likely to be controlled), a counter-coup may be staged. If successful, this will result in the arrest, trial, and execution of many of the known leaders of the uprising, forcing the others to go underground and putting at least a temporary end to revolutionary action.

In general, coups take three forms which may be described as *personal, army,* or *national.* In a *personal coup* a strong leader decides he wants to run a country and, if he has the power to do so by force, he pushes out the old government and takes control himself. His motives, however, are personal power rather than any interest in changing the political, economic, or social structure of the country. This type of violence is usually associated with Latin American revolutions during the past 150 years.

The newly independent states of the Near and Middle East have, since 1945, seen many examples of the form of political violence known as the *army coup.* For instance, late in 1948 after Syria had been defeated in the war against Israel, violence broke out between pro- and anti-government mobs. When it became clear that the military would suffer if the country collapsed, Colonel Husni al-Zaim, the Commander-in-Chief of the Syrian Army, imposed martial law and installed a new cabinet. The disorders continued and Colonel al-Zaim, in March, 1949, overthrew the President and the Prime Minister and became the real ruler of Syria. He made only minor attempts toward social change but worked to strengthen the Army, partly to "preserve" it and partly to strengthen his own position. Soon he was comparing himself to Napoleon and when his sense of grandeur proved too much for even his brother officers, he was assassinated in another army coup.

The most sophisticated form of quick political take-over may be referred to as a *national coup,* a sudden and violent change of government which often liquidates the previous leaders and then produces at least some change in governmental policies. The leaders of national coups are usually military men who believe, or say they believe, that the government in power is destroying the nation, that elections are impossible, and that the only way to save the country is to use the army to put in a new regime by force and then change governmental policies.

A striking example of a national coup occurred in South Vietnam in the autumn of 1963 when grievances against President Diem and his all-powerful and overbearing family had reached the breaking point. Months of intrigue, pressure, rioting, and suppression involving Nationalists, Catholics, Liberals, Radicals, Buddhists, and Communists finally culminated when infantry tanks and artillery took over control of Saigon. Diem and his brother were captured the next morning and executed. Control of those parts of South Vietnam not dominated by the Communists was assumed by a Military Revolutionary Council of twelve generals. Most of the officers involved acted in the belief that the only way to save themselves, the army, and more broadly, the whole of South Vietnam was to get rid of the Diem regime through a national coup. Unfortunately, however, *coup d'etats* whether personal, army, or national are habit-forming and South Vietnam saw eleven such violent changes brought about by the military within the next eighteen months.

The Interrupted Revolution

No matter which side stages a coup, observers should look for "dress rehearsals". Trotsky showed the usefulness of such action in Petrograd during the autumn of 1917. When a band of communists was given the assignment of capturing the railway station, they broke up into small groups and, wearing civilian clothes, spent several days wandering around the station until they were completely familiar with it. Thus when the time for action came they could move with speed to take over the vital parts of the installation. So successful was this technique of rehearsals that it is frequently used today, not only by the Communists but by all kinds of revolutionaries, and may be a tipoff that a coup is pending.

If disorders lead to a pro-government coup which is successful, its leaders must take steps toward ending the grievances behind the revolt. If this is not done, bitterness will continue to smolder, further uprisings are to be expected, and what is known as an *interrupted revolution* will result. This, then, in most cases is the last cut-off point for a government in power to end the grievances behind a revolt. From this time on the situation will deteriorate so rapidly that the party of revolt will insist on dealing with some group other than the original government.

If the coup by the party of revolt has been unsuccessful, the party will probably be declared illegal at this time. If the movement is run by amateurs, being forced underground will largely destroy the party's ability to make trouble since most of its members will be arrested and most of its activities shut down.

If, however, the movement is run by professionals, or by communists, they will be well prepared for such a development. Plans will be in existence designating who remains "above ground" and is therefore soon arrested; who goes underground and continues to work secretly; and who flees the country, possibly to set up a government in exile. South Africa today is an example of such a situation, where the amateurs have largely been arrested while the professionals are growing in effectiveness in their underground roles.

Underground Operations

A successful shift to underground operations will mean that the party of revolt will turn to terror, which is apt to take three forms:

1. *Material terror* against facilities such as railway bridges, power lines,

or public buildings. This is usually not meant primarily to kill or to injure people but to advertise the fact that the party is "going strong". Even a "token" bomb set off somewhere in a capital city each night for a week will keep the police on the run and let the populace know that the cause is alive. However, revolutions are not won by material terror, nor is it likely even to lead to negotiations for the settling of grievances. Almost without exception it is just the first step toward . . .

2. *Personal terror.* This involves assassination of opponents of the revolt such as police chiefs, village headmen, outspoken members of the government, well-known writers, popular teachers, and businessmen. The Communists frequently send in specialists to carry out a regime of personal terror, often people who have been trained behind the Iron Curtain or who have received practical experience in other revolutions. Such terror, if properly carried out, is hard to combat. Thus, in conflicts like Vietnam, Algeria, or the Congo, the losses of known supporters of the regime occurring night after night had a serious effect on public morale. If for instance a village has lost six headmen in six weeks, the government will find considerable difficulty in getting still another headman to volunteer for the job. In such a situation it may well be that the only candidate to step forward will be a person who is secretly working with the Communists and therefore knows that he will not be killed by them.

3. *Total terror.* This involves the employment of both material and personal terror, plus acts against the general public calculated to undermine morale. There was considerable general terror during parts of the Algerian rebellion, with bombs and explosives placed in theaters or stores or thrown into cafes. This undermined confidence in the French regime, slowed up business activity, and stimulated the flight from the country of white settlers, or Colons. In Vietnam, both under the French and in the current phase of the cold war conflict, the Communists have used material terror, personal terror, and total terror with varying degrees of effectiveness.

During the underground phase and possibly even earlier, observers should watch for political robbery, one of the means through which a party of revolt gets needed funds. Stalin developed this technique for financing revolution back in 1917, when he carried out several highly successful bank robberies in the city of Tiflis, kept the Bolshevik party in funds, and gained Lenin's favorable attention as well. There were several political robberies in Algeria during that rebellion, and they are to be met with in every revolution today in which professionals are involved. A Far Eastern variation of this form of money raising is a political kidnapping of the child of some wealthy businessman who is apt to come through with ransom money.

Also during the underground phase, although it may well occur earlier, observers should be on the lookout for political jailbreaks. By now many of the leaders of the party of revolt are in jail, probably being kept in a special prison other than that reserved for common criminals. Such a jailbreak may be engineered through bribery or by help from inside supporters, some of them high up in the government. It can result in the escape of a substantial number of important party members, who may then go underground or else flee the country. Governments are particularly loath to admit that a political jailbreak has happened, and they try to dismiss such a happening as "the escape of a few pickpockets". But, once the persons involved have reached safety, news is spread among the faithful or leaked to the press, thus strengthening the revolt considerably.

Obviously the government in power cannot allow various forms of terror, robbery, and jailbreak to continue unchecked and will organize a wave of suppression which will grow into counter-terror. This will involve rougher handling of crowds and widespread arrests, plus more aggressive police action of all sorts including third-degree excesses. Such police action against persons being arrested or already in jail may result in deaths under violent circumstances. This is a development to be deplored by most persons, but it provides the hardened revolutionary with martyrs who are highly prized as political assets.

If some student is shot down by the police while marching in a demonstration or dies later while being beaten in jail, the party of revolt can then stage a funeral with the widest possible publicity. All the faithful will participate along with large numbers of interested bystanders, and the best orators of the revolt will work up the crowd to a state of wild emotion. This may lead to protest marches against police headquarters or the palace, and if the tension can be maintained for several days, the party of revolt may be able to attract sufficient followers from the security forces to carry out a successful coup.

The Communists feel that martyrs are so useful that if none are developed during the regular course of a revolt they do not hesitate to manufacture them. There are several well-recorded cases in which communists have purposely sent young men or women on assignments which they knew would lead to their deaths in order that they could be used later for propaganda purposes.

The Guerrilla Phase

If there have been no successful negotiations, no clarifying elections, and no coups or counter-coups, a stalemate will develop. When this occurs the party of revolt may change its tactics and begin to use guerrillas. Essentially the guerrilla phase of a rebellion or revolution is military and has been examined in detail by a series of military writers ranging from Mao Tse-tung through Lucian W. Pye to Charles Thayer.

The emphasis in this book, however, is on the political, economic, and social aspects of revolt. It is an effort to examine the grievances most likely to cause uprisings, the types of men that lead them, and the course or pattern which such upheavals can be expected to follow.

SOCIETAL REVOLUTIONS

LOOKING back over the past fifty years future historians will probably note at least three important characteristics of the international scene. First, the unprecedented proliferation of *societal revolutions*. Second, the virtual ending of the European-dominated empires through various forms of *independence rebellions*. Third, the growing clash between the Communist and non-Communist powers in a series of what have come to be called *cold war conflicts*.

From the long range point of view it is probable that the most important of these will be the expansion and frequency of violence aimed at bringing about basic political, economic, and social change. Whereas *societal revolutions* had sometimes occurred previously, as in England in 1648 and France in 1789, the changes now are not only frequent but worldwide. The practice of reorganizing society by violence has spread from Europe to the Far East, the Near and Middle East, and Latin America. In a few instances, as in Egypt, the change was relatively peaceful. In others, as in Cuba, it was carried out in part by trickery using a technique often referred to as a *revolution betrayed*.

But the two most important revolutions of the twentieth century were the Bolshevik seizure of Russia in 1917 and the Communist victory in China in 1949. Both had certain aspects in common, but the techniques used differed widely. In Russia, success for the professional Communist organizers came largely through the workers in the city with much help from military elements and a little from the peasants. In China, on the other hand, after several failures based on the Russian pattern, the Communists finally won through the use of guerrilla-type peasant armies, aided by economic self-sabotage by the Nationalist regime. The Russian Revolution developed techniques which we might expect to see copied if further revolts break out in the urbanized western world. The Chinese Revolution was the proving ground for techniques suitable for use in the rural areas of the Far East and Southern Asia, some of which are being used today in Vietnam.

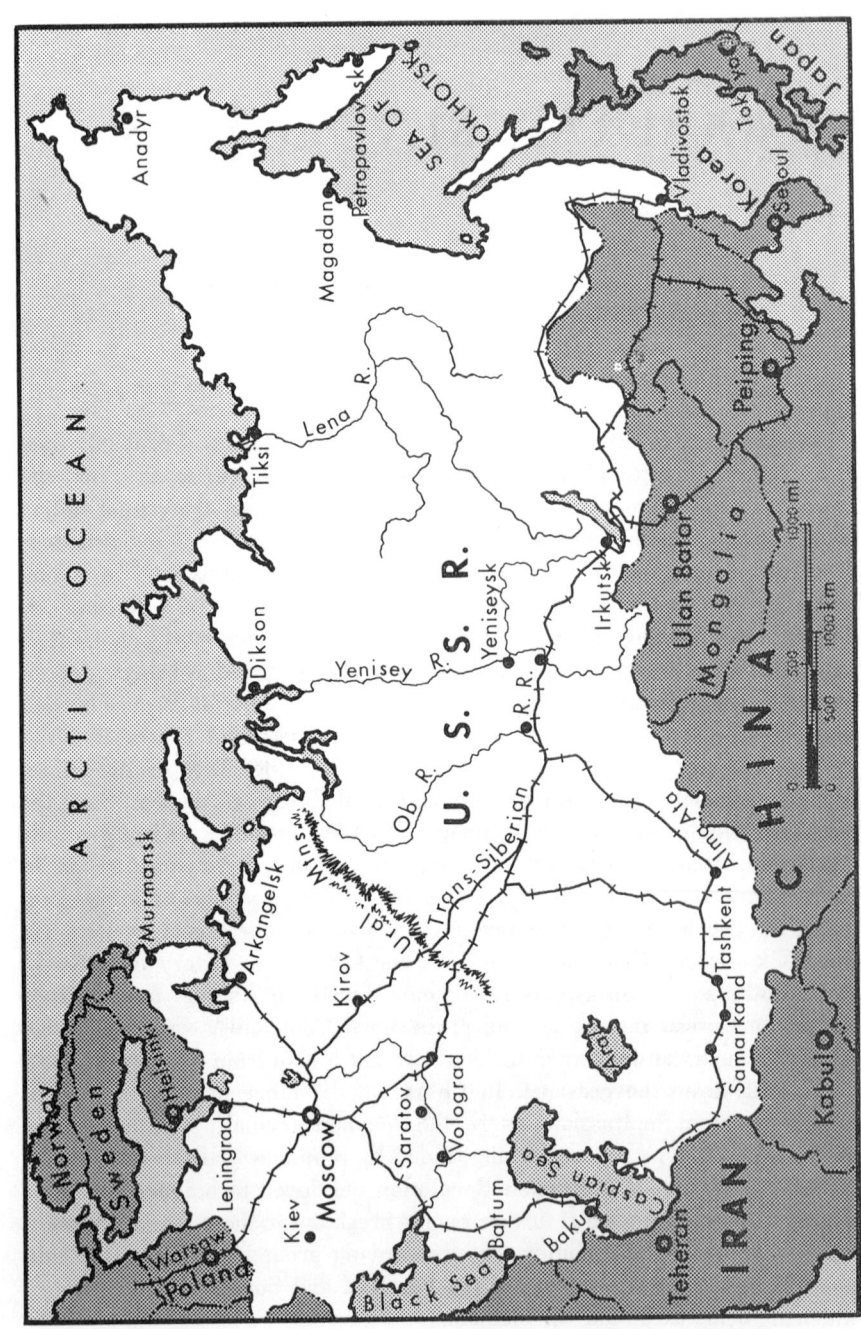

CHAPTER II

RUSSIA AND CHINA: DIFFERENT PATHS TO COMMUNIST VICTORY

RUSSIA

By 1914 Russia was a country in deep political and economic trouble. The workers, soldiers, peasants, and intellectuals all had grievances. There was a wide gap between those running the country and the majority of the people. The unsuccessful Revolution of 1905 should have brought about basic changes, but little was done and in fact some conditions worsened.

The immediate cause of Russia's collapse was the inability of her government to deal with World War I. Food production fell off sharply, factory output dropped, transport broke down, and the soldiers found themselves trying to fight the German war machine, often without guns, ammunition, or even shoes. In March, 1917, riots broke out in the breadlines of Petrograd. When ordered to fire on the rioters, the troops in the city not only refused but many of them joined the demonstrators. Realizing he had no support, Tsar Nicholas abdicated on March 15, 1917, and was replaced by a provisional government under Kerensky which included aristocrats, officials, and bourgeois. At the same time, liberal, socialist, and radical groups organized a council known as the Petrograd Soviet of Workers and Soldiers Deputies. At first there was no intention of overthrowing the provisional government, but the Soviet won the support of the workers and soldiers, and soon Russia had in effect two governments.

The Seizure of Power in Russia

In April, 1917, the Germans arranged to have the Communist leader Lenin transported from Switzerland to Petrograd. He immediately started working to put his Communist followers, known as Bolsheviks, into control of the government. The Bolsheviks developed the short and simple platform of "peace, land, bread! All power to the Soviet!" Whereas the other leaders were confused,

Lenin had a specific plan which included rapid and widespread organization of worker, soldier, and peasant soviets. Actually the role of the peasants was not too important during the seizure of power, but they gave the movement breadth and general support.

Lenin put great emphasis on having the Communists active in the armed forces where a series of soviets were organized. In addition, Communists set up units of Red Guards, a form of "People Militia" which they controlled. As the Russian fighting front against the Germans fell into collapse, more and more soldiers moved back into the cities. Petrograd, Moscow, Kiev, and other centers became jammed with bitter and hungry troops, most of whom still had their rifles. To strengthen the Red Guards further, the Communists formed soviets in the munitions factories. Because most Russian goods moved by railway, the Communists also emphasized the growth of soviets among the transport workers. Communist organization of the peasants increased the general disintegration as they took over the estates of wealthy landowners.

In July, the provisional government tried to smash the soviets, but the railroad workers sabotaged the effort; few anti-Communist troops reached Petrograd, and Kerensky and the provisional government were completely discredited. A meeting of the All-Russian Congress of Soviets was scheduled for early November, and although the Bolsheviks controlled the Petrograd Soviet they did not have a majority in the Congress. Lenin's followers therefore planned a coup with tactics which were largely the work of Leon Trotsky. Units of the Red Guards and groups of workers or soldiers who supported the Bolsheviks were given targets such as the railway station, the telegraph office, and important government buildings. For almost a week they quietly visited their respective goals and familiarized themselves with approaches and other essential features. Then, just before the All-Russian Congress of Soviets convened, these soldiers and workers carried out a sudden coup which, in spite of resistance from supporters of the provisional government, was largely successful.

Thus, when the Congress of Soviets convened on November 6, the Bolsheviks were soon able to announce that they controlled most of the city of Petrograd and had pushed out the provisional government. The Congress of Soviets thereupon declared itself the real government of Russia. It established a Central Executive Committee of 110 members, more than 60 of whom were Bolsheviks. It also organized a Cabinet, the Council of People's Commissars, to which all the leading Communists were elected with Lenin as Chairman and Trotsky as Commissar of Foreign Affairs and War. Many of the non-Communist members in the Soviet walked out of the hall, leaving overwhelming power to the Bolsheviks. Before long, with his famous remark, "We shall now proceed to construct the Socialist Order," Lenin began to put into effect the Bolshevik platform.

During November and December the Bolsheviks used these same tactics to take control of various other major cities. It was many months, however, before they gained anything like efficient control of the vast Russian countryside. Meanwhile, in March of 1918, their government signed a treaty of peace with the Germans and moved the capital to Moscow.

During the next three years, thanks largely to the genius of Trotsky, the Red Army fought off no less than five different attacks by non-Communist forces, which included conservatives, liberals, socialists, Cossacks, and British, French, American, and Japanese troops.

The counter-revolution was marked by widespread arrests, executions, and atrocities by all factions. But by the beginning of 1921, the Communists were securely in control of most of the former Russian Empire. The tactic of taking power through the workers and soldiers with some support from the peasants had proved successful in Russia, and the new rulers in Moscow saw no reason why it should not prove equally successful elsewhere.

CHINA

By the end of the 19th Century, China's population had passed 500 million persons and the shortage of good land was acute. Class differences were sharply drawn and there was little motion from one class to another. Seventy-five percent of the population were peasants who worked small tracts of land; a man with three acres was considered well-off. Communications were primitive, disasterous floods were frequent, schools were backward, and medical facilities scarce.

Nevertheless, to many foreigners China appeared prosperous. The great powers had economic concessions in the coastal cities such as Shanghai, and fortunes were being made by western business interests and by the Chinese, known as "compradores", who worked with them. There was a small but growing number of industrial workers making a living in the docks, the railroads, the textile mills, and other light industries. But they worked for long hours at low wages and were in general unorganized or belonged to company unions.

A group of intellectuals was also beginning to make itself felt. Some of them had classical Chinese educations, others were educated by missionaries, and a few had gone to school or college outside of China. They realized that the social pattern of China must be changed and that she had to emerge both from feudalism and from her semi-colonial status.

With the breakdown of the old patterns, graduates of the military academies formed another center of power. They began to occupy top positions, not only in the army but in the regional and central governments. Since they had the force of their troops behind them, they could play extremely important roles.

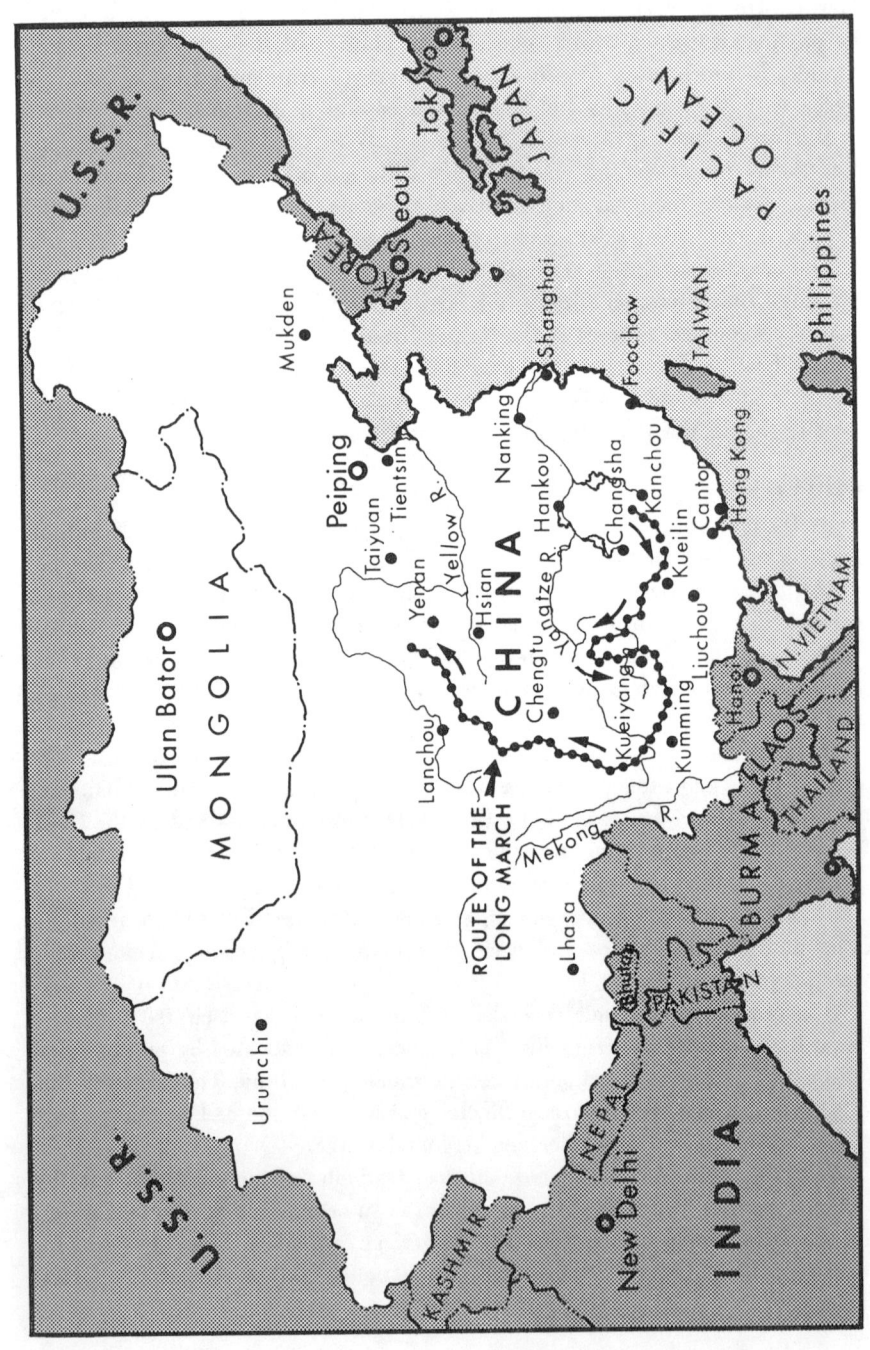

In 1894, Sun Yat-sen, a liberal Chinese Christian doctor, with a few relatives and friends forming the Society for the Regeneration of China, tried unsuccessfully to upset the Manchu dynasty. A second attempt during the Boxer Rebellion in 1900 also failed. Inspired by Sun, revolution broke out again in 1911, and the Emperor Piu I abdicated the next year. Yuan Shih-k'ai was elected premier and controlled the north, while Sun Yat-sen held power in the south. Yuan objected to Sun's plan to make China a liberal republic. Sun moved his Nationalist Party, known as the Kuomintang (KMT), to the southern city of Canton, but after a brief period of dominance it was pushed aside by a local warlord. Sun Yat-sen thereupon sought help from foreign powers, including the United States and the recently established Soviet Republic.

Start of the Chinese Communist Party

A Society for the Study of Marxism was formed in Peking in 1918, and the movement spread. The First Congress of the Chinese Communist Party was held in mid-1921 in an empty girls' school in Shanghai. When that building was raided, the Party members hired a boat and continued their deliberations under the guise of a social outing.

The next year the Chinese Communists proposed a united front with the Kuomintang against warlords, feudalists, and foreign exploiters. Sun Yat-sen turned down this proposal, but the Communists adopted the policy of joining the Kuomintang individually. Before long, a rising young army officer named Chiang Kai-shek was sent to Moscow for a few months' inspection tour and to arrange aid.

In mid-1923, a well-trained Moscow Communist agent using the name of Michael Borodin arrived in Canton. Borodin guided the reorganization of the KMT. He persuaded the Kuomintang to form a Central Executive Committee, to cooperate with the Chinese Communist Party and to start an army training center, the Whampoa Military Academy, commanded by Chiang Kai-shek after his return from Moscow. As head of the political department of the new school, Borodin chose a Chinese intellectual, Chou En-lai.

The growth of leftist influence became so obvious that by mid-1925 a group of conservatives in the Kuomintang charged that its policies were being made by communists. After a struggle for power, the conservatives were expelled and communist-trained Chiang Kai-shek, backed by the cadets of the Whampoa Academy and some 10,000 leftist workers from Hong Kong, took complete control. A network of soviets was started, including groups among the transport and dock workers. It seemed that the tactics which had succeeded so well in Russia would work again in China.

Borodin, however, had misjudged Chiang Kai-shek and his beautiful and ambitious wife. In February, 1926, while Borodin was absent, Chiang Kai-shek announced that he had discovered a communist conspiracy in Canton. He arrested the Russian advisers still in the city, shut down the trade unions, disarmed the Workers' Militia, and purged the Central Executive Committee of communists.

Borodin was also a resourceful man. In October, 1926, he persuaded the leaders of the Kuomintang to move their headquarters to the interior towns of Hankow and Wuchang where the Communists were strong and Chiang's followers were weak. Before long Chiang resigned as leader of the Kuomintang and of the Nationalist Army.

But Chiang was not finished. Before daylight on August 12, 1927, armed squads swept through Shanghai arresting communists and radical labor organizers, smashing soviets, and liquidating such Red Guards as they met. Soon China's greatest city was firmly in his hands. After a final effort to stage a counter-coup, Borodin and some of his followers fled westward across the Gobi Desert in an old Dodge sedan.

Mao Tse-tung and New Uprisings

After this reversal Moscow sent two new Communist agents to China with instructions to reorganize and expand the network of soviets, build up the Red Guards, and strengthen the Communist Party among city workers. Thanks to their efforts revolts broke out in the cities of Nanchung and Swatow, followed by a revolt in the city of Changsha, known as "the Autumn Crop Uprising". After considerable bloodshed it also was crushed, partly because one of its leaders, Mao Tse-tung, failed to produce the strength he had promised among the local peasants. Mao was then stripped of much of his power in the party. Realizing that he had little or no future in the cities, Mao collected his peasant supporters and led them to a remote part of Kiangsi Province. There, in a former bandit hideout, he began forming soviets among the peasants and organizing a rural Red Militia.

In spite of these three defeats, the Moscow-trained advisers continued to work for a successful uprising of workers and soldiers along Russian lines in the cities of China. Utilizing leftist cadets from the Whampoa Military Academy and radical trade union groups among the workers, the Communists seized the city of Canton and set up a soviet government which promptly executed many anti-Communists.

The bulk of the Nationalist forces in the area were anti-Communist and they forced their way into the city. For the next five days a "white terror" reigned in Canton, during which more than six thousand Communists and their supporters were shot, beheaded, or thrown off riverboats in the bloodiest anti-

Communist reaction seen in China up to that time. It was a bitter defeat for the Moscow policy of trying to bring about revolution in the cities. The Soviet Union, however, continued its interest in revolution in the cities of China, though at a lower key. In 1930, another wave of Communist advisers known as the *Returned Student* clique soon dominated the Central Committee of the party, and continued agitation for the Russian pattern of takeover.

Since March of 1929, Chiang Kai-shek and the Kuomintang had controlled China's main seaports, some of her interior cities, and the neighboring farm areas. His strength, however, did not extend far inland nor to mountain areas such as south Kiangsi, where Mao controlled a force of about 10,000 men. Although only about 2,000 men were well-armed, they were thoroughly indoctrinated and Mao used them to organize a series of soviets. In almost every village they entered, the poor farmers supported these "agrarian reformers". Mao's cadres took over the farms of the richer landlords, announced that the debts of the peasants were null and void, and confiscated stores and some small factories. In July, 1930, Mao led a raid against the town of Changsha, where some 2,000 anti-Communists were killed before Mao's guerila forces were driven back by the soldiers of Chiang Kai-shek.

This raid awoke the leader of the Kuomintang to the danger presented by the guerrillas, and he tried to get rid of them in three separate "campaigns of extermination". In each case, however, Chiang's regulars were ambushed by Mao's guerrillas who were perfecting their hit-and-run tactics. According to one estimate, they captured more than 30,000 rifles plus much ammunition from Nationalist troops, who either fled before the surprise attacks or surrendered and went over to Mao's side. These victories strengthened Mao greatly, and the areas he controlled expanded. As a result, the Communists held the first All-China Soviet Congress in Kiangsi Province in November, 1931. A central Soviet Government was set up, a Soviet Congress was established, party discipline was tightened, and a school for guerrilla fighters was organized. In all of this Mao emphasized that the role of the peasants was much more important than that of the workers.

This "following of the peasant road" was still not pleasing to the Moscow Communists, and Mao had several years of in-fighting with the Returned Students and the city Communists in China. Yet, the area under his control grew year by year, and when the second All-China Congress was held by the Communists in January, 1934, Mao was listened to carefully. Explaining his success, he said: "Our class line in the agrarian revolution is to depend upon the hired farmhands and poor peasants, to ally with the middle peasants, to check the rich peasants, and to annihilate the landlords. The correct practice of this line is the key to the success of the agrarian revolution . . ."

The Long March

Much of the world still discounted Mao and his "agrarian reformers"; but Chiang Kai-shek recognized them for what they were. Aided by a German general, he moved into the Communist-held territory in 1934 with substantial strength. By now the leaders of the Moscow-trained Returned Students thought that they were strong enough to meet the Nationalist Forces head-on. Abandoning Mao's guerrilla tactics of hit-and-run raids, they tried to stop the advance of Chiang Kai-shek's troops in conventional battles.

Untrained in such warfare, the peasants were beaten back, day after day, with heavy losses until it appeared that the Red Army would be wiped out and the whole Communist-controlled area overrun. In desperation, the assembled Communist leaders telegraphed Moscow for permission to take the Red Army and their chief supporters to a *safe haven* in a remote part of western China.

Then, with the greatest possible secrecy, some 125,000 members of the Red Army, the party leaders, and their chief followers, were organized into mobile columns. Moving at night, the Communists broke through the Nationalist lines and marched night and day, spending four hours on the road and four hours at rest, until Chiang's troops lost contact with them. Continuing westward at a slower rate, the columns moved on until January, 1935, when, in the province of Kweichow, they halted to rest and reorganize their political structure. Mao chose this occasion to strengthen his position within the party by blaming the Returned Students both for giving up guerrilla tactics and for wasting the energy, time, and money of the Chinese Communists in unsuccessful efforts to bring off a revolution in the cities. His arguments proved telling and were repeated at the next halt made by the columns in northern Szechwan. There, various other Communist leaders lined up behind his policy of victory through the peasants. At last, after a difficult crossing of the Yellow River, the Communists reached Shensi Province on the border of Inner Mongolia, where they established permanent headquarters in the city of Yenan.

Although still in China, Yenan was well beyond the control of Chiang Kai-shek, and thus afforded a true safe haven for the Communists. In October, 1937, there was a final showdown on Communist policy in China. The Comintern in Moscow at last gave Mao its rather half-hearted support, and Mao became the dominant figure in the Chinese Communist Party.

Mao's Background

Mao came from a small village in Hunan Province where as a boy he quarreled with his father and was much influenced by a liberal school teacher. An avid reader, Mao became ashamed that China should have been dismembered by the western powers. He studied the careers of various world leaders including Peter the Great and George Washington and became so excited by the Chinese Revolution of 1911 that he spent some time with the rebels.

After graduating from a local college, Mao went to Peking where he got a job as assistant librarian at the National University. Influenced by leftist contacts and studies, by 1920 Mao had become a Marxist, and the next year he went to the meeting in Shanghai which organized the Chinese Communist Party. He was accused of putting too much emphasis on the role of the peasant and was sent back to Hunan Province for "reasons of health". There he was able to put his theories into practice, organizing more than twenty peasant unions, a series of soviets and several groups of peasant militia. Returning to Canton to escape arrest, he ran a Communist school for the training of peasant organizers. He repeatedly tangled with the orthodox wing of the Chinese Communist Party which believed in giving the city workers and soldiers the main role in a revolution.

Mao studied the writings of various Chinese military leaders, and partly from them, but more particularly from experience, he evolved his own pattern for successful guerrilla operations. This pattern has been summarized as follows:

> When the enemy advances, we retreat!
> When the enemy halts and encamps, we trouble them!
> When the enemy seeks to avoid battle, we attack!
> When the enemy retreats, we pursue!

In essence this meant that guerrillas should always know the strength and location of their enemy, should never fight unless sure of their numerical superiority, should if possible attack from ambush, and should fall back if counter-attacked.

Unity Against the Japanese

While the Reds and the Nationalists were fighting each other in the hinterland, the Japanese had been pushing down from Manchuria, capturing cities, and acquiring some control over the countryside. After a series of negotiations, during which Chiang Kai-shek was held for a time as a prisoner of two of his warlords, Mao's Communists agreed to stop working against the Kuomintang. They promised to join forces against the Japanese and to "abolish" the soviets in favor of "democracy based on the people's rights", a phrase of doubtful interpretation. In exchange, Chiang agreed that the Red Army would be merged with his forces. Mao's guerrillas were rechristened the Eighth Route Army and he was made Deputy Commander of the second war zone within the Nationalist army area. As a result, from 1937 to 1940, the Eighth Route Army received both cash and munitions from Chiang Kai-shek and grew steadily in strength.

While Chiang's frontal attacks on strong Japanese positions resulted in a series of defeats for the Nationalists, the Eighth Route Army, using Mao's guerrilla tactics, defeated the Japanese in battle after battle and collected large amounts of guns and ammunition from both the Japanese and Nationalist troops who had been defeated. Meanwhile Mao continued to pose as an "agrarian reformer", while the Soviet Union gave little support and openly assisted Chiang Kai-shek.

In order to strengthen his organization, Mao started what he called Cheng Feng, a course of carefully-controlled mass indoctrination. Beginning in February, 1942, more than 30,000 Communist leaders were put through this ideological course, thus producing a cadre of faithful adherents which later made possible the indoctrination of many millions of Chinese.

While the Communists were consolidating their hold on the remote parts of China and training their hard core of leaders, Chiang Kai-shek was not idle in putting forward his plan for a New China. This included a revival of the teachings of Confucius, a return to the system of party cells within the Kuomintang, the reorganization of a regimented youth corps, the designation rather than election of many members of the National Congress, and the expansion of the secret police. To many forward-looking Chinese, this pattern seemed a "leap backward", and they began to lose faith in the Kuomintang. Their feelings were strengthened as it became clear that in the areas controlled by the Chinese Nationalists the rich were getting richer, the middle classes were being squeezed by inflation, and the poor were no better off.

Corruption and Economic Subversion

Graft and corruption among some of the leaders and many of the traders of Nationalist China were becoming widespread. The amount of arms, commodities, and money pouring into the non-Communist areas was enormous, and so were the opportunities to make profits on the side. Obtaining contracts, shipping goods, storing items, and their eventual distribution, all offered chances for "squeeze" on an unprecedented scale. In a highly uncertain world such chances were irresistible, and scores of new millionaires appeared, while rumors of graft touched thousands of lesser figures and a multitude of small traders. A spirit of "make the most of it while you can" permeated many official, business, and even military Nationalist circles.

All this gave Mao and his Communists, particularly those in the big seaports of China, the chance to push economic subversion within the areas controlled by the Nationalists. Thus, observers of the Nationalist scene began to discover that by western standards very curious things were happening in Shanghai and the other non-Communist cities of China.

A shipment of arms from the United States would arrive on the China seacoast, be properly cleared, and move into the interior, where duly signed receipts would show that it had arrived at a town controlled by Chiang Kai-shek. However, further investigation would run into difficulty and, if finally pinned down, the local officials would say that most of the shipment had then been lost or stolen. In any case, the arms would soon turn up in the hands of Mao's guerrillas or the People's Militia fighting for him. Other items which mysteriously ended up on the side of the Communists included hard-to-obtain drugs, trucks and transport equipment, gasoline, communication items, and winter clothing.

Just as serious as the movement of the material was the fact that there grew up a wide network of persons who were either Communist sympathizers or more usually "neutral Chinese" who could not resist sharing in the large amount of money involved in this traffic. Persons accepting "cuts" included masters and crews of coastal ships, harbor pilots, dock workers, warehouse superintendents, railroad officials, and business leaders.

Another aspect of the economic subversion was that it compromised hundreds of officials who, after taking their first bribes, were in no position to work against the Communists. The extent of this subversive economic network was known to only a few, but rumors of it spread, sometimes pushed by the Communists themselves. Thus more and more Chinese came to feel that the government of Chiang Kai-shek was rotten.

In contrast to this situation among the Nationalists, such news as reached the outside world about Mao and his followers made them appear honest, dedicated, democratic up to a point, and truly forward-looking. Thus many people in and out of China came to think that the choice was between a reactionary and corrupt Nationalist regime and a progressive and honest government which contained some Communists.

The Collapse of Chiang

As the population controlled by Mao grew from about 1,500,000 Chinese in 1937 to over 85,000,000 in 1944, the United States sent a series of high-level emissaries to China to strengthen the war effort against the Japanese and to curb the graft and corruption. Several of them, particularly General George Marshall, returned and attacked the "dominant group of reactionaries in the Kuomintang". The General stated he felt that the only way to reverse the deterioration in that organization was for the "liberals in the government and in the minority party, a splendid group of men" to take over its leadership.

But, with the ending of the war against Japan, liberals in and out of the Kuomintang were not given a chance to lead, and the moderate cause in China began to wither steadily in spite of U. S. aid which ran into billions of dollars. Inflation spread rapidly, Nationalist morale in the cities fell, and the will to fight among the troops sank so low that there were widespread surrenders and desertions. Chiang's army was large and well-equipped with American arms, but he became overextended and the intelligence received by his officers was not as good as that reaching the Communists.

Mao's forces, on the other hand, were now supplied with substantial amounts of arms captured from the Japanese, recovered from the fleeing Nationalists, or received directly through the underground via economic subversion. Thus they were able to make good use of Mao's proven guerrilla tactics, attacking only when their chances of winning were good and always retreating in the face of overwhelming force.

In four successive battles in the autumn of 1948, Chinese Nationalist forces were reported to have lost 33 divisions, about 400,000 rifles, and a vast store of ammunition, most of which ended up in the hands of the Communists.

Unable to match the Communist troops in the mobility and surprise attacks of guerrilla warfare, Chiang Kaï-shek's heavily-armed troops began retreating into the cities. The Communists were free to move about in the countryside, liquidating their enemies and taking over the farms and villages as Nationalist strength further eroded.

Evidence that the end was near came in October, 1948 when the Nationalist defenders of Mukden, a key city in Manchuria, defected *en masse* and went over to the Communists, taking with them their weapons and much heavy equipment. Afterwards, the Nationalist-held cities went down like tenpins. Tientsin surrendered in January, 1949, Peking fell a month later, and by April the Communist armies, which by now were far more than guerrilla bands, had crossed the Yangtze River. Shanghai went over to the Communists in May after which Chiang Kai-shek left the Chinese mainland and set up his headquarters, including what was left of his government and his army, on the island of Formosa. Canton fell without resistance. The Communists had won their long fight for the Chinese mainland.

The People's Republic of China

At the gate of the former Imperial Palace in Peking, on October 1, 1949, stood Mao Tse-tung, who for three decades had staked his life on the theory that communism could be brought to China through the use of guerrilla tactics by armed and disciplined peasants. He announced that the Central People's Political Consultative Council of the People's Republic of China had just taken office.

"The People" thus referred to were defined by Mao as the working class, the peasant class, the *petit bourgeois*, and the *national bourgeois*. They were united under the Communist Party "to carry out a dictatorship over the lackeys of imperialism, the landlord class, the bureaucratic capitalist class, the Kuomingtang reactionaries and their henchmen representing these classes . . ."

This relatively broad base was in line with standard Communist procedures, which until sure of its power incorporates as many elements as possible into the first revolutionary government, thus making it appear democratic and nationalist, rather than communist. Then, as the years passed, the national bourgeois, the petit bourgeois, and the richer peasants and some shopkeepers were found "to have gone over to the enemy" and were liquidated one by one. By then Mao had at his command a thoroughly reliable People's Militia, a secret police, the hard core of the Communist Party, and a chain of informers which extended down to the Chinese children. Once securely in control, Mao and other Communists were able to proceed with the modernization and industrialization of China, a process carried out with disregard for past Chinese traditions or the feelings and lives of its people. In spite of widespread famines, mass arrests, and a falling standard of living, Communist control of China has continued.

* * * * * * * * * * *

In winning his revolution, Mao did more than take over some 500 million persons and pour them into a communist mold. He developed a new technique of revolution which he and his followers feel is better suited to the conditions of Asia, the Middle East, and Africa than is the Moscow approach. In essence this involves utilizing peasant guerrillas in order to pave the way for a campaign of setting up soviets among the farmers, which at first are based on all but absentee landlords, moneylenders, and their associates. Then, as time passes, "the tallest branches on the economic tree" are lopped off until only the poorer elements remain to be collectivized.

Equally important, Mao and his followers note that in the "rural" world are to be found weak and inexperienced governments which have only recently emerged from colonial rule. Such governments are far different from those in the west, many of which have a long history of sovereignty and some experience with democracy. Thus, Mao feels that in colonial or rural areas it is not necessary to have two-stage revolutions. [The first of these stages ends feudalism and brings in a regime run by the national bourgeois, and the second does away with capitalism and brings about communism.] He believes that, as was done in China, revolution can be achieved in a single step.

Revolutions, like people, have a definite life span and as they get older they become more conservative. This is happening in the Soviet Union which, although in no sense conservative, is not as radical as it was thirty years ago. Thus, Moscow is ready to work with national bourgeois regimes and believes that progress through socialism to communism may in some cases be brought about by the ballot.

Mao, on the other hand, seeks to keep his revolution at white heat, partly through the device of the "Great Proletarian Cultural Revolution". Whereas Moscow is willing to settle for eventual world communism, Peking wants it now, believes it can only come through violent revolution, and is quite ready to run the risk inherent in pushing "wars of national liberation" to free the masses, not only from colonial powers but from local national bourgeois regimes. It is not very surprising, therefore, that there is a serious Sino-Soviet split, a division of theory and practice which may well continue to deepen.

While such a concept dominates the thinking of China, we can expect her aggressively to export communist revolutions of her own one-stage peasant-guerrilla type. If necessary she will do this directly, but from her point of view it is more desirable to use an intermediary state such as Vietnam.

It is unlikely that the drama of a violent communist take-over will again be played on so vast a stage as was the case in China. It appears certain, however, that a repetition in related forms will occur in other eastern countries—countries where modernization has moved too slowly, where flagrant graft and corruption exist and can be made worse by Communist subversion, and where peasant guerrillas can trade space for time and expand village by village in hope of a complete Communist victory.

CHAPTER III

EGYPT:

THE ARMY BRINGS SOCIAL CHANGE

THE Egyptians are not Arabs; rather they are Arabic-speaking Mediterraneans who adopted Islam. Along with some 200,000,000 other followers of Mohammed, they stretch in a great arc from western Africa through Pakistan to Indonesia, China and the Philippines. They have encountered religious and social problems whenever they try to modernize, and these difficulties spring from two aspects of Islamic history.

Islam was and is a complete way of life. Through the Koran and the example and sayings of the Prophet and his immediate followers, every problem of life for the inhabitants of Arabia was answered simply and definitively. It was a case of: "This is all ye know and all ye need to know."

Though Islamic thinking changed and developed in the first centuries after Mohammed's death, it crystallized about 1200 A.D. and changed little thereafter. For 500 years, when Europe was progressing rapidly, the Islamic world stood relatively still. Followers of Islam found themselves guided and dominated by a way of life which was not suited to the problems of the 19th and 20th centuries. Although a few Islamic leaders over the past two centuries realized the problem, they were unsuccessful in finding acceptance for modernization. New sects tended to become more conservative, and the followers of Islam found no bridge to take them from medieval to modern times.

Breakdown of Old Patterns

Even at best, Islam had produced not political peace, but a system of balanced tensions in which its followers were given detailed guidance on their relationship with God and with their fellow men. By the 19th century, this "structured world" began to come apart. New tensions developed and the old system of balances no longer sufficed.

Since there was no organized church in Islam, there had never been a hier-

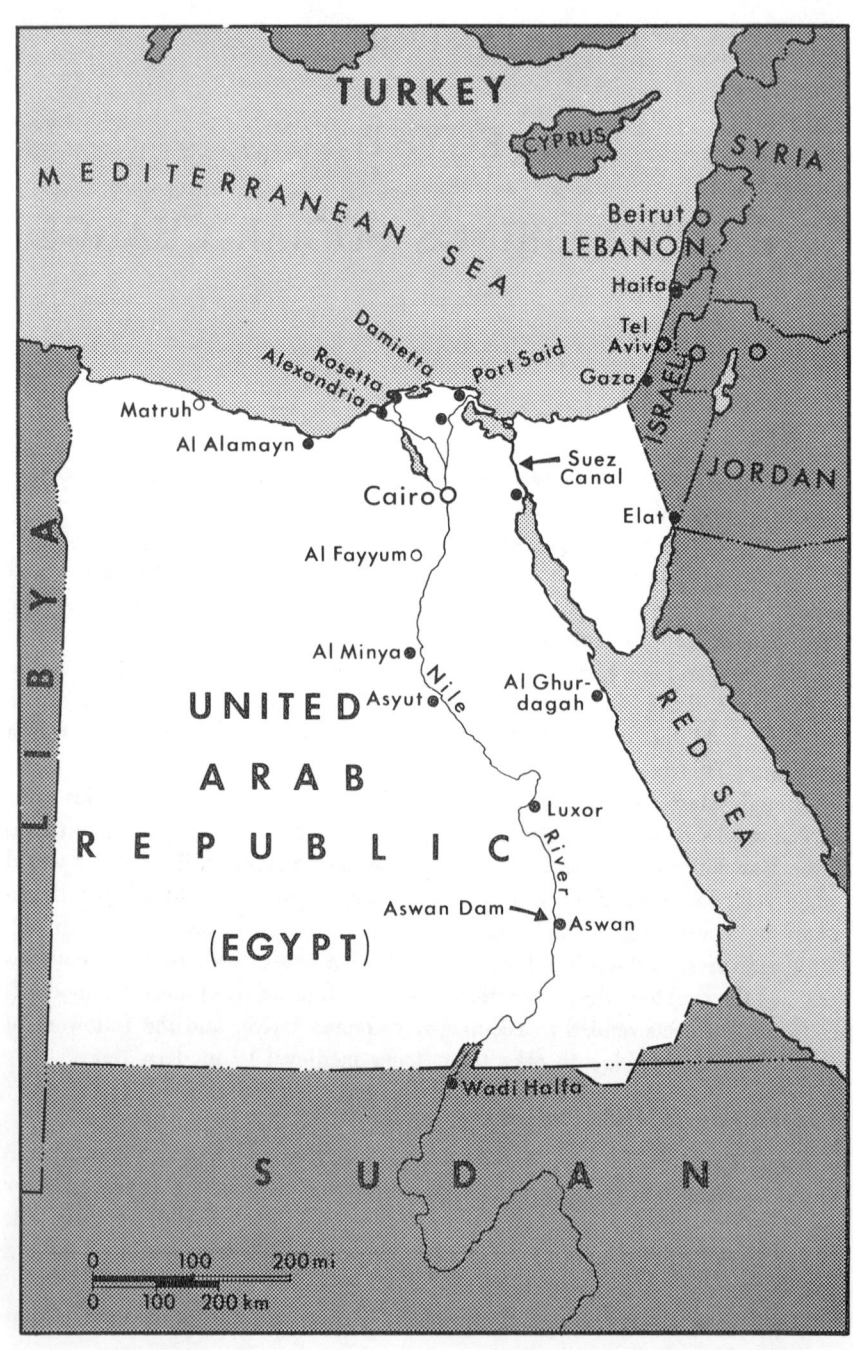

archy comparable to that in the Roman Catholic or Protestant worlds. The Caliph was both the spiritual and temporal head of an Islamic community, but he did not have a religious chain of command down to his individual followers. There were Ulema, or learned men, in each Islamic community who served as the interpreters of Islamic doctrine and law. Since about 1800 A.D., the Ulema are no longer the teachers of Islam, and today remain largely its guardians of tradition.

The Islamic Empire which had given a certain cohesion to Islam came to an end. Egyptians in general, and Nasser in particular, look back on the great days of the Mameluke Empire of the 15th Century as "the Golden Period" when Egypt was the power center of Islam. In spite of efforts by Nasser and others, the Empire has not been revived. In fact, the trend has been in the opposite direction towards more independent nation states.

Because so many of the traders in Egypt were Copts, Greeks, Armenians, and Jews, the Moslem bourgeoisie was weak by European standards. When the old order began to change, these bourgeois elements, which were largely non-Moslem, turned to the British for support after 1800. This was viewed with suspicion by the Egyptian middle and lower classes.

It has been said that the societal revolution which swept Egypt in 1952 was really started by Napoleon when he conquered that country in 1798. After his scientists and experts had scrambled over the ruins and waterways of Egypt, and his soldiers had put an end to Turkish power there, Egypt seemed to roll over from its medieval slumber. Following Bonaparte's visit, Egypt was never the same, for he left a legacy of unrest.

The British and Turks, using Ottoman forces, threw the French out of Egypt in 1801. Then the Ottomans chose one of their Generals, Mohammed Ali, to be Pasha of Cairo and then made him Viceroy of Egypt in 1806. This son-of-a-Macedonian-tobacco-merchant-turned-Pasha ran Egypt as his own personal property, determining even what crops would be sown and in how many acres. Under him there was little enlightenment, but considerable economic change.

Egypt was given another rough shove into the modern world in 1869 by the completion of the "two seas canal" from Port Said to Suez. With it came free trade, open markets, and a great expansion of business, accompanied by wild market speculation. The economic bubble burst in the crash of 1879.

Lord Milner wrote of "the complete dissolution of Egyptian society" during the summer of 1882 when peasants rose against their landlords. Angered and upset by the wave of military dismissals following the financial crash, and by benefits given Circassian and Turkish army officers, Colonel Arabi and other Egyptian officers revolted against the Khedive, who had British backing.

For a while they were successful. The Armenian Prime Minister of Egypt was dismissed, a liberal constitution was granted, a national assembly of notables was called, and two British ultimata were rejected. The British thereupon landed an expeditionary force which defeated the Egyptians, captured Colonel Arabi, and banished him to Ceylon. From the time of his capture Ahmed Arabi was a forgotten man, but in 1881 and 1882, he was the leader, spokesman, and image of an Egypt awakening to demand justice at home and abroad.

It took the British about 10 years to get Egypt back on its feet. They set up an administration that worked with some efficiency, and put finances on a reasonable basis. Most important were the changes made in Egyptian irrigation, including the Delta barrage, the three main canals in lower Egypt, and the first Aswan Dam. After 1899, the British joined the Sudan to Egypt in a condominium, thus assuring Egypt a proper share of the waters of the Nile. Thanks largely to these changes, the output of Egyptian cotton doubled and the establishment of an agricultural bank in 1902 made it possible for the peasants to get loans at reasonable interest. Thus a superficial observer passing through Egypt just before World War I might well have concluded that the country was prosperous and contented.

Broader education, the beginnings of a free press, and somewhat greater distribution of wealth were all beginning to have their effects. A small push would have been enough to change the political and social pattern, but Egypt got a big push in the form of World War I.

That struggle broke the last ties with the Turkish Sultan and began a British protectorate. Many British officers and men were stationed in the country, industry expanded, cotton prices rose sharply, and much new wealth resulted. On top of these changes there fell on Egyptian ears the intriguing ideas about self-determination and independence to be found in President Wilson's Fourteen Points. Furthermore, in November, 1918, the British and French issued a declaration which promised independence to many parts of the Turkish empire, but did not mention Egypt. As a result, a spirit of revolt began to spread.

The Revolt of 1919 and Aftermath

In Egypt in 1919 there appeared an Egyptian with a typical peasant broad face, strong frame, and much good humor, ambition, and eloquence. His name was Sa'd Zaghlul. He had graduated from El Azhar University, had fought in the Arabi revolt in 1882, and had been in the government under the British as Minister of Education.

Believing that the British Protectorate in Egypt was temporary, he led a delegation before the British High Commissioner and asked that Egypt be granted her independence. He spoke for almost all the people of Egypt, but London ordered that the demands be met with firmness. In March of 1919,

Zaghlul and his supporters were deported by the British to the Mediterranean island of Malta.

This was the spark. Up and down the length of the Nile there were riots, demonstrations, strikes, and sabotage. Thousands of students marched in Cairo and five were shot. Smaller towns, and even villages, followed suit, and the revolt became a national movement. But the British declared the movement a Bolshevik plot and moved forcibly when a group of nationalists took over the town of Minieh and set up a government along the lines of a Communist soviet. The rioting was soon put down, but discontent simmered.

At this time, the India leader Gandhi was showing the world the power of passive resistance and non-cooperation. The Egyptians began to copy his techniques. Civil servants staged a strike in March, 1919, and other workers followed suit. The most effective example of non-cooperation was shown in Egyptian relations with a British commission of inquiry headed by Lord Milner. Once the Egyptians concluded that this commission would not do anything constructive, they simply refused to talk to its members. The commission could get no facts on which to write a report. Met everywhere by silence, Lord Milner advised Britain to end the protectorate.

Finally, in February 1922, the British government issued a declaration which recognized the independence of Egypt, subject to reservations over communications, defense, and the status of the Sudan. Sultan Ahmed Fuad became King Fuad I, and the Egyptians elected a chamber of Deputies in which the returned nationalist leader, Zaghlul, and his Wafdist followers received a tremendous majority. As a result, every aspect of Egyptian life was dominated by the Wafd party, which became the political expression of the entire people. In the Wafd, Egyptian leaders found a vehicle to power. Both the local landowners and the imperialist British recognized its usefulness. Despite its corruption and decadence, the Wafd proved to be an invaluable political asset to the Egyptian nation for over a generation.

Grievances

With the coming of World War II, Egypt at first remained non-belligerent. Then, as opinion in Egypt moved toward the Axis, the hard-oppressed British sent a tank crashing through the gates of the palace to force Farouk, King Fuad's son, to come out on the side of the Allies. Neither the King nor the people of Egypt ever forgot this move, and that day, February 4, 1942, a number of officers in the Egyptian army resigned. Among them was Mohammed Naguib, of whom more was to be heard later.

In addition to straining relations with the British, World War II pushed the economic life of Egypt into a spiral of war profits. The number of Egyptian millionaires rose from 50 to 300. Cotton planters, owners of sugar refineries, and hotel owners saw their profits double or triple each year. The price index also tripled, while wages and farmers' profits increased only slightly. Early in 1942 a hungry mob attacked wheat shipments in Cairo.

After the war boom, many industries closed down and at least 300,000 unemployed roamed the streets of Cairo. The continued presence of large numbers of Allied troops, including some Americans, who lived far better than most Egyptians, added to the discontent.

On top of all of these grievances came anger against the new state of Israel which was born in May, 1948. Anti-Jewish feeling developed and the Egyptian police began a wave of arrests and beatings. The Egyptian Communist movement was smashed and the Moslem Brotherhood was hit hard. The feeling spread that King Farouk, his close followers, and many politicians were using the police to hold down resentment against graft, corruption, and decay in the palace and government.

Anyone studying Egypt at that time could not fail to note that change was overdue. The King had great power, wealth, and little social consciousness. The "power elite" included a few industrialists, but for the most part consisted of large landholders, 10,000 of whom owned 37% of the available land, and some 200 of whom had average holdings of 2,600 acres.

Many of them, though they took their wealth from the valley of the Nile, had little use for Egyptian culture, and poured out their gains in "conspicuous consumption" in Cairo, Istanbul, or Paris. These landowners spent little time on their holdings, but were happy to pocket the excessive profits wrung from the soil and from the backs of the poor *fellahin*. These peasants, who comprised more than 70% of the population, lived in mud-brick villages and most of them owned less than half an acre. Even by Near Eastern standards, their living conditions were poor.

There was virtually no movement in or out of the ranks of the fellahin, or of the great landowners, but able men could move up in the middle class. Careers in religion or the army provided the best avenues for social advancement, along with some openings for teachers.

The Egyptians were about 90% Moslem with the rest belonging principally to the Coptic branch of Christianity. Since the government maintained the mosques and was responsible for the appointment and payment of preachers and other Islamic officials, it is not surprising that few of the religious elements in Islam were active in liberal politics at that time.

The King not only had much executive authority, but also had unusual legislative power over the Chamber of Deputies and the Senate. According to the Constitution of 1923, the cabinet was responsible to the parliament, but actually it had to answer to the King, who appointed its members. Even the Prime Minister was controlled by the King, who appointed him, and could dismiss him for his own reasons or to satisfy the great landowners.

With the coming of the 1950's, the chief political party was still the Wafd, which had gained a majority in almost every election during the preceding thirty years. The King, however, frequently formed his cabinet from persons who were not members of the Wafd or from members whom he knew would do his bidding. From an all-powerful and truly representative party of the people of Egypt, the Wafd had degenerated by 1952 into a political machine of patronage.

In opposition to the Wafd was the Moslim Brotherhood which was strongly anti-western and anti-modern, and whose fundamentalist teaching appealed to illiterate peasants and the semi-literate proletariat. The Brotherhood had been outlawed in 1949 after a series of assassinations, but it continued to function nevertheless. A growing Young Egyptian Party was also important. Beyond these, the only political force known to most Egyptians was the Communist movement whose 7,000 members were split into factions, with most leaders in jail.

Although Egypt was nominally independent from Great Britain after 1922, British business interests were important and British military forces were prominent throughout the country until 1947 when they were confined to the canal zone. The 1936 Anglo-Egyptian treaty, which gave the British the right to occupy the Sudan as well as the canal zone, was unilaterally abrogated by Egypt in 1951. When the British refused to leave the canal zone or the Sudan, anti-British demonstrations broke out in several major cities.

Because most of the people of Egypt were disturbed by the danger which they thought Israel represented, the government adopted a strong pan-Arab policy. This led to a worsening of relations with Great Britain and the United States and to Egypt's making overtures to various communist countries.

After World War I, the British were able to reduce the Egyptian death rate, but they could do nothing about the steady increase in births. Consequently the country developed one of the world's highest ratios of population density to arable land. By the early 1950's there were 20,000,000 people crowded into the 14,000 square miles of land in the Nile Valley, and in a few main cities such as Cairo (population 2,000,000). Added revenue was much needed, but the only real source of wealth was cotton, which constituted nearly 90% of Egypt's exports. Under these circumstances, the peasants and the masses in the cities lived just above the subsistence level. Inflation was so rampant that from 1945 to 1950 the cost of living went up 400%.

After 1950 there were some efforts at reform. Ministers of Social Affairs and Education were appointed and rural social centers were established in some villages. Labor unions were permitted to organize more freely, and a series of promotions were made in the ranks of the military. Then, in a final effort to silence the rising opposition, early in 1952, the King appointed as Prime Minister an honest and popular former Minister of Education who announced that he would "purify" the government.

Unfortunately such elections as were held produced only delegations of malcontents. Elections were followed by demonstrations which grew into riots, usually aimed at foreigners and their holdings. The worst of these outbreaks occurred, January 26, 1952, when mobs, partly organized by terrorists, swept through the streets of Cairo and centered their attacks on hotels, stores, apartments, and other places known or believed to be owned by foreigners. Twenty-six persons were killed that day, many hundreds were wounded, and more than 700 buildings were burned or sacked including the world-famous Shepheard's Hotel.

When the Wafdist government did little to check these riots, the King dismissed it and appointed a series of Prime Ministers who did not have the support of the Wafd or of the people. Thus by the spring of 1952, the people of Egypt had serious grievances, and efforts to improve the situation through the ballot had failed. All that was needed for an explosion was a leader, a movement, and a spark.

The Society of Free Officers

The first two elements were supplied by the appearance on the scene of a vigorous and calculating young army officer named Gamal Abdul Nasser, a popular front man, General Mohammed Naguib, and an organization known as the Free Officers Movement. This group started in 1939 as a secret society inside the army whose goal was to free Egypt from British control. It consisted of a series of small cells whose members used secret signs and who were controlled by a central committee. The society had informal contacts with the Moslim Brotherhood during World War II, and at one time carried on negotiations with the German Army with a view to organizing a revolt against the British. Little came of this beyond the arrest of pro-German members of the society.

Early in 1945, the society was reorganized into two parts, military and civilian. Except for the central committee which ran both of these groups there was little contact between the parts, and the civilian side never became important.

Under Nasser's direction, the reorganized movement had four principal subdivisions, including Economic Affairs, which handled the society's finances; Personnel, which recruited and indoctrinated; Security, which enforced secrecy; and Propaganda, which put out pamphlets and worked through the spoken word. A second reorganization took place in 1950 and the name "Society of Free Officers" was adopted. Nasser, who by now was a 29 year-old major, was elected President of a new executive committee. Although dedicated, most members of the Free Officers Society appear to have been politically naive. They believed that if King Farouk and his unsavory following could be removed from the political arena, Egypt would be "purified" from

EGYPT: THE ARMY BRINGS SOCIAL CHANGE

British neo-colonialism and from exploitation by feudal landlords and unscrupulous industrialists. Nasser himself thought that once the corrupt monarchy and its political supporters had been driven from power, the people of Egypt would rise up and go forward to make Egypt a great, independent, and progressive nation.

Thus, the top activists in the Society, the Revolutionary Command Council, expected to carry out a coup and then hand over the power to a group of "honest patriots". This group would then make the changes Egypt needed for economic progress and social justice, including agrarian reform, more industrialization, changes in the tax structure, and an adjustment of wages and prices.

The first of the two officers who played particularly important roles in the Egyptian Revolution, Mohammed Naguib, was the son of a graduate of the Egyptian Military Academy. He was born in Khartoum in 1901, attended Gordon College in the Sudan and then went on to the Military Academy. In spite of this educational background, he had bitter differences with the old line military command, which contributed to his decision to join the Free Officers Movement in 1949. He had little to do with planning the revolt, but he was given the front role once it was successful.

Behind Naguib was Major Gamal Abdul Nasser, the real head and driving force of the revolution. Born into a middle-class family in upper Egypt in 1918, Nasser graduated in 1939 from the Royal Military College. In addition to service in the field, he taught at the Military College in Cairo. In 1948-49 he served in the Palestine campaign. Disillusioned by the poor state of Egyptian preparedness, he blamed corrupt civilians, particularly the politicians, and the King. He was intelligent, methodical, and a persuasive orator, with a personality which attracted support.

The existence of the Society of Free Officers became quite well known after World War II, but the identity of its members was not disclosed. In contrast to such terrorist organizations as the Moslem Brotherhood and Ahmad Husayn's Socialist Party, the Free Officers did not go in for violence or guerrilla operations. Their goals, however, were paralleled by the Communists and, after January of 1952, by the Wafd Party. The Farouk regime retained little popular support and this five-fold attack by the Socialists, the Brotherhood, the Communists, the Wafd, and the Free Officers began to produce results.

According to the usual pattern followed by the Free Officers, they contacted leaders but never sought wide popular support. They left the task of spreading mass discontent to organizations such as the Moslem Brotherhood. However, being military men themselves, the Free Officers knew well that a coup could not succeed without the support of at least a substantial part of the army, and their propaganda efforts were centered on winning over key officers.

King Farouk

By 1952, King Farouk had become the symbol of what was wrong with Egypt, but this had not always been the case. In his youth, Farouk had been carefully groomed for kingship and taught to meet people "in a royal but friendly way". Unfortunately, however, he was weak and impressionable. When his father died and he had to take over the throne at the age of 18, his character was not firmly developed. Soon he was taking advice from the palace guard, large landowners, rich industrialists, conservative generals, and the most reactionary religious groups. They showed him advantageous loopholes in the constitution. Gradually cabinets became more reactionary, political freedom in Egypt lessened, and even the Wafd Party lost contact with the people.

There had been some improvement in the political climate in 1944, when Ahmad Maher became Prime Minister, but he was assassinated in January, 1945. His two successors continued the liberal trend, even allowing limited street demonstrations. When the popular will showed signs of exploding, the Palace forced the government to put into effect a series of repressive measures including the suppression of various newspapers. A large number of persons were arrested at this time, including not only communists, but many progressive leaders.

An additional source of discontent was the widely-held belief that the King, the Palace Guard, and the Ministers were making fortunes out of the Palestinian War. Eventually the Palace clique and the King himself were held responsible for Egypt's defeat in that struggle.

After this, a wave of terror broke out. The Commandant of the Cairo Police and the Prime Minister were assassinated. The Moslim Brotherhood was blamed; however, the Supreme Guide of the Brotherhood was in turn assassinated, and hundreds of its members were arrested and beaten. General elections were held in January, 1950, as a safety valve for pent-up popular feelings. The corrupted Wafd party was defeated, but the elections were far from honest, and bitterness against the government continued to increase.

After these events, palace domination in political matters became even more open. Farouk appointed high officials without consulting his ministers, he gave titles and decorations to sycophants, and he sidetracked all who opposed him. Next he involved himself in the decisions of the courts and tried to hush up the scandal growing out of the arms shortage at the time of the Palestinian War. He could not, however, suppress the gossip regarding his numerous mistresses, his frequent attendance at nightclubs, and the wild parties which he gave. The people of Egypt are normally quite tolerant about the private

EGYPT: THE ARMY BRINGS SOCIAL CHANGE

lives of their rulers, but they felt that Farouk's actions had passed the bounds of permissable taste.

The spark igniting Egypt in the summer of 1952 was the decision by Farouk to dissolve the Executive Committee of the Officers' Club, a committee on which the Free Officers were heavily represented. General Naguib was President of the Club, a post which he had won earlier in the year through the support of the Free Officers against the King's hand-picked candidate. Thus, Farouk's move against the Committee was really a test of strength between the King and the senior officers of the army. Many of the Free Officers thought he was about to arrest General Naguib and several other leaders of the Club. In these circumstances the Society of Free Officers decided that if they did not move rapidly against Farouk he would move against them. Less than four days were devoted to putting the finishing touches on plans for a military take-over.

About midnight of July 22, accompanied by the troops under their command, the leaders of the Free Officers marched to the general headquarters of the army where a meeting of high officers was in session. Most of them agreed to join the revolt. Throughout the rest of that night and the next morning the Free Officers and their expanded military following took possession of key points in Cairo. These moves were accomplished in a matter of hours and with so little bloodshed that most Cairo inhabitants were unaware that anything out of the ordinary had occurred. At 7:30 the next morning, Naguib broadcast a statement explaining that the coup was necessary to counter corruption in the army, which, he said, was the main cause of their defeat in the Palestinian War.

During the first hours of the coup, Nasser guided the revolution. On July 23, however, he told Naguib that members of the Command Council wanted Naguib to be the new Commander-in-Chief. Naguib accepted and, during the ensuing days, it was he who deployed the forces and directed the military moves necessary to complete the coup.

A new cabinet was picked by the army, and it was headed by Ali Maher. In choosing its members, all persons connected with the royal household and with the ruling palace clique were excluded. The King was forced to accept the new cabinet against his will.

As head of the new government, Ali Maher then presented an ultimatum to King Farouk, which set forth clearly the grievances of the Free Officers, ordered the king to abdicate in favor of his son, and then leave the country.

At about 6:00 a.m. on July 26, King Farouk, in the uniform of a naval commander, left his palace for the last time. Behind him his flag was lowered and he received the last royal salute of 21 guns.

Even though most of his fellow officers objected, General Naguib went on board the royal yacht to say goodbye to the King. It is reported that

Farouk told the General he hoped the Egyptian Army would be properly taken care of, to which Naguib replied, "that it would be, since it was now in honest hands."

After Farouk left the country, a regency Council was established, laws were passed against corruption, and political parties were told to purge themselves. Then the Free Officers sat back and waited for the "better civilian elements" to come forward and modernize Egypt. The Free Officers, however, soon discovered that entrenched office holders do not fade away overnight and vested interests are uninterested in social change which will affect them adversely.

In *The Philosophy of the Revolution*, Gamal Nasser wrote:

> After July 23rd I was shocked by the reality; the vanguard (the military) performed its task; it stormed the walls of the fort of tyranny; it forced Farouk to abdicate and stood by expecting the mass formations to arrive at their ultimate object. It waited and waited. Endless crowds showed up, but how different is the reality from the vision! .... The holy march towards the great goal was interrupted. A dismal picture, horrible and threatening, then presented itself. I felt my heart charged with sorrow and dripping with bitterness. The mission of the vanguard had not ended. In fact it was just beginning at that very hour.

A Two-Stage Revolution

The years after 1952 were eventful ones in Egypt. Friction developed among the Free Officers, Naguib was pushed aside, and Nasser became Prime Minister and undisputed ruler of Egypt. A "deal" was made with Czechoslovakia and Russia involving the acquisition of substantial arms. The last British troops left the canal zone, and Egypt moved into a position of "positive neutrality". A great deal of wealth was expended on the building of a High Dam at Aswan with Russian assistance. Following Nasser's announcement in July, 1956 that he was nationalizing the Suez Canal, a crisis with international implications occurred.

From the point of view of social revolution, however, it would seem more pertinent to note that the early years of the revolution in Egypt showed two stages in the economic and political thinking of its leaders. During the first four years, the economic moves of the new government, although they seemed extreme to persons affected, were relatively orthodox efforts to stabilize the economy, expand production, and to improve social welfare. Foreign capital, for instance, was allowed to acquire a majority control of companies operating in Egypt and profits could be transferred abroad with relative ease. New companies which were judged to promote the economic development of the nation were encouraged and freed of taxes for seven years. New mining and petroleum concessions were granted to foreigners as well as Egyptians.

From 1956 the new rulers of Egypt were pushed by both internal and external circumstances into less orthodox actions from the western point of view. These included closer control of business, nationalization or sequestration of foreign and domestic property, intensified industrialization, and higher taxes on larger incomes. Particularly, since 1961, there were cooler relations with the west and wider use in speeches and state documents of Socialist, Marxist, and class-conflict phraseology.

When the Free Officers came to power, the government of Egypt was taking only about 20% of the national income, the State's role was not important in the economy outside of railroads and irrigation, taxes were low, and foreigners played an active part in the economic life of the country. By 1962, however, although it lacked the party structure to be found in communist states, Egypt had become a state-controlled society. State ownership was widespread in industry, transport, finance, and foreign trade, while the government budget accounted for 60% of the gross national product. Foreign ownership of the means of production was practically eliminated and the number of foreigners working in Egypt was much reduced.

Looking at the Egyptian Revolution in retrospect, one finds considerable progress balanced by serious defects. The "humiliation" of the Egyptian people, which General Naguib claimed as the cause of the seizure of power, no longer exists. The very great inequalities of wealth have been reduced by limits on the extent of land ownership, more social services, the fixing of salaries, and by higher taxes on the wealthy. In 1949, the income tax ceiling was 50% on earnings of 100,000 Egyptian pounds and above. In 1952, the figure was raised to 80% on earnings above 50,000 pounds, and by 1961, it was again increased, this time to 90% on incomes above 10,000 pounds.

Foreign troops have left Egyptian soil, the Suez Canal Company has been nationalized, work is well advanced on the High Dam at Aswan, education is much expanded, and opportunities for advancement within the society are broadened.

As is the case in all regulated societies, however, political and intellectual freedom has been much reduced, politics are now state-guided, while the press and the radio are state-controlled. Furthermore, the series of spy trials, arrests, prison sentences, and some executions and expulsions from the country have affected many Egyptians as well as foreigners, giving them a feeling of insecurity and fear. The bold and optimistic pronouncements of the new government have raised the expectations of the masses on the one hand, while various economic realities, including the "need" for armaments and, above all, the rapid increase in the Egyptian population, have resulted in a negligible increase in the national standard of living.

To achieve the progress that has been made, Egypt was forced to mortgage her economic future largely to the communist bloc, private initiative has been discouraged, and the rapid nationalization has resulted in a loss of efficiency.

Nasser Seeks A Middle Way

The result of Egypt's policy has been a series of swings from west to east and then back again, as Nasser and his advisers tried to find a "middle way". Like several other successful revolutionary groups since World War II, the new rulers of Egypt did not start with a clear-cut political or economic blueprint, but had to work their way step by step towards their goals. In Nasser's case these goals are called "Arab Socialism", a pattern based on nationalism and socialism blended to form a cooperative society in which the state acts as trustee for the people until they are ready to govern for themselves. In the search for an economy that is neither capitalist nor communist Nasser felt that national planning would provide the answer internally, coupled with a policy of international non-alignment. As it has evolved, Arab Socialism has looked for ideas in all parts of the world including Khrushchev's Russia, Mao's China, Tito's Yugoslavia, Gandhi's India, and Sukarno's Indonesia, plus certain aspects of politico-economic development in the west.

Because of its history, the Arab world is not particularly disturbed by the fusion of state and church, and the sanctity of private property is weaker there than in the west. The Moslems, like many Europeans, are not troubled by the state having an extensive role in education. Thus a pattern of government which seems socialistic and totalitarian troubles the people of Egypt far less than would be the case in the United States.

Internally, however, the revolution has, in general, continued to have at least the acquiescence of the Egyptian masses. Nasser knows he cannot swing too far either to the right or to the left, but he also knows his people and how far he can push them. In taking power with a grievance but not a program, hammering out a political-economic pattern which suits his people, and keeping a balance between capitalism and communism in the process, Nasser is typical of a group of revolutionary leaders who have assumed power in the emerging countries since World War II. Thus developments in Egypt are watched closely everywhere as an example of a new pattern for societal revolution.

CHAPTER IV

CUBA: A REVOLUTION BETRAYED

OF the insurgencies since World War II, few are more dramatic and more important to the United States than Castro's seizure of Cuba, an island only 90 miles from Key West and 220 miles from Miami. Cuba was the "brightest jewel" in the Spanish colonial crown and control of the island, which began with Columbus, lasted long after most other countries in Latin America had become independent. The Cubans were far from happy with Spanish rule. From 1848, they made a series of violent efforts to obtain freedom. One of these began in 1895 and was still in progress in 1898—a bloody stalemate which had exhausted both the Spaniards and the Cuban rebels. The United States was moving toward involvement when the U.S. battleship Maine blew up "mysteriously" in Havana harbor. This development acted as a catalyst in encouraging the United States to declare war. Defeat of the Spaniards in Cuba took four months.

The island was extremely backward, with almost no transport, and such industry as existed was at a standstill. U. S. military occupation conferred many benefits on the island, ranging from better roads and drinking water to a real improvement in public health and education. It took four years to get the economy moving and to lay the basis for a broader school system. An important development of that period was the drafting of the country's first constitution by a convention of eminent jurists. That document included a section known as the Platt Amendment, which gave the United States the right to intervene in Cuban affairs if necessary to keep law and order on the island, or to insure Cuban independence. The amendment, which also enabled the U.S. to lease naval bases, was accepted reluctantly by most Cubans.

Castro's Early Days

In 1924, a Cuban lawyer named Gerardo Machado was elected President and prolonged his term in 1928 by a constitutional amendment. The next

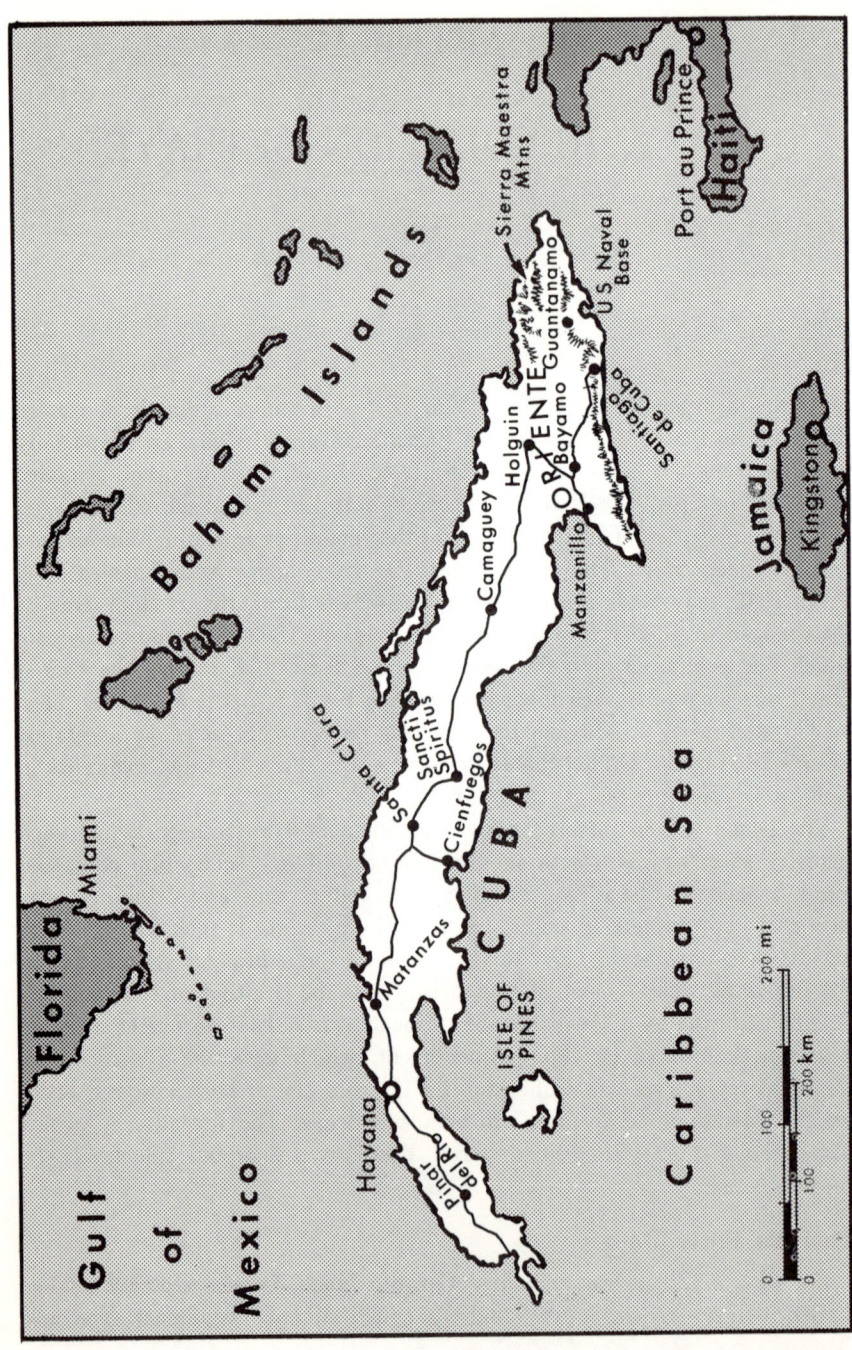

years saw worldwide economic depression, including a catastrophic drop in the price of sugar. This led to so much disorder in Cuba that President Machado resigned in 1933 and was succeeded by a weak caretaker government. Then, September 5, 1933, five sergeants headed by Fulgencio Batista carried out a successful coup. A series of presidents followed over the next six years, some good and some not so good, but all held office at the pleasure of Batista.

In line with the growing popular demand, Batista allowed a convention to be held in 1940 which produced an elaborate national constitution. It included such progressive ideas as nationalization of public utilities, limitations on the amount of land which foreigners could own, and universal suffrage with the secret ballot for all Cubans.

Batista ran for president under this constitution, was elected, and served from 1940 to 1944. He then picked a successor who, rather surprisingly, was beaten by Grau San Martin, a popular professor and the idol of many of the Cuban people. In contrast to most defeated Latin American dictators, Batista bowed to the election results and left Cuba peacefully. After serving four years, San Martin was defeated in 1948. These regimes included many able and devoted Cubans and were reasonably democratic by standards of that time; nevertheless, they were also marred by political gangsterism and corruption. Financial excesses finally aroused the more educated Cubans to the need of political change, and new parties and leaders appeared.

One of these new leaders, and a graduate of the University of Havana, was Fidel Castro. Born in 1926 to the family of a moderately wealthy landowner in the Province of Oriente, Castro attended two Jesuit secondary schools, where he found that his interest lay in politics. At the University of Havana, Castro gave long speeches to his fellow students, or to anyone else who would listen. He held various offices in undergraduate and graduate organizations. While still at the University, he showed his talent for convincing forcefully those whom he could not sway by oratory; he was known to carry a pistol, and on several occasions presided at student meetings flanked by henchmen with machine guns.

Castro's revolutionary zeal came to the surface when, from the university, he helped plan an invasion to rid the Dominican Republic of its dictator, Gen. Rafael Trujillo. Cuban government sources found out about the movement, and the proposed expedition was stopped before it was underway.

A more controversial incident during Castro's undergraduate years occurred when he was in Colombia in April of 1948. This was the time of the bloody riots which followed the death of Jorge Eliecer Gaitan, a popular leader of the Liberal Party. There are those who cite Castro's presence during the violent days of the "Bogotazo" as showing that Castro was a communist even at that date and the uprising was part of a carefully-laid communist plot. The Communists participated in the riots to be sure, but there was no firm evidence that they organized the uprising or that they profited much from it.

After graduation from the University of Havana, Castro was trained as a lawyer. However, he did little towards advancing this side of his career; rather, he became more deeply involved in revolutionary politics. He joined the Ortodoxo Party, under the leadership of Senator Chibas, whose platform was opposition to the corruption of President Grau San Martin. Chibas was notable for his dramatic radio addresses, but he overdid this role one day, in 1951, and committed suicide while he was on the air.

Castro took advantage of this opening and was soon the party's leader in Havana. National elections were scheduled to take place in 1952, and Castro had hopes of winning a place in the new government.

Batista and His Opposition

By then, Cuba had quite accurate public opinion polls. Shortly before the elections, these polls indicated that Fulgencio Batista, who had returned to Cuba, did not have a chance of winning and would, in fact, come out a poor third. This probability was more than his concept of democracy, or his ambition, could take. On March 10, 1952, he carried out a well-executed military coup in which only two men were killed. The army rallied behind their old comrade Batista, and the Cuban people seemed undisturbed.

In 1934 the United States had signed a new treaty with Cuba, which had the effect of abrogating the Platt Amendment. Later treaty commitments reaffirmed U.S. policy not to intervene in the internal affairs of any Latin American country. Thus, when the Cuban people accepted Batista's coup with calmness, the United States went along with them and recognized his government.

As a result of Batista's illegal return to power in 1952, a series of opposition groups formed. One of these was led by Fidel Castro, who made one of his rare appearances as a lawyer to plead before the Supreme Court of Cuba that the Batista regime was unconstitutional and its acts illegal. In view of the nature of the new Batista government, it was not surprising that Castro's plea was rejected.

The young revolutionary, now 26 years old, then decided to capitalize on the experience he had gained working against the Trujillo dictatorship. He organized about 150 followers into an attack group, some of whom had been with him at the University and all of whom felt frustrated under the Batista regime. Under Castro's direction, they worked out a plan to take the military headquarters in the important seaport of Santiago de Cuba. From it they planned to march on Havana, after occupying the Province of Oriente, which was believed to be anti-Batista, and ready to rise against him.

While Castro master-minded the operation from a command post two blocks away, on July 26, 1953, his followers attacked the military clinic and some of the outlying sleeping quarters. They then tried to enter the central barracks. The attack failed, casualties were high on both sides, and Castro fled to the protection of the Catholic Archbishop of Santiago, who handed him over to an army court. Thanks to the intervention of the Archbishop, Castro's life was saved, and he got off with a sentence of 20 years in prison on the Isle of Pines. A year later Batista decreed an amnesty for all political prisoners, and Castro became free again to carry on his plotting.

It is unclear how much Batista really tried to make his regime legal. In any case, Grau San Martin agreed to run against Batista in 1954, but his political followers were so threatened and harassed that he dropped out of the running seven days before the election. With no opposition at all, Batista won easily, making him seem more of a dictator than ever.

The early months of 1956 saw an effort by a number of respected Cubans to find a constitutional way out of the dictatorship. Its failure probably marked the point of no return for democracy in Cuba.

A serious effort to get rid of Batista was made by the army in April, 1956. It might have succeeded, but Batista's informers learned of the plot the day before the coup was scheduled. Its organizers, all of them old friends of the dictator, were promptly put in jail.

A year later, in September, 1957, the Cuban Navy decided to try another anti-Batista coup. Because of security leaks, the Admirals decided to call it off at the last minute, but the naval unit at Cienfuegos, a town on the south coast of Cuba, did not get the word and revolted on schedule. After two days of bloody fighting, Batista had the situation under control.

Not to be outdone, the officers of the Cuban Air Force secretly held meetings at about this time and tried to organize several conspiracies of their own. Lacking support from the other services, nothing came of these plots. Batista, however, learned what his airmen were thinking and purged the Air Force just as he had purged the Army and the Navy. It meant that the abler and more popular officers in all three services were jailed, retired, or otherwise removed from power. These developments were topped by an arms embargo from the United States and were severe blows to the morale and efficiency of the military forces of Cuba. Later, when they were called upon to oppose Castro, their fighting ability was far below normal.

In addition to opposition from the military, various civilian groups also wanted to have Batista out of the way. It has been estimated that by 1957 some three-fourths of the Cuban people felt he had been in office too long. Normally, labor would have been a center of such opposition, but Batista had made a series of deals under which the unions obtained many of the things they wanted in exchange for staying neutral towards the Batista regime. As a result, demonstrations, strikes, and riots, which could have been expected from hostile labor groups, did not occur.

The students, however, were in no sense neutral, and the University of Havana became a center of anti-Batista feeling. With the Army, Navy, and Air Force purged, and labor tamed, Batista feared the students more than any other group on the island. They demonstrated, they rioted, and they carried out acts of assassination and terror. To hold them down and to check other elements of the opposition as well, Batista's police and secret service became increasingly more aggressive and brutal. Hundreds of homes were raided, scores of arrests were made, and many of the persons who disappeared in the night were never seen again. Furthermore, those who did leave or escape from Batista's prisons were sometimes so beaten or tortured that they were crippled for life. The growing "government terror" in Cuba became one of the chief grievances held by the people against their dictator, and the lengthening list of martyrs gave the anti-Batista forces some of their strongest ammunition.

Castro Returns

After he had been amnestied from prison in 1954, Castro went into voluntary exile in the United States. His presence stirred considerable interest among groups working against Batista in Miami and in New York, but the only visible result was the raising of some money and endless "paper conspiracies". Castro loved talk, but he was also a man of action who decided that he could not get results from a beach in Florida.

Before long, therefore, with some of his closest friends and supporters, he went to Mexico where they rented a deserted plantation and began recruiting followers. They were trained in guerrilla warfare by a man called General Bayo, a Cuban Communist who had previously fought on the Republican side in the Spanish Civil War.

While Castro's forces were training in Mexico, those of his supporters who had remained in Cuba formed the "26th of July Movement", which became part of a more general resistance. The name was taken from the date of that first unsuccessful attack on the Santiago military headquarters in 1953.

Anti-government progress in Cuba proper was slow and difficult because of Batista's extensive network of informers. However, little by little, cells were activated either by Castro's followers, or by other opponents of Batista, among students, the labor unions, the bureaucracy, and even in the Cuban military itself. This overall apparatus for rebellion became known as "the Civic Movement of Resistance."

By the fall of 1956, Castro's force of guerrillas had completed their training in Mexico, and his organization in Cuba had reached what he thought was an adequate state of readiness. The striking force had acquired a small yacht called the "Granma", and this unseaworthy craft sailed in November, 1956, with 82 men, one of whom was lost overboard on the trip.

The plans called for an uprising in Cuba on the last day of November, which did occur on a small scale. However, it was not until two days later that the "Granma" reached the south coast of Cuba. She had been spotted on the way by Batista's Air Force, which was probably tipped off by traitors within the Castro movement. As a result, government planes strafed the yacht, and only thirteen of the party struggled ashore through a mangrove swamp to the comparative safety of the Sierra Maestra mountains. Havana radio announced that all the attackers, including the leader, had been captured or killed.

For a month, Castro and the other survivors wandered about some of the roughest terrain in Cuba. Most people they met there were fugitives from justice, and the law of the mountain was "live and let live". Gradually, the group gained the confidence of the mountaineers and, since Castro had plenty of money, their food and clothing situation was soon solved.

The expedition had left Mexico well-armed, but most of the weapons had been lost during the disastrous voyage and landing, forcing Castro's men to build up their armament according to guerrilla pattern. This meant they bought what they could, stole what they could not buy, and by surprising small patrols of isolated police stations, picked up enough rifles, machine guns, and ammunition to develop limited fire-power. As time passed and it became clear that they had not been wiped out, but were living in the mountains and growing strong, recruits began to join them. These included outlaws from the hills, police or soldiers who were captured or deserted to them, embittered peasants from nearby farms, and intellectuals and liberals who came from the cities. In public, the communists at this time referred to Castro and his band as "adventurers".

After they had been in the Sierras for a year, the Castro forces were divided, and brother Raul went east to another range of rugged mountains, putting out the word that he was taking 5,000 men with him. By then a myth had grown up about Castro and his "large band of rebels", a myth pushed by Castro's followers, but the number with Raul was certainly nearer 500 than 5,000.

The image of the "freedom-loving rebels" received support from many different quarters. One of America's most distinguished correspondents, Herbert Matthews of the *New York Times,* was able to visit Castro's hideaway in February of 1957. When he came out, Matthews published several articles which read in part as follows:

> At last one gets the feeling that the best elements of Cuban life, the unspoiled youth, the honest businessman, the politician of integrity, and the patriotic army officer are getting together to assume power. . . . Communism has little to do with the opposition to the regime. There is (in Cuba) a well-trained, hard core of Communists that are doing as much as they can and that naturally bolster all opposition elements, but there is no Communism to speak of in Fidel's 26th of July Movement.

This is what people in Cuba and throughout the liberal world wanted to hear about Castro, and it became his image for several years thereafter.

At the time of Castro's landing in Cuba, Batista had announced that the whole expedition had been wiped out. When this proved wrong, the dictator said that the Sierra Maestra Mountains were ringed by loyal police posts and that Castro and his men would soon be starved into submission. This was equally untrue, and, before long, porters carrying supplies on their backs, mule trains, and even truckloads of goods were moving through the "blockade" to Castro's outposts in the lower foothills.

As far as is known, only one plane brought in supplies from the outside, coming from Costa Rica early in 1958. It crashed when making a landing attempt, but the supplies were rescued. Except for a few parachute drops, the idea of supplying the rebels by air was given up in favor of more reliable ground methods.

Meanwhile, Castro's 26th of July Movement was growing in the cities, particularly among liberals and student groups. On March 12, 1957, a suicide squad of students, known as the "Directorio Revolucionario", broke into Batista's palace and came within an ace of killing or capturing the dictator. The scheme had been worked out in such great detail that the attackers had copied plans of the palace to show where Batista could be found. By the irony of fate, however, when the copies of the palace plan were being run off, the prints came out in reverse. Thus the students, after charging through the gunfire of the palace guards, turned right instead of left and Batista escaped.

Almost all of the Directorio students were killed in this attempt or shot down in cold blood immediately afterwards. A few survivors later joined Castro's guerrillas in the mountains. After this affair, bitterness against the dictator rose to new heights.

By coincidence, the American Ambassador and a group of American businessmen were the first non-Cubans to be admitted to the palace after the attack. The purpose of the call involved rates to be charged by the Cuban telephone company. Word of the visit spread, and it increased the feeling in Cuba that the United States was pro-Batista.

As time passed, the rebel areas expanded, and, in addition to military units, an organization developed which had its own departments, police, schools, hospitals, and postal service. Events were going so badly for Batista that, by July, 1958, he felt that he had to make an all-out effort to wipe out Castro and his guerrillas. The plan was to have one reinforced batallion move in from the north, while another landed on the steep southern coast, thus catching Castro in a pincer. Guerrilla strategy dictates that rebels do not stand up against superior forces; so Castro and his men fell back, ridge by ridge, until there was less then two miles left at the top of the mountains between the two battalions. Just as it appeared the guerrillas would be wiped out, supplies stopped reaching the force which had come up the southern side of the mountain from the sea. Castro's men surrounded them, and they surrendered. When the government troops coming from the north found that "Castro's back door was open", they turned around. It was a close call for the rebels, but it strengthened the myth that Castro could not be beaten. After this, Batista never again seriously tried to smash Castro's mountain base.

The technical reason for the failure of the joint expedition is probably unimportant, but it shows the weak state of Batista's forces and morale by that time. From then on the dictator was on the defensive, and Castro began to move down through the foothills and out onto the Cuban plains.

Less than two months after the government forces had left the mountains, Castro sent two columns up the island to cut the central Cuban highway and the main railroad, which came together in the town of Santa Clara. An idea of how small Fidel's forces really were can be gained from the fact that one column under the strategist Che Guevara consisted of 120 men, while the other under Camilo Cienfuegos had 119.

The leader of Camilo's rear-guard made the mistake of tangling with one of the few local commanders who was willing to fight and he lost 24 men, a fifth of his force. Books written later by Castro's followers attribute the success of this first northern thrust to their great skill as guerrillas and to their high morale. These were factors, but another important factor was money. Garrison after garrison along the way let them pass unopposed, either because the commanders were pro-Castro, or because they liked the look of his coin. Later evidence showed how lavishly the guerrillas distributed gold; the commander of one post received $200,000 to let the guerrillas through.

The money even influenced the behavior and the loyalty of the government reinforcements sent out from Havana. Sometimes they surrendered immediately, sometimes they took their gold and melted away. In the case of the town of Sagua la Grande, the garrison of government troops held off a detachment of over 300 guerrillas under the command of Fidel's brother, Raul. Rebel forces were suffering heavy casualties, and the picture looked black for them when bombing planes of the Cuban Air Force appeared overhead. Their bombs, however, landed not on Castro's few guerrillas but inside the town, and Raul scored one of his most striking victories. It is interesting to speculate whether the pilots were poor marksmen or pro-Castro.

Thanks to such incidents, the Castro forces were able to cut Cuba in two and to close in on the town of Santa Clara in the heart of the island. By now, Batista could not send supplies or reinforcements up and down Cuba, while Castro controlled the three eastern provinces. The town of Santa Clara, the key to central Cuba, finally fell to him on the last day of 1958.

When word of this event reached Batista, he realized that the end had come. It was his custom to hold a New Year's Eve dinner for his close friends at the Presidential Palace. That night the gathering was held as usual, but when the time came for Batista to make his after-dinner speech, to everyone's amazement, he announced that he was leaving the island at once. There was a stampede to the airport as three plane loads of Batista's followers flew out with him and his family before dawn.

On New Year's Day, 1959, Castro was master of Cuba. His underground supporters in the 26th of July Movement took over Havana and other main towns, while Fidel himself moved slowly up the island from Santiago to Havana, accompanied by his victorious guerrillas and greeted by crowds that went wild at the sight of the liberator. The people of Cuba had deep and real grievances and almost all of them believed that Castro was the man to cure them.

The New Cuban Government

The revolutionaries soon formed their first cabinet, a coalition of the leaders of the 26th of July Movement, plus some other opponents of Batista. Jose Miro, former head of the Havana Bar Association, became Prime Minister. Once in power, the new regime set out to punish those responsible for Batista's reign of terror and to clean out corrupt elements in the government. Military courts were established and at their direction over 600 people were executed during the first quarter of 1959.

During these three months, thousands of government workers, charged with corruption, were cut from the public payroll. Other early and worthwhile reforms included a reorganization of the tax structure, modernization of the social security system, and the streamlining of various retirement funds. It was also decreed that future proceeds of the national lottery be used for low-cost housing. Most of these changes were constructive and Castro's popularity continued. From this base he proceeded step by step to make Cuba into a totalitarian state.

Even after he had taken over Havana, Castro did not talk about communism. He continued to emphasize that he would solve the grievances of the Cuban people by democratic means.

Slowly but steadily he took care to strengthen his position and to make sure that the numerous non-communist elements in the July 26th Movement were pushed aside. Persons favorable to him and to communism were given key positions. These included members of town councils, city governments, regional leaders, and the cabinet itself. The mass of the members of the July 26th Movement were not communists, for that movement was a united front of all who opposed Batista. As time passed, however, Castro followed the accepted communist pattern of cutting off the top limbs of the coalition which had brought him power.

At first when communist leaders began replacing well-known but moderate figures in the 26th of July Movement, Castro blamed his brother Raul or Che Guevara, his chief leftist advisers. By the beginning of 1960 it became clear that although Raul and Che may have been the hatchetmen, they were acting under Fidel's orders in pushing the communization of the movement.

During his exile and guerrilla days, Castro had frequently promised that when he came to power he would restore the rights of Cuba's political parties. When he took over control of the country, action was put off time and again, and the old parties languished except for the PSP, which was the Communist vehicle. In July, 1961, all Cuban political parties were combined into a United Party of the Socialist Revolution, which Castro supporters dominated. Faced with this development some leaders went into exile, while the rest reluctantly went along with the "Maximum Leader".

In this process another group, the regular military, had the ground cut out from under them. The military units were in part "dissolved" when Castro came to power, while his Peoples Militia (the rebel army and former guerrillas) was given new armament, largely Russian and Czech. Before long this militia had become more powerful than the regulars.

Castro Becomes the Law

In order to move further towards complete control of Cuba, Castro next set out to dominate the judges and lawyers. Cuba had developed a modern legal system during the previous fifty years and had educated an outstanding group of jurists. These men had been most unhappy about Batista's regime and soon objected also to the arbitrary acts of Castro and his followers. As early as May, 1959, Castro reportedly told a respected Cuban jurist, Dr. E. R. Alvarez: "We need not violate the laws because we ourselves make the laws."

Before he had been in power for a month, Castro had begun by setting up a series of revolutionary tribunals reminiscent of those established in France during the terror and in Russia after the Communist Revolution. These courts were given power to judge, condemn, and execute "the enemies of the people", and they did so with little regard for normal legal processes. In February, 1959, Castro had enacted a fundamental law which centered power in the judicial fields in the hands of the Executive, namely himself. He thereupon took most of the remaining powers from the regular judges and gave them to the revolutionary tribunals.

Then, in May, 1959, Castro put across an agrarian law which expropriated the properties of the many larger landowners without due process of law. In early 1960 an urban reform law was "passed" which overrode the legal rights of city property owners. Other legislation prescribed the death penalty for almost anything opposed to the pattern of the revolution, including the "damaging of the public treasure", and the right of *habeas corpus*, a right for which the western world had struggled for centuries, was ended.

Obviously, many judges and other legal leaders opposed these unconstitutional moves and set out to break or bypass them. Those who did not go along with his way of thinking were attacked in the press, were shadowed by the secret police, were arrested without proper charge, and, in extreme cases, were shot. This meant the liquidation of some important Cubans. As a result, about 400 members of the Cuban judiciary, many of them progressives, are now in exile, in prison, or dead.

Cuba was and is basically Roman Catholic. However, the Church had strong class connotations and was weak in labor and peasant circles. Many of the hierarchy were thus conservative, but a considerable number of Cuban Catholics were forward-looking and ready to support political, economic, and social progress. They, therefore, disagreed sharply with Batista and welcomed Castro as a man who could lead Cuba forward. But soon some Catholics began to doubt Castro's sincerity and to worry about his ties with communism. They realized that Castro was aware of the influence the Church had on the people of Cuba and they saw that he and his followers were out to curb it. Outspoken bishops or priests were attacked by Castro in his long speeches, in the controlled press, or by extremist members of their congregations. Some of the clerics were threatened and jailed.

In the first three years under Castro almost half of the Roman Catholic clergy of Cuba were pushed aside or silenced, and many non-Cuban priests were forced into exile. The Castro regime spread the word that the future of Cuba lay in breaking loose from the Catholic and other churches and putting faith instead in "political, economic, and cultural revolutionary progress".

These moves naturally aroused opposition, which was led by the Cuban press and radio. Although Castro on his way to power had repeatedly guaranteed that the freedom of the press would be maintained, he now moved to stifle it. If an editor wrote against him, he was called in and lectured on the error of his ways. If the man persisted, strikes broke out in his newspaper plant. If this warning was not enough, advertising withered away. The real tip-off came when a group of Castro supporters held a mock funeral solemnly carrying an open coffin through the streets containing a copy of the rebellious paper. If all this did not bring the publication into line, pro-Castro mobs would wreck the plant. Furthermore, owners, publishers, editors, and important writers found themselves hounded by the police, their bank accounts closed, and their actions constantly attacked in the pro-Castro press. Such persons were likely to be attacked by "armed robbers" who beat them while the police stood idly by. Thus, one by one, Cuba's newspapers and magazines were forced to shut down while the people running them ended up in jail or in exile. By the middle of 1960 there was no written or radio criticism of Castro in Cuba.

Castro then moved against labor, which had been one of his early supports. Labor had shown great independence in its policies and elections during Castro's early days. Top ranks of the labor unions were penetrated and tricky elections gave communists key posts on the reorganized executive committee of the all-important Confederation of Workers of Cuba. A purge committee was established in the Confederation, supposedly to get rid of pro-Batista elements, but actually to drive out enemies of communism. Leaders in a series of unions ranging from maritime to construction workers were then arbitrarily dismissed. The Ministry of Labor was reorganized and given power to "intervene" in any labor dispute. Next, it was decreed that the only way a worker could gain employment was through the employment service of the government itself, an agency dominated by communists. Even the right to strike was "temporarily" ended. All of this resulted in continuing low wages and higher work "norms", both supposedly in the interests of the state.

On his way to power Castro talked frequently about encouraging legitimate business enterprise. But in mid-1960 the Cuban government took over one British- and two U.S.-owned oil refineries when the companies refused a request that they refine a quantity of Soviet crude oil. Soon it was announced that all United States-owned property in Cuba would be expropriated, a total investment of about $1,000,000,000. This involved not only the property of oil and sugar companies but investments in utilities, transports, hotels, and a number of small enterprises. These actions were to a large extent triggered by the U.S. decision to suspend the balance of the Cuban sugar quota. Informed observers felt that Castro welcomed these decisions as facilitating his socialist and pro-Soviet plans.

Next Castro's followers moved against rich Cubans, accusing them of being enemies of the revolution and made it so difficult for them to continue in business that they were forced to give up or flee. Then, having lopped off the highest branches, the government took over middle-sized Cuban business until gradually the state owned or controlled most of the means of production. In these circumstances Cuba's gross national product decreased sharply. Instead of looking for better incentives Castro blamed the troubles on "counter-revolutionaries and Yankee saboteurs" and proceeded to sign a series of trade agreements, many of them on a barter basis, with Russia and Communist China.

The same "turn to the left" was seen in the field of agriculture. Cuba needed land reform and higher agricultural wages. Soon after he was firmly in power, Castro adopted a new farm policy. Almost no one could own more than 1,000 acres and expropriated properties were divided among the landless and paid for by government bonds in the amount for which the land had been previously taxed. However, rather than build up a strong group of lower middle-class farmers who were reasonably independent, less than 5,000 landless peasants actually received acreage. Almost all the rest of the landless peasants were "encouraged" (and the pressure on them was considerable) to become members of cooperative farms. At first these cooperatives were run by the peasants themselves. However, they were soon put under the control of directors who were party members picked by the Institute of Agrarian Reform, a government-run and Communist-dominated organization. Those working on the cooperative farms were not allowed the right of collective bargaining but were told what to plant. They received an amount set by the central government for their produce. Thus the peasants of Cuba came under the complete domination of the party, and the slogan "Land to the Peasants" for which they had fought became a mockery.

Students in Latin America have an especially privileged position, for they are expected to take part in politics. In addition, they are allowed unusual freedom on their campuses and have a strong voice in selecting or firing their professors. Castro was particularly careful in moving against them, waiting until he had control of the army, the police, the press, and part of the Church before he acted. Then he arranged for new elections in the various student committees which resulted in putting his followers in key positions. Student leaders who objected were then voted off the committees and before long the important posts, such as secretary, were in the hands of the Communists. In the case of some student groups there was physical violence and intimidation. In still others, rival student organizations were set up and given financial backing.

Castro's followers moved into the nationwide organizations, bypassing the true liberals, subverting the rank and file, and finally taking over control of the movement. It was one of Castro's most skillful operations and many honest young liberals went to jail before it was finished. Before long, Castro and his communists were in complete control of the schools and universities, for along with the change in student leadership, he carried out a purge of non-communist college officials, school principals, professors, and teachers.

The extent of this purge of teachers was shown by a *New York Times* story in January, 1962, which stated that "402 out of 500 former faculty members of the University of Havana were in exile, having been forced out by pressure from the Castro-controlled Student Federation." It was also reported that a series of "Revolutionary Instruction schools to teach Marxism-Leninism" had been set up and were graduating some 30,000 students a year, elite cadres who in turn would take over the guidance of other pupils.

One of the most popular points in Castro's early speeches when he was seeking power, and again as a guerrilla leader in the Sierra Maestra, had been his assurances that he would give the people honest elections. Even when he first gained control in Havana, Castro said he was "preparing" for elections. As the months passed, something always came up to make it necessary to put off the voting. To date, no democratic elections have been held nor are they likely to be held in Communist Cuba. Castro explains this by saying that during his lengthy speeches, which are often listened to by as many as 100,000 people, he asks for reactions from the crowd; thus his listeners are able to "vote" on the policies which he is proposing without the cumbersome paraphernalia of "bourgeois elections".

The direction of the movement was seen in the field of foreign policy. The conservative faction favored closer ties with democratic parties in other parts of Latin America, but the extremists sought a break with the United States and the adoption of a policy close to that of the Soviet Bloc. For some months Castro did not make his position clear, but in November, 1959, he sided with the Communists. That year, Castro made a series of attacks on the United States, its policies in Cuba and other parts of Latin America. In addition, he recognized all the countries of the Communist Bloc, backed the Soviet position at the United Nations, and economically tied Cuba closely to the Soviet Union.

Many of those who had supported Castro in his early days or even during his first ten months in power, found themselves unable to go along with these aspects of Cuban foreign policy. Thousands began leaving Cuba for the United States, and by the beginning of 1962 there was a sizeable community of exiled Cubans in Florida and smaller groups in other parts of the Caribbean.

Changing Castro's Image

With the 26th of July Movement purged, the military bypassed, the law taken over, the Church subdued, the press stifled, business brought to heel, agriculture harnessed, elections suspended, and the student movements dominated, Castro was in a position to run Cuba as he pleased. Actually, he and the Communists around him were faced with only one major problem, namely, how to fit Castro into the leadership of a Communist Party.

Since Castro could not join the Moscow-dominated PSP without appearing ridiculous in view of his early anti-Communist speeches, a new organization had to be developed which would appear as Castro's own party. Blas Roca, a professional who had been Secretary General of the PSP since 1934, was well-prepared for such a maneuver. First, the semi-official party newspaper ran a story about a meeting in Guantanamo at which the 26th of July Movement, the Student Revolutionary Directorate and the PSP were "merged" at the local level. Then a new party was born in two stages, first under the name of "Integrated Revolutionary Organization" and then as the "United Party of the Socialist Revolution", referred to as PURS. Late in August, 1961, a spokesman announced that the United Party would be built on Marxist-Leninist principles. In a striking example of Communist phraseology, the spokesman explained the dictatorial pattern under which the United Party would function when he said:

> Democratic centralism is the method which Lenin discovered for the application of true democracy. It is the only method for applying democracy. It consists of democracy being applied by a central leadership. An idea approved by the masses is applied by a centralized leadership, by the leadership of the workers vanguard which is the Party.

The final fitting of Castro into the role of a communist revolutionary took another twelve months and involved a great show of humility on Castro's part. In a series of speeches he admitted his past mistakes and even his earlier ignorance, largely growing out of his "bourgeois background" and prejudices. As obfuscation grew more frequent in his speeches, Castro indicated that he had believed in Marxism when he led the unsuccessful coup on July 26, 1953, and again on several later occasions, but that he had not understood it. Finally in a speech, December 1, 1961, he indicated that his understanding had increased to a point where he could cry out: "I am a Marxist-Leninist, and I will be one until the last day of my life."

Thus, step by step, Castro worked to convince the people of Cuba that in spite of a record of anti-Communist declarations he had now become worthy of being Secretary General of a Marxist-Leninist organization. In a frank explanation of why he used the technique of the *revolution betrayed*, Castro said that he had kept his communist beliefs hidden for years "because otherwise we might have alienated the bourgeois and other forces which we knew we would eventually have to fight".

Leaving aside the fascinating but obscure point of when Castro became a communist, it is clear that the Cuban Revolution followed a pattern well-known to Moscow, Peking, and other centers of communist thinking. This is the strategy of arranging to have a leader, or group of persons, come to power on the basis of a truly popular program, and then when they are firmly in control of the apparatus of government, proceed to turn the country into a communist state. Castro's phenomenally charismatic personality was ideal for just such a technique as the post-accessional revolution, or, in simpler terms, the revolution betrayed.

If well done and led by a man like Castro, such a scheme is almost impossible to stop until the trap has been sprung. If it is unsuccessful, the Communists can slip away, perhaps to the mountains, perhaps overseas, always ready to fight again some other day—when the odds are in their favor. This is a pattern of communist take-over of which we are likely to see more in the future.

INDEPENDENCE REBELLIONS

IN addition to observing the spread of *societal revolutions* to all parts of the globe during the past fifty years, future historians will also note that this period was marked by the virtual ending of the European-controlled Colonial Empires. Whereas, in 1917, a high percentage of mankind was ruled from London, Paris, Brussels, the Hague, or Lisbon, by 1967, only a few remnants remained of these once widespread sovereignties, and it appeared likely that these areas would soon join the more than three score newly independent states sitting in the United Nations.

In a certain number of cases, particularly areas under British rule, such as Nigeria, and the states of British East Africa, the change to independence was relatively peaceful and was achieved legally. These cases do not fall within the scope of this book, which is essentially a study of current political strife. In a few others, such as India, independence involved "non-violent" pressure. But in parts of other empires, the road to freedom was long and bloody.

The next two chapters, which are devoted to *independence rebellions*, describe, therefore, the way the Communists increasingly dominated the violent anti-French independence rebellion which ended in 1954 in Indochina. The following chapter examines the highly emotional and theoretically non-violent rebellion led by Gandhi in India against the British raj, a movement which succeeded in June, 1948.

CHAPTER V

INDOCHINA: THE COMMUNISTS DOMINATE A VIOLENT REBELLION

INDOCHINA is a dramatic example of communist exploitation of anti-colonialism. Events there—particularly in Vietnam—have shown the Communist skill in accelerating and controlling a nationalist independence rebellion. Using guerrilla tactics, they wear down an opponent's will to fight through *protracted conflict*. If necessary they will move to the conference table and temporarily settle for half a loaf. The details of these events are important in two ways. First, for the light they cast on how a bloody guerrilla-type independence rebellion can succeed against a modern and well-equipped army. Secondly, as needed background for the understanding of our limited war in Vietnam today.

Historical Background

The struggle for independence is nothing new to the descendents of the Kingdom of Viet, which according to legend was founded in 2879 B.C. The earliest historical records available on the area come from Chinese sources and state that in 111 B.C. the soldiers of the Han Dynasty overthrew the Viet ruler. During the next 900 years, Viet was under Chinese domination, although at first the local rulers were given considerable authority. In 39 A.D. a rebellion led by two warrior queens was initially successful, but when the Chinese rallied their superior forces, the revolt was put down, and the two queens drowned themselves. The Chinese established a more direct and onorous regime, collecting taxes, policing the area, and making the Chinese language and culture dominant. The centuries that followed saw other unsuccessful revolts against the Chinese overlords, producing a number of national heroes and heroines.

At last, in 938 A.D., a successful uprising drove out the Chinese and the victors established a virtually independent kingdom which lasted almost a thousand years. Viet rulers, however, paid tribute until the late 19th century to the Chinese Emperors. The people rejected Chinese political rule, but they accepted many aspects of Chinese culture.

The people we know as Vietnamese actually started near the present Chinese border in Tonkin, whose modern capital is Hanoi. Spreading southward into warmer and more productive areas, they defeated the people known as the Cham and took Annam, which now makes up the central part of Vietnam. Continuing their drive southward, the Vietnamese pushed back the Khmer tribesmen of Cambodia and, about the middle of the 18th century, occupied the southern part of Cambodia including the Mekong Delta. This segment of present Vietnam was known as Cochin China. South Vietnamese think of North Vietnam, or Tonkin, as their original home, and some of the inhabitants of Tonkin as distant cousins.

A crescent curving along the Gulf of Tonkin, Vietnam (North and South) is a thousand miles long with a variable width of 50 to 250 miles. Much of it is sparsely populated. Most of the 32 million-odd inhabitants live in the rich lowlands of the deltas of the Mekong and Red rivers. Apart from a few minority groups, such as the Thais and the Khmers, the people all speak Vietnamese.

In 1787 a French missionary, the Bishop of Adran, saved the life of a prince named Nguyen Anh. The bishop then worked out an alliance which resulted in Anh being made Emperor, the first of the Nguyen Dynasty which lasted down to the end of World War II. The French were given commercial concessions and granted the port of Danang.

After the death of Nguyen Anh, his successors turned against the French missionaries, killing many of them. Partly because of this, and partly because by the middle of the 19th century colonialism had become the accepted pattern for a great European power, the French decided to conquer Vietnam. After a second massacre of Catholic missionaries, French troops landed in Vietnam in 1858 as the strongest element in a Franco-Spanish punitive expedition. The Spanish soon left, but the French stayed on, expanding their military, political, economic, and religious positions until they had established a well-ordered and prosperous colony.

Two treaties in 1883 resulted in French protectorates over Tonkin (northern Vietnam), and Annam (central Vietnam), while the southern part of the country, Cochin China (around Saigon) became a French colony. The Emperor and his court were allowed to continue at Hue in Annam, but French civilians and military controlled them and actually ran the country. In 1885, Chinese troops tried to move back into the Tonkin area. They were defeated in battle, after which China recognized France's paramount position in Vietnam. Chinese Communist historical atlases today show all of Indochina—as well as Thailand and the Malay peninsula—as part of "Greater China" until the years 1885-1895.

When Japan defeated Russia in 1905, a wave of nationalism swept over Asia and various anti-French societies sprang up in Vietnam, one of which even went so far as to organize a government-in-exile. This early phase of nationalist activity reached a peak in 1916, when, with France involved in World War I, a rebellion took place in Vietnam. Nonetheless, the French regime proved stronger than expected. French agents penetrated the rebel messenger service and the rebellion was quickly put down. Many of the rebels, including the Emperor Duy Tam, were sent into exile. In his place, the French chose another member of the royal family whom they believed could be controlled. He died in 1925 leaving as his heir a 12-year old king who took the name of Bao Dai.

Communism Comes to Vietnam

Nationalists in Vietnam had watched the communist revolution in Russia with great interest, particularly because of its anti-colonial propaganda and its offers of racial equality for oppressed or colonial peoples. One of these was a man who called himself Nguyen Ai Quoc, meaning Nguyen the Patriot, a name which he later changed to Ho Chi Minh, or "Ho, the Enlightened One". Born in northern Annam in 1892, he made his way to Europe on a merchant vessel just before World War I, working first in the kitchen of the Carlton Hotel in London, and later in Paris, where he lived when the war ended. Deeply impressed by Woodrow Wilson's Fourteen Points, he rented evening clothes and went to Versailles to make an appeal that Indochina be given independence. However, the statesmen assembled there had other things to think about, and the Vietnamese nationalist was unable to see Wilson or anyone else of importance.

Discouraged, Ho Chi Minh stayed on in Paris for several years earning his living by retouching photographs and devoting his spare time to meeting French Communists, and reading or writing on revolutionary subjects. When the French Communists held their first congress in Marseilles in 1921, he made a speech to the delegates urging that the Party give more attention to the problems of France's colonies. Afterwards he wrote a book on this subject, copies of which were smuggled back to Vietnam. In addition he set up an Inter-Colonial Union as a rallying place for leftist representatives from the French colonies, and published an anti-colonial newspaper known as *Le Paria*.

In 1923, Ho Chi Minh went to Moscow as a delegate to the Congress of the Peasant International and remained in Russia learning the techniques of revolution. When he left there in 1925, Ho travelled to southern China where he served as a translator at the Russian consulate in Canton, working under Michael Borodin, the top Soviet agent in the Far East.

In line with accepted Marxist thinking of that period, Ho Chi Minh preached that the revolution in Indochina would have to come in two stages: first, independence under a bourgeois regime; then a true Communist government. To start this revolutionary process Ho Chi Minh collected a group of Vietnamese living in Canton, taught them Marxist philosophy, and organized them into the Association of Vietnamese Revolutionary Youth. Once their training was completed, Ho Chi Minh sent them back to Vietnam with instructions to create the hard core of a revolutionary movement. One task was the selection of promising young leaders, who were in turn smuggled out to China for further training.

The position of the Communists in China took a turn for the worse in 1927 when Chiang Kai-shek forced them out of a coalition with his Kuomintang Party. Borodin, who had urged Stalin to support the KMT, was recalled to Moscow, and Ho Chi Minh followed him.

The Association of Revolutionary Youth held its first and only congress in Hong Kong in 1929, issuing an appeal to the peasants, workers, and students of Vietnam to revolt against the French imperialists. Soon afterwards the movement split into three parts, and Ho Chi Minh came back to try to bring peace between the warring factions. As a result of his persuasion, a single Indochinese Communist Party was organized with various affiliated bodies such as a Woman's League, a League Against Imperialism, and several other front organizations.

By now other groups were also working for Vietnamese independence, including one called the Vietnam Nationalist Party. On the night of February 9, 1930, its members staged an uprising in northern Vietnam during which French officers were killed and French property destroyed. The revolt was soon put down, however, and most of the members of the Nationalist Party were either executed or given long prison terms. There is some reason to believe that the Communists knew of the planned uprising, pretended to support it, but actually tipped off the French and thus got rid of a number of "bourgeois nationalists".

To capitalize on the resentment caused by the ruthless way the French put down the Nationalist revolt, the Indochinese Communist Party, in May, 1930, organized a series of mass demonstrations. The peasants began destroying village tax rolls in the mistaken belief that they would then get the land for their own use. The extent of these riots took the French by surprise, but once they had recovered the initiative, hundreds of persons suspected of being Communists were rounded up. Cooperating with the French, the British in Hong Kong arrested a number of Communists, including Ho

Chi Minh himself. "The Enlightened One", however, who even then had become something of a legend, was soon set free; some said because of a previous deal with the French secret police. After he left jail in Hong Kong, Ho Chi Minh went into hiding and, before long, detailed and convincing reports were spread that he had died.

Emperor Bao Dai finished seven years schooling in France and returned to his capital in Hue in 1932. There he tried to modernize his administration and persuade the French to give him and his officials greater freedom. Many French liberals favored such a development, but the conservative military and the colonists showed little interest in turning over any real power to the Vietnamese. When this became clear, the young Emperor relaxed his political efforts and concentrated on enjoying himself. Many of his more able advisers, including Ngo Dinh Diem, who was later to play an important role in the history of Vietnam, resigned in disgust.

As soon as the Communists began to recover from their setbacks they started "study groups" in Saigon, which they expanded until they had a skeleton organization of cells in many parts of Cochin China. In 1935, several Vietnamese attended an important meeting of Asian Communists which was held in Portuguese Macao. There, under pressure from Moscow, the Vietnamese delegation reluctantly agreed to support the new worldwide Communist Party line and to work with non-Communists to combat Fascism. This meant that in Vietnam the Party temporarily dropped its opposition to French colonialism, a tactic which gained it some minor advantages.

When the Popular Front in France fell in 1938, the Communist parties there and in the French possessions overseas were again outlawed. Thanks to their excellent ties with Paris political circles, the Communists in Vietnam received advance warning and went underground. Thus, when World War II broke out, the secret structure of the Communist "apparat" in Vietnam was virtually intact.

France fell to the Germans in 1940 and the Japanese moved into Tonkin, the northernmost section of Vietnam. Because they were "stretched too thin" the Japanese let the French do the detailed running of the country. Had the French government made a strong offer of independence, the Vietnamese might have supported it. Instead, Vichy France ordered a crackdown on Communists everywhere. With the Japanese standing on the sidelines, the Communists started a revolt which spread from southern Vietnam to the Chinese border.

The colonial French were still powerful. Soon the uprising was smashed and a number of its leaders were jailed or exiled. After this defeat, the Communists once again moved into China and set up an external "safe haven". To it flocked Marxist intellectuals, soldiers, workers, and peasants who began preparing for the next phase in the struggle to liberate Vietnam from outside control. Their leader was none other than Ho Chi Minh who, after ten years in hiding, openly took control of the communist movement in Vietnam.

The Viet Minh

Wiser and more crafty than ever, Ho told his fellowers that they must keep communism in the background and put emphasis on gaining national independence. Furthermore, he said that they should temporarily forget their hatred of class enemies and push for a "united front" in which virtually all Vietnamese could join as patriots in the freeing of their homeland. The Communists in China then organized a League for the Independence of Vietnam, whose long name was shortened to Viet Minh. To no one's surprise, Ho Chi Minh was "elected" as its Secretary-General.

The League grew so fast in strength that Chiang Kai-shek became worried, arrested Ho Chi Minh, and started a non-communist Vietnam Revolutionary League. This new organization looked impressive on paper but found little support. Consequently, in 1943, Ho Chi Minh was released from prison, and the Viet Minh was supplied with arms and guerrilla training as a section of Chiang's Revolutionary League. Taking advantage of this cover of respectability, the Viet Minh leader first made overtures to the American representatives in Kunming and received some weapons from them. Then, when he felt strong enough, Ho cut his ties with the Kuomintang. In addition, he reduced the strength of the non-communist Revolutionary League by betraying some of its leaders to the French police in Vietnam.

Once they were strong enough, the Viet Minh began active recruitment in northern Tonkin. By 1945 they were estimated to have some 10,000 guerrillas under the leadership of a young lawyer named Vo Nguyen Giap, who had studied guerrilla tactics in China under Mao Tse-tung. Giap showed a genius for unconventional warfare, and his forces were able to push back the French and the Japanese and to establish a "liberated zone" in northern Tonkin. It was these troops which later grew into "the People's Army of the Democratic Republic of Vietnam".

By August, 1945, the communist advance into Tonkin had progressed far enough to permit Ho to move his headquarters back from China into North Vietnam. From there he sent Communist agents into the Red River Delta. They found the peasants bitter against Japanese-French rule. Consequently they were able to set up a pyramid of revolutionary cells running from the villages through the provinces to a central committee. At a meeting, August 16, 1945, representatives of these groups established an overall People's National Liberation Committee with Ho Chi Minh as its chairman.

The Viet Minh then began a campaign to convince the people of northern

Vietnam that, once the Japanese had been driven out, the choice would be rule by French imperialists, or by the Viet Minh—"patriots, dedicated to gaining independence for Vietnam". For most Vietnamese there was little doubt about the choice. When Giap's army moved into Hanoi there was widespread celebration, and Bao Dai's viceroy in the north handed over his power to the National Liberation Committee.

By now the tide of independence was so strong that Emperor Bao Dai sent a message to General De Gaulle which read in part, "even if you come to reestablish a French administration here, it will no longer be obeyed." But Bao Dai soon found himself with little government and less support. As feeling against him grew, Bao Dai informed the leftist regime in Hanoi that he was prepared to abdicate. On August 26, 1945, Bao Dai stepped down from his throne and urged his people to consolidate their national independence under a democratic republic. To show how far he had moved with the times, Bao Dai then shook hands with representatives of the Viet Minh, the first such democratic act by an Emperor of Vietnam in almost a thousand years.

Although eight of the fifteen members of the National Liberation Committee belonged to the communist Viet Minh, enough moderates were included to quiet many suspicions. Addressing a large crowd in Hanoi, in September, 1945, Ho showed the impact of the American Revolution on his thinking, for the first paragraph of the new document read in part: "We hold these truths to be self-evident, that all men are created equal." A high percentage of the Vietnamese were happy on that historic occasion. For them not only was the war against the Japanese over, but they believed that their struggles with the French were past and that they had at last won real independence.

Meanwhile, the situation in Cochin China was becoming steadily more confused. The only group there with a clear-cut platform were the Viet Minh, who moved about organizing secret communist cells and open People's Committees. Fanned by the Viet Minh, who stressed the need for genuine independence, anti-French feeling grew and French houses and businesses were attacked.

The bitterness and chaos increased when Paris announced that it planned to form a Federated Indochina under a French High Commission and within the French Union. The French expanded their military and police forces while a growing wave of French civil servants poured into Indochina. After a period of widespread rioting and the massacre of several dozen French men, women, and children, the French military gained the upper hand. So many communists were either arrested or killed that the Viet Minh were forced to go underground while their leaders fled to the north.

The Communists were steadily strengthening their hold in the north.

After the Indochinese Communist Party, which Ho Chi Minh himself had organized, was "dissolved", its members had quietly joined non-communist parties. The Viet Minh had organized a United Front, which included communists, liberals, and even middle-of-the-road nationalists along with Buddhists and Confucianists. Many Catholics, however, saw what was going on and refused to join the coalition.

The Viet Minh next moved into the villages where they replaced the Councils of Village Notables, time-honored links between the villages and the central government, by People's Committees in which the Communists held key positions. A campaign for literacy was carried so far that peasants had to prove they could read a communist newspaper before they were allowed to sell their produce. A drive was also made against gambling, prostitution, and the use of alcohol, while unpopular taxes such as those on salt were abolished. In place of taxes the Viet Minh encouraged "voluntary contributions", which actually produced more money than the French had been able to collect.

Another basic reform pushed by the Viet Minh in the north was the establishment of universal suffrage, after which the country's first general election was held in January of 1946. There were many irregularities, but the result was widespread support for those who had been most active in gaining independence—a result which helped the Viet Minh particularly. The elected National Assembly contained people from all walks of life, ranging from Ho Chi Minh to the former Emperor Bao Dai.

This National Assembly of the Democratic Republic of Vietnam met in a Hanoi theatre. Following communist technique it remained in session just long enough to hear some patriotic speeches and to give Ho Chi Minh a vote of support. Then its members went home, leaving "interim" decisions to be made by a Permanent Committee. All the members of this Permanent Committee were members of the Viet Minh.

Distressed as they were by these developments, the French had little choice of action because of their weakness in the northern part of Vietnam. Therefore, in March of 1946 they signed an agreement with Ho Chi Minh recognizing the Democratic Republic of Vietnam as "a free state, with its own government, parliament, army and finances, forming part of the Indochinese Federation and the French Union." The French also agreed to the holding of a referendum to determine whether Tonkin, Annam, and Cochin China should be joined in a single nation.

In order to pave the way for a favorable vote on unity in this referendum, Ho Chi Minh sent some of his best communist organizers into the Saigon area. There, through a combination of oratory, widespread use of funds, and terror, Ho's representatives were able to bypass the non-communist resistance movement and organize a communist-dominated Central Committee for the south. Guerrilla units were also formed, supposedly for use against the French, but actually to bring pressure on anyone who opposed Viet Minh control.

As tension grew, two conferences were held between the French and the Viet Minh, one in Vietnam and the other in Paris. In spite of Ho's presence at the latter gathering, little was achieved. It was clear that there was no meeting of the minds on the future of Vietnam. Both sides, therefore, prepared for a showdown. By autumn the Communists had some 60,000 regular troops and 40,000 guerrillas serving under General Giap. In order to rally all possible elements in the population to his side, Ho then presented the country with a reasonable and forward-looking constitution which guaranteed freedom of speech, assembly, and religion, help for the aged, and free compulsory education for all. Then, riding a wave of popular support, Ho Chi Minh formed a new cabinet in which he and other communists held the key positions.

The Shooting Starts

As the autumn of 1946 wore on, the French became increasingly alarmed at the extent of communist influence behind the government in the north. French police activity increased and there were incidents and riots. Finally, on November 20, widespread shooting broke out in the port of Haiphong. When the Viet Minh refused to withdraw from the French and Chinese sections of that city, the French went into action with artillery and airplanes, flattening large areas of Haiphong and reportedly killing over 6,000 Vietnamese.

The incident was the turning point in the struggle for control of the country. Few Vietnamese now believed that further cooperation with the French was either possible or desirable. The French landed more troops including elements of the French Foreign Legion. Both sides began putting up road blocks and digging deeper trenches. When the French, on December 19, sent an ultimatum to Ho Chi Minh insisting that the People's Militia of the Democratic Republic be disarmed, the Viet Minh shut off Hanoi's water and electricity and attacked the French garrison with machine guns and artillery. The French responded and the fighting spread throughout much of Indochina. The Vietnamese fought fiercely but they were no match for the better-trained, better-armed French forces in open combat. The French proclaimed martial law on December 23 throughout Tonkin and northern Annam. Ho secretly slipped out of Hanoi, leaving behind him a nationalist movement which was well-organized and had both overt and covert elements. Although informed observers knew that it was communist-oriented, many patriotic Vietnamese felt they had little choice but to close ranks behind the resistance movement of the Viet Minh.

The years that followed saw the struggle for the control of Vietnam carried on both at the conference tables and in the jungles and rice paddies —a struggle in which both sides were handicapped by divided political viewpoints. Most French liberals sympathized with the idea of Vietnamese independence and thought it should be encouraged. On the other hand, French colonial elements, including planters, business men, government officials, and soldiers argued that Vietnam was not yet ready for freedom and that giving the country liberty at that time meant handing it over to the Communists.

The people of Vietnam also were politically divided between those who were willing to work, or were forced to work, with the communist Viet Minh against the French, and those who felt that they should side with the French until the communist threat was checked. The latter element organized a Provisional Central Government under a Vietnamese career soldier called General Nguyen Van Xuan.

The Communists continued to strengthen their control over much of Vietnam; the party structure was tightened; front organizations became more active; and persons known to oppose communist rule were threatened, beaten, or killed.

By autumn, 1949, the victory of Mao Tse-tung's Communists in China was virtually complete and, in December, their advance units raised the Red Flag at the north end of the International Bridge linking Vietnam to China. The Viet Minh promptly recognized Mao's new regime, which in turn recognized the Democratic Republic of Vietnam. Viet Minh guerrillas now had a completely safe haven to the north where they could recuperate, organize, train new units, and receive arms, ammunition, and medicine.

Growing numbers of Viet Minh guerrillas streamed northward in worn-out uniforms, carrying antiquated weapons. In autumn of 1950 these men were marching south again, dressed in new clothes, and carrying reasonably modern rifles and machine guns. Behind them came artillery battalions, many of which were equipped with American-made recoilless rifles, and 75-mm and 105-mm howitzers captured by the Chinese Communists from Chiang Kai-shek's American-equipped troops. In addition, the guerrillas had a new spirit and morale, for they had been given exhaustive training in the successful techniques of Mao Tse-tung.

After working underground for five years, the Viet Minh held a Congress, in March 1951, and announced the formation of a Worker's Party (Lao Dong). The Communist Party of Indochina had been reborn under a new title. Along with growing political strength, the Viet Minh expanded their fighting forces until by the end of 1953, the army, plus regional troops and the People's Militia, totalled 350,000. Their actual strength was even greater than this because of the effective way in which they persuaded or forced Vietnamese men and women to act as porters.

The French had about 420,000 troops including elements of the regular army, the Foreign Legion, African regiments, and Indochinese levies. Fighting with them were an additional 200,000 Vietnamese. The real problem, however, was not numbers, but motivation and morale. The Viet Minh felt they were fighting for their freedom, while the nationalist Vietnamese often suspected that they were fighting to keep the French in control.

The pattern of the French resistance to communist guerrilla attacks went through several phases. At first small patrols were sent along roads and trails where the Viet Minh were known to be operating. The Communists, however, soon learned to ambush these patrols, which suffered heavily. The French and their Vietnamese allies then started sending out larger units, but the Communists melted away at their approach, hid their weapons, and turned into peaceful peasants until the French had moved on.

The French next established a network of hundreds of armed strong points from which they believed that they could control the countryside. When the Communists found out the size of these garrisons, they hit them selectively with superior strength, wiping out position after position.

To combine the tenacity of a strongpoint with the mobility of a large patrol the French put in the field several heavily-armored mobile groups, which were expected to fight their way through any ambush and also be able to move deeply into enemy territory. One of the strongest of these was Groupe Mobile 100 which was made up of about 3,500 French veterans plus jungle-wise Vietnamese and Cambodian regulars. Equipped with tanks, armored cars, armored troop carriers, and jeeps, it was a formidable striking force with high morale. The French command decided to use it to defend the plateau area in the central section of South Vietnam. As the weeks passed however, GM 100 began to run into ambushes which became progressively more serious. Sometimes the lead vehicles would be wiped out by guerrillas who slipped away into the jungle when the main elements of the column reached the spot. At other times, the Viet Minh would cut off and destroy the rear vehicles. Often attacks were made at night, attacks which put tanks and armored cars out of action before the sleeping crews could get into them.

Because of Viet Minh raids in widely separated areas, GM 100 was kept on the march "putting out the fires" until its men became exhausted, its ammunition ran low, and its vehicles bogged down in mudholes caused by the winter rains. The Viet Minh concentrated their fire on the French officers, until many units were led by sergeants or corporals. When the French formed their vehicles in hollow squares, the Viet Minh used suicide attacks to break through the weakest part of the perimeter. Then they placed explosives which put the tanks and half-tracks out of action. The French and their allies fought bravely, but by April they were decimated. Furthermore, the Communists had cut the roads from the coast to the central highlands. GM 100 could receive new supplies and personnel only by air, and few planes or helicopters were available. At last the day came when the Viet Minh surrounded what was left of Groupe Mobile 100 and opened up on the stalled convoy with mortars and recoilless cannon. Groupe 100 ceased to exist as a fighting force and only a handful of Frenchmen were able to fight their way to the safety of the nearest French camp.

Dienbienphu

The Viet Minh guerrillas began infiltrating Laos as well as moving down into South Vietnam, and the French decided the best way to stop them was to establish an impregnable strongpoint which would control the trails running in both these directions. They therefore chose a valley deep in the hills and jungles of Tonkin and set up a great fortified camp there. The fortress was named after the nearby village of Dienbienphu. It was garrisoned by 12 infantry battalions, supported by artillery and tanks. The French spent much of the winter of 1953-54 digging trenches in the plain, improving an airstrip, and fortifying two low hills, which they called "Gabrielle" and "Beatrice." The French generals hoped that the Communist guerrillas could be lured into attacking this fortress. This hope was fulfilled.

The French and the Communists had agreed to hold a conference in Geneva in the spring of 1954, and General Giap was ordered to take Dienbienphu at all costs before that meeting. Tens of thousands of the best Communist troops and guerrillas were secretly moved into the jungles surrounding the fortress. Even greater numbers of porters were mobilized to bring up food and ammunition. The French felt secure for they knew there were no roads from the north over which truck convoys could carry needed supplies. But where the roads ended, the Viet Minh put their cargoes in bicycle baskets, or on the heads of porters, who then crossed the mountains on foot trails. The French were also convinced that artillery could not be brought within range of their fortress. But the Communists disassembled artillery and mortars and, using innumerable peasants, dragged the 75's, 105's, 180-mm anti-aircraft guns, and Soviet rockets to the hills overlooking Dienbienphu.

On March 13, a tremendous artillery barrage was directed at the strongpoint, Beatrice. The French artillery, which was concentrated too far to the south of the main fort, could not reach the Communist batteries and the French artillery officer in charge committed suicide that day. After the shelling, wave after wave of Viet Minh infantry attacks beat against the outpost from trenches built secretly during the preceding nights. When Beatrice fell there was not a French officer left alive on the hill.

Then, the fortifications on the other hill, Gabrielle, were reduced to rubble, and the few survivors from its garrison fell back into the main camp. After this onslaught, the Communist artillery was moved forward until it could reach the airstrip. With the roads cut, the airfield out of action, and almost no helicopters available, the defenders were isolated and soon began to run out of ammunition. Against them more than 40,000 select Communist troops pushed forward around the clock, supplied by porters with an apparently endless amount of ammunition. The French fought bravely, but the weight of the Communist artillery plus limitless manpower was too much. Day by day the size of the French-held area shrank. At last, on May 8, the artillery fire reached a climax, after which special assault teams charged what was left of the fortress from all sides. By nightfall the red flag flew over the bunker that had housed the French headquarters at Dienbienphu.

Of the 20,000 Frenchmen who began the battle, plus those who were dropped by parachute, or flown in while the airfield was still operational less than 7,000 lived to surrender. Only 2,000 of these ever saw France again.

* * * * * * * * * * * *

The loss of Dienbienphu was more than the fall of a fortress; it was more than the capture of some of the best troops and equipment which the French had in Indochina. It was a psychological blow which broke the French will to resist. A few more skirmishes followed, and then, August 1, 1954, the seven-year French effort to keep control of Indochina ended in an armistice. When word of the defeat at Dienbienphu reached the negotiators at the conference in Geneva, it was clear that the Communists held the strong cards and that the independence rebellion against French colonial rule in Indochina had triumphed.

CHAPTER VI

INDIA: GANDHI'S NON-VIOLENT VICTORY

In India, the largest and most populous of all the colonial areas, independence came about through a pattern of "nonviolence". There was bloodshed, but the concepts of unity, nonviolence, and noncooperation dominated the rebellion.

The politically-alert Indians had a grievance: they did not wish to be ruled by foreigners different from themselves in race, religion, and culture. The British sincerely believed they were doing a superior job in maintaining order and encouraging progress in so vast an area, but the Indians, both elite and masses, were nevertheless resentful of British rule. Starting in a small way, the leaders of the rebellion organized parties which grew steadily and sought to obtain their ends through negotiation and the ballot. When these failed, violence began. It might well have spread to unimaginable proportions, but at this point the Indian rebellion departed in three main ways from the path normally followed by independence movements.

1. Nurtured by the British colonials, India had developed an unusual depth of political institutions, with a large number of leaders well-trained in various aspects of government.

2. Many elements of the British ruling class, particularly the liberals in England, had lost their will to govern India as a colony, although not their desire to remain there economically.

3. Into this complex scene came a unique leader, Mahatma Gandhi, a religious politician and mystical showman who, in the drive for independence, stressed noncooperation, nonviolence, and "soul force". Ghandi was only one of many Indian leaders, but his unique methods left a lasting imprint on India's independence rebellion. He was a man of action who radiated inner peace, and who, in Nehru's words, personified the "majesty of the meek".

Gandhi's Background

Mohandas Karamchand Gandhi was born October 2, 1869, in Porbandar, a state of western India, where his father was its Prime Minister. Gandhi's father, following Hindu custom, arranged the early betrothal of his son, and at the age of 13 Mohandas Gandhi married Kasturbai.

Gandhi later wrote in his memoirs: "I see no moral argument in support of such a preposterously early marriage as mine." Nevertheless, Kasturbai bore him four children and was his partner in a happy marriage lasting 60 years until her death in 1944.

Against the wishes of his family, Gandhi journeyed to England to study law. He was called to the bar at the age of 20, and shortly afterward he left England for Bombay. His practice in the Bombay High Court was not successful. During this period he had several unfortunate experiences with British officials, developing a dislike of all bureaucrats, particularly members of the British civil service.

In 1893, Gandhi left India for South Africa, where he soon built up a very lucrative practice as a barrister. During the Boer War in South Africa, he served in the British forces with an ambulance corps, which he helped organize. This service was repeated in 1906 during the campaign to put down the Zulu revolt.

Many Indians lived in South Africa, and racial discrimination against all "nonwhites" already was widely practiced. Early in his stay, Gandhi was thrown out of a first class compartment of a train because of his brown skin. This upset him so deeply that he began to make speeches against racial discrimination and often took to fasting.

The more he thought about the restrictions against his people in South Africa, the more he became convinced that the solution did not lie in either physical or political force. Rather, he felt it must come through *Satyagraha*, a word which he developed from *Satya*, meaning truth or love, and *Agraha*, meaning firmness. Thus, the full concept meant truth or "soul-force".

To Gandhi soul-force meant: "the vindication of truth, not by causing suffering to one's opponent but by the affliction of suffering on one's self." This, he felt, would wean the enemy from error by patience and sympathy.

In August, 1906, Gandhi tried out soul-force in South Africa when he opposed an act requiring all Indians there to be registered and fingerprinted. Before long, Gandhi was in jail, along with hundreds of his followers.

In the end, his effort to force repeal of the Registration Act failed, and Gandhi withdrew to a farm in Natal where he went through another period of soul-searching. He concluded the answer lay in soul-force, plus "non-cooperation" with the authorities. Soon he was in jail again, but this time he determined that though his body was in prison, his soul was free. Forever afterwards he had no fear of prisons.

Noncooperation turned out to be no more effective than soul-force and, after further meditation, Gandhi decided the missing factors were unity and discipline. He developed still another technique for publicity—cross-country mass marches to dramatize a simple injustice. He set out with some 2,000 of his followers from Natal to the Tolstoy farm in the Transvaal. Gandhi was arrested, but the march gained world publicity. There were meetings of support in India and much was written about the march in the liberal British press. Before long, thousands of workers in South Africa, both Indian and African, went on strike; then railroads stopped running, martial law had to be declared, and the economy of South Africa was seriously affected.

At last Gandhi had an effective technique for use against a government willing to follow democratic practices. At that time the leader of South Africa was General Jan Christiaan Smuts, a most understanding man. After a number of talks, the two men reached an agreement which Gandhi called "the Magna Carta for Indians in South Africa". Now he was ready for struggle in a larger arena.

Gandhi returned to India in January, 1915. He had left as an unsuccessful lawyer; he returned as a well-known leader. To western eyes, he was small, homely, and far from being an orator. He was not rich and he had held no important office. But by now he had developed a political-emotional technique which would eventually break the power of the British raj in India.

In order to maintain his inner peace, Gandhi went to a religious retreat in a group of whitewashed huts under a grove of trees beside the Sabarmati River. There he lived for 16 years in a simple cell; a room to which, as the years passed, most of the leaders of India beat a path.

Gandhi's political mysticism tends to make one forget that he had many co-workers and disciples with him during the thirty-odd years of struggle for independence. As in virtually all successful political movements, these co-workers fell into several categories: politicians, many of whom had their own followings; financiers or fund-raisers, who provided the money for the movement; organizers and administrators, who bound the leadership together and built his following at various levels, from city machines down to remote villages; men and women of ideas, the "braintrusters" who took Gandhi's broad concepts and made them understandable ideals for which thousands were willing to work, to go to jail, and to die.

Gandhi's co-workers included nationally-known politicians such as Pandit Metilal Nehru, a strong-willed and highly successful lawyer who abandoned his lucrative practice to devote himself to the independence movement. A proud, sensitive aristocrat, he was the father of Jawaharlal Nehru who, in turn, worked unceasingly for independence and who became the first Prime Minister of the new Republic. The son went to jail time after time, often for his work as secretary of the All-India Congress Party.

Also working for the cause at various periods, sometimes closely with Gandhi and sometimes in opposition to his methods but not his goals, were the militant nationalists, Bal Gangadhar Tilak and D.C.R. Das.

Gandhi's personality, austere way of life, and philosophical approach to independence and salvation strangely enough appealed to many businessmen, financiers, and other wealthy Indians. Among these were G. D. Birla and Seth Bajaj who, from their own large fortunes or through contacts with wealthy friends, financed the independence movement not only when it was going well, but also during periods of doubt and discouragement.

Another of Gandhi's aides was Vallabhbhai Patel (called Sardar), a strong-minded lawyer from Ahmedabad, who was much influenced by Gandhi's theory of the use of nonviolent action to correct flagrant wrongs. A solid, serious man, he became one of the chief organizers among the Mahatma's close followers. Partly through him, others with organizing ability at the provincial, district, and village levels were brought into the movement to give it "a skeleton to which the people could cling".

Around him too there gathered many intellectuals, writers, and persons of deep religious faith. In this group was Vinoba Bhave, a leader in the application of individual soul-force, who thought of Gandhi as personifying the holy men of ancient India. It was he who, in the fall of 1940, took the lead in the movement against World War II.

Other "idea" men included subtle lawyers such as the politically moderate Chakravarti Rajagopalachari, who pushed Gandhi's cause in Madras and eventually became the first Indian Governor General. Then, there were humanists like Dr. Rajendra Prasad, who later became the first President of India. Helpful in tying the theme of the independence movement to the ancient Indian philosophies was the scholar Maulana Azad, writers such as the poets Rabindranath Tagore and Sarojini Naidu, and the Irish theosophist, Mrs. Annie Besant.

The world currents were such that India probably would have obtained independence sometime during the mid-twentieth century. However, without the support of such politicians, financiers, organizers, and thinkers, Gandhi's success would have been much slower and might not have come at all during his lifetime. He was the spark, but they were the tinder who kept the flame of independence alive, caused it to spread, and eventually to consume the British raj in India.

Moves Toward Independence

The more he studied India, the more Gandhi became convinced that strength and power lay in the 700,000 villages where 80 percent of its inhabitants lived. They were poor, discouraged, diseased illiterates, but they were the soul of India.

In 1916, a peasant from the state of Bihar, not far from Nepal, came to Gandhi to say that he and his fellow sharecroppers were having trouble with the British settlers. After weeks of pleading, Shukla, the peasant, won over Gandhi and together they went to the Champaran district of Bihar.

In Bihar, Gandhi found more than a million peasants forced to pay higher land rents in spite of a sharp drop in the price for indigo, their chief cash crop. He and a few disciples travelled widely, developing close personal ties with the people. His program of unity, discipline, non-cooperation, nonviolence, and soul-force, aided by Patel's organizational genius, gained him thousands of followers. The British became concerned. To check the spread of the movement, the British arrested Gandhi. Popular outcry was such that the British soon realized that if Gandhi was convicted, he could bring the local economy to a standstill. After a few days the case against him was dropped. It was a relatively small test in terms of the whole of India, but a most successful one, for it showed that the new technique was particularly applicable to the minds and feelings of the Indian people.

After his release, Gandhi stayed more than seven months in the Champaran district. Aided by Patel, whom the peasants christened *Sardar* (leader), he brought in a doctor and some teachers and improved health conditions among the indigo workers. He did this partly to help the peasants, and partly because of his faith in the overall moral integrity of the British. He believed that if the Indians showed enough inner discipline and unity to prove that they deserved more freedom, the British, in their wisdom, would grant it. Using the same technique in Guyerat, in western India, he again helped the peasants against the landlords and strengthened his organization considerably.

An important aspect of Gandhi's requirement of unity was better relations between the Indians and Moslems. Thus, there was widespread satisfaction, when, in December, 1916, the two largest political groups in India, the predominately Hindu Indian National Congress and the Moslem League signed the Lucknow Pact, an agreement on a broad program of moderate political reform which would benefit both communities.

The feeling of hope which this pact engendered was raised still further when the new British Secretary of State for India, Sir Edwin Montagu, declared, in August, 1917, in the House of Commons, that Britain had a new policy toward India which meant "the progressive realization of responsible government in India as an integral part of the British empire". Hindsight shows that this statement was made at a time when the British fortunes of war were very low, and the British needed support from all parts of the Empire, including, of course, the millions of India. But for a time the declaration was taken at face value.

Then, with the coming of peace, disillusionment set in. To the surprise of many Indians, the restrictive measures which the British had imposed on India during the war were continued under an act which was termed by Gandhi "unjust, subversive of the principle of liberty, and destructive of the elementary rights of the individual". As he campaigned against the act, he developed further his Satyagraha organization which was pledged to peaceful disobedience.

The Indian leaders sought some way in which their people could make their grievances clear to the world, and Gandhi's mind turned to the success he had achieved in South Africa through nonviolence. Then, as he told a friend, the idea came to him in a dream that the Indian Nationalists should meet their British challenge through a general *hartal*, a complete suspension of the economic life of the country.

After administrative preparation and a good deal of publicity, the hartal was begun. It proved tremendously successful, for India's economic life came to a virtual halt. Like other leaders of later peaceful movements, Gandhi did not appreciate the capacity for violence of his countrymen, and they, in turn, did not yet understand the real nature of soul-force. Thus, along with the peaceful aspects of the hartal, such as non-cooperation, there was widespread violence; British shops were burned, trains wrecked, and Englishmen were attacked.

Realizing that the movement was out of control, Gandhi fasted for three days and asked that his followers end the hartal and themselves fast for a day.

The Amritsar Massacre

The Nationalists had sown the whirlwind. In April, 1919, when two nationalist leaders, a Moslem and a Hindu, were banished from Punjab province, a mob surged through the streets of Amritsar. Much damage was done and three prominent Englishmen were killed.

By an unfortunate coincidence, an extremely tough, old-school British officer, Brigadier General Reginald E. H. Dyer, took command of the Amritsar garrison two days later. He issued a proclamation forbidding the holding of meetings or processions. There is reason to think that this proclamation was not widely distributed and certainly it was not widely read.

In any case, the nationalist leaders of Amritsar decided to hold a political meeting next day in a place called *Jallianwalla Bagh*, a square surrounded by buildings or walls through which there were few exits. From a raised platform at one end of the Bagh, orators began to address a crowd of perhaps 15,000 persons. On some raised ground at the other end of the square, General Dyer lined up about 100 Gurkhas, Baluchis, and other troops who were not residents of Amritsar.

Soon after they were drawn up, General Dyer appeared and looked over the crowd which was meeting in spite of his formal proclamation. There are varying reports of what happened next, but apparently the General, without waiting for its leaders to move the crowd, ordered his troops to begin firing. Ten minutes later, according to official reports, there were 379 dead and 1,137 wounded.

As General Dyer later explained to his superiors, he was trying not merely to disperse the crowd but to produce "a sufficient moral effect not only on those who were present, but more especially throughout the Punjab". He added, "There could be no question of undue severity. I thought I would be doing a jolly lot of good." In a classic understatement, the official report of the investigation later said: "this was unfortunately a mistaken concept of his duty."

As the news spread, a wave of indignation swept over India. The answer, Gandhi said, was to boycott British goods, refrain from taking British jobs, refuse to be tried in British courts, take Indian children out of British schools, and do everything possible to bring the British-controlled economy and society to a halt.

The British, in a document known as "the Montagu-Chelmsford Reforms", responded by granting Indians a number of concessions and the British king stated that "a new era is opening". Believing these reforms were a real step in the right direction, Gandhi abandoned his campaign of non-cooperation and persuaded the Indian National Congress to do likewise. But, as the British had expected, the new concessions divided the Indian nationalists.

In contrast to Gandhi, Mohammed Ali Jinnah, Tilak, and other Indian leaders opposed the reforms, while many of the Moslems were adamant in their opposition to working with the British. Time showed that the reforms were far from basic or adequate.

One of Gandhi's characteristics was that he was always ready to take advantage of new developments, or at least to take a new look at old ones. Thus, once he realized the limitations of the Montagu-Chelmsford reforms, he agreed with the extremists and supported the decision of the Congress Party to vote against collaboration. Gandhi even sent the Viceroy two South African medals given him for service during World War I, along with a letter which read, in part: "I can retain neither respect nor affection for a government which has been moving from wrong to wrong in order to defend its immorality."

It was a turning point in Gandhi's thinking, the end of his belief that he could obtain independence for India through cooperation with the British.

At a Congress Party meeting in December, 1920, Gandhi told members of the Party that if the pressures could be controlled, and if India's program of non-cooperation could remain nonviolent, self-government would come in twelve months.

Prominent Nationalists such as Jawaharlal Nehru left the British courts, professors left the universities, and students left their classrooms. Singly or in groups they went to the villages and preached nonpayment of taxes in order to reduce the revenues of the government, plus the nonuse of liquor for moral reasons. During the next seven months, Gandhi and his co-workers moved about the Indian countryside talking to crowds which numbered sometimes a thousand and sometimes a hundred thousand. Often his admirers would not let him pass through their town without his making a speech; night and day Gandhi exhorted and prayed.

These meetings of Gandhi's were a strange combination of politics and religion. He urged his listeners not to wear foreign clothing, both because it was non-Indian and because Indian sales meant so much to the British textile industry. If the crowd applauded, he had them strip off items of apparel that had been made abroad and place them in front of him. When the pile was big enough, Gandhi set fire to it and told his fellow Indians that in the future they should weave their own clothing. He personally spent half an hour each day spinning, calling it a "sacrament". Hundreds of thousands of spinning wheels were distributed to build up the economy of the villages. When the masses again learned to make their own cloth, as they had done in ancient times, the villages became more self-sufficient and the British textile firms suffered.

The British officials were at first amused, then puzzled, and then angered by this nationwide campaign against taxes and British goods. Furthermore, the solid front of the British elite began to disintegrate. All they could do was to make more arrests, and by January, 1922, ten thousand Indians, many of them political leaders, were in jail.

Gandhi felt that with a little more pressure the British would give in and would grant India its independence. In February, 1922, he wrote the new Viceroy, Lord Reading, that he was going to start an intensive campaign of civil disobedience in an area called Bardoli, near Bombay. He believed that if he showed the British he could bring about a complete economic stoppage in a small area, they would realize that he could do the same all over India.

Civil disobedience in Bardoli got off to a good start with virtually all political and economic contacts with the British stopped. But a few days later a riot occurred some 800 miles away in the United Provinces and twenty-two policemen were killed. To the amazement of most Indians, and the dissatisfaction of many of his co-workers, Gandhi stopped the campaign in Bardoli, told his fellow countrymen they were on the wrong road to freedom, and forbade further violence in the cause of independence.

The Indians followed him reluctantly and, for the time being at least, Gandhi's threat to British India had passed. As the crisis eased, however, Lord Reading had Gandhi arrested on March 10, 1922, on charges of preaching sedition.

Speaking in his own defense, the Mahatma said that he had been a loyal cooperator with the British until the end of World War I. Events since then, however, had convinced him that the only road to independence for India was through non-cooperation. He, therefore, requested "the severest penalty" and was sentenced to six years in prison. When the court adjourned, most of the Indians present fell to the ground and wept; tens of millions of Indians did likewise when they heard of the sentence. Several times after this the British put Gandhi in jail, but they were wise enough never again to try him.

In January, 1924, Gandhi was operated on for acute appendicitis and because he recovered slowly the British released him from jail. Moving about India again, Gandhi concluded that, during his almost two years in jail, much strength had gone out of the independence movement. Indian lawyers were again practicing in British courts, Indian children had gone back to government schools and colleges, Indian politicians were again taking part in government, and the boycott against British products, particularly liquors and textiles, was weakening. Furthermore, relations between the Hindus and Moslems had taken a turn for the worse and violence appeared likely.

Gandhi realized he must recapture the leadership of the independence movement, and to do this he must once again stir the conscience of India. He, therefore, announced that he would fast for 21 days so that Hindus and Moslems might think more clearly about their relationships and move closer together. He had come to the conclusion, that unless there were better relations between the Hindus and Moslems, the British would not grant independence. He did not have the political, economic, or military power to influence these two great communities. Furthermore, he was not much of an orator and felt that a speaking tour of India would produce few results. A fast, however, was something which both Hindus and Moslems understood, and he gambled that his apparently frail body could survive twenty-one days without food. As the foodless hours went by, Gandhi wrote pleas for unity, prayed frequently, talked to chosen friends, and maintained much publicized silences.

On this and later occasions, Gandhi developed the politico-religious fast to its highest level. It was for him a new method of communication, a new way of reaching men's hearts and minds.

Millions were awed by the emotional drama of Gandhi's fast, but when it ended, October 6, 1924, apparently the effort had little lasting effect on most Hindus and Moslems. After careful analysis, Gandhi and his inner circle came to the conclusion that the people of India were not yet unified and tolerant.

India's Grievances

By 1928, India was rife with unrest, bitterness, and violence. The feeling against Great Britain's rule was so strong, many younger members of the Congress Party wanted an immediate declaration of independence from Great Britain, even at the risk of war.

Indian hopes rose when the British Labor Party took office and announced that a Round Table Conference would be held, but the talks proved unproductive. Following Gandhi's lead, the Congress Party instructed its members to withdraw from state and national legislatures, to practice civil disobedience, to push economic non-coopeation, and to cease the payment of taxes. In one of the most unusual letters ever addressed to a viceroy, Gandhi wrote:

> Dear Friend,
>
> . . . and why do I regard the British rule as a curse? It has impoverished the dumb millions by a system of progressive exploitation and by a ruinously expensive military and civil administration which the country can never afford. It has reduced us politically to serfdom. It has sapped the foundations of our culture . . . . I fear . . . there has never been any intention of granting . . . Dominion status to India in the immediate future. . . .

To dramatize India's grievances, Gandhi chose to make an issue of British control over salt—a product used by every Indian. For 24 days Gandhi and a growing group of supporters marched across India, following back roads from village to village. Then after an all-night prayer, Gandhi and his marchers walked into the ocean and picked up some salt left on the sand by the waves. By this act he focused world attention on the absurdity of the British salt monopoly and the immorality of the political pattern which allowed a small and distant nation to regulate the internal affairs of over 300,000,000 people down to the last grain of salt.

Thousands of peasants began gathering their own salt, contraband salt was sold in most of the cities, and the jails once again became crowded. Within a month Gandhi himself was arrested, but the campaign continued without him. It reached a terrible climax in a march on the Dharsana Salt Works when 2,000 volunteers moved toward the salt pans guarded by 400 policemen.

Advancing in absolute silence, the marchers walked up to the police line where they were knocked down by the blows of steel shod staves. Not one of the marchers struck back or even raised an arm to fend off the blows. As soon as the first group of demonstrators lay writhing on the ground, their places were taken by another column, which, in turn, was beaten flat without a struggle. Hour after hour stretcher bearers carried off the wounded and more demonstrators advanced to the sacrifice.

After several such marches and brutal beatings the Indian philosopher Tagore wrote: "Europe has completely lost her former moral prestige in Asia. She is no longer regarded as the champion of fair dealing . . . but as the upholder of Western race supremacy. . . ."

The British realized that a new approach was needed. Most Indian leaders were released from jail, and the Viceroy held a series of meetings with the Mahatma. From these meetings the "Delhi Pact" was issued. Under it the British agreed to free political prisoners, to permit the local making of salt, and to hold a round table conference in London. The rebels, for their part, agreed that civil disobedience would end.

In August of 1931, Gandhi went to London as the only delegate of the Congress Party. He talked with many of the British leaders but no agreement resulted. When he returned to India he found most of the leaders in jail. Gandhi soon followed them to prison.

A new issue was needed to publicize the independence rebellion. After weeks of soul-searching, Gandhi came to the conclusion that he must make a "fast unto death" on behalf of the untouchables. Gandhi had become profoundly concerned over the conditions of these 50 million Indians who stood so far below the four main Hindu caste groups that they were considered socially and physically untouchable. Furthermore, he and the other leaders of the rebellion realized that thousands of untouchables were ceasing to be Hindus and turning to religions such as Islam or Christianity, in which they hoped to find equality.

Once again Tagore spoke for thinking India when he said: "The penance which Mahatmaji has taken upon himself is not a ritual but a message to all India and to the world. . . ."

India got the message, and in many places Hindus and Harijans, or "Children of God" as Gandhi called the untouchables, began to fraternize. While Gandhi was losing strength, the leaders of the caste Hindus and the Harijans worked out a series of social and political agreements which the British Prime Minister, MacDonald, hurried to accept. Then, and only then, did Gandhi break his fast. There is still caste in India, but it will never be what it was before the "Epic Fast".

Afterwards the leaders of the rebellion were again released from jail and Great Britain came forward with new proposals known as the Government of India Act of 1935. It was essentially a plan for a federal government in which the Indian States and British India would be joined. In 1905 its proposals would have been widely hailed, but, by the mid-1930's, most of the Hindu and Moslem leaders in India felt that it did not go far enough.

With the coming of World War II, the British, in August 1940, pledged that "after the war" they would give India a new constitution. The Indian leaders, however, had become skeptical of British promises and remained cold to the proposal. As political cooperation decreased among the nationalist leaders, in the spring of 1942, the government in London sent Sir Stafford Cripps, who was known for his pro-Indian views, to the Indian subcontinent. Even his proposals failed to interest the Indians. Soon after Cripps left the country, nationalists came out for the immediate termination of British rule. If this did not happen, the English were told that they might expect "a mass struggle on nonviolent lines and on the widest possible scale". Once this news reached London, the leaders of the rebellion were put back in jail where they stayed until the end of World War II.

The years immediately after the war saw further conferences and another cabinet-level mission to India. From these efforts there came a certain amount of understanding between the British and the Hindus, but the Moslems of India led by Mohammed Ali Jinnah feared that an independent India would be completely dominated by the Hindus. As a result they sought a separate Moslem state—Pakistan.

Jinnah and his followers would not yield on this point. As unrest mounted throughout the country, Lord Wavell, the new British Viceroy, in August, 1946, called on Nehru to form an interim government without the Moslems. Nehru took office early in September, and in October the Moslem League partially reversed its stand and agreed to participate in the government. Prime Minister Nehru then introduced a resolution to make the Indian Union an independent sovereign republic. Once again political friction blocked Hindu-Moslem agreement. As the tension rose throughout the country, British Prime Minister Clement Atlee, in February, 1947, announced that his government would transfer sovereign power to Indian hands in June of 1948. In essence, Britain was saying: "Here is your independence, it is up to you to solve your domestic problems."

Lord Mountbatten was then sent out as new Viceroy to guide the progress towards independence. He quickly realized that the friction between the Hindus and Moslems had reached dangerous proportions in 1947 and that the transfer of power had to be moved up to August of that year. With unprecedented speed British officials ironed out details of the greatest decolonization in history. There was, however, nothing they could do to hold back the pent-up bitterness between Hindus and Moslems. In cities, towns, and villages, both Hindu and Moslem demonstrations turned into riots, the riots grew into pillaging, and tens of thousand were massacred.

To Gandhi, the apostle of nonviolence, such madness was unthinkable. In an effort to stop the slaughter he travelled widely through some of the regions where the worst atrocities were taking place, constantly preaching the theme: "Love your enemies, Bless them that curse you, Do good to them that hate you. . . ." He prevented hundreds of deaths, but not he or anyone else could stop thousands more from occurring.

An effort on his part to convince Lord Mountbatten to resist partition was unsuccessful, as were his efforts to persuade the leaders of the All-India Congress Committee to stop the move towards separate states. On June 15, 1947, by a vote of 153 to 29 it was agreed to accept the idea of partition. For the Mahatma it was his greatest tragedy. "Thirty-two years of work," he said, "have come to an inglorious end."

Independence

It terms of obtaining its overall goal and gaining independence from Great Britain, the "end" was both successful and glorious to most Indians. As Nehru said in a dramatic speech to the Constituent Assembly:

> Long years ago we made a tryst with destiny, and now the time comes when we shall redeem our pledge . . . at the stroke of the midnight hour, when the world sleeps, India will awake to life and freedom. A moment comes, which comes but rarely in history, when we step out from the old to the new, when an age ends and when the soul of a nation, long suppressed, finds utterance.

Thus, after some thirty years of struggle, the largest colonial area in the world became free, took its place as an independent nation in the British Commonwealth, and was granted the former seat of British India in the United Nations. In terms of nonviolence, however, the bloody clash which developed and grew worse over the next few months was indeed "inglorious". The partition of the new nation into the two separate states of Pakistan and India caused a drastic, major population movement of eleven million people. Some estimates place the death toll at more than half a million killed and five times that number injured in the tragic slaughter that resulted.

Crushed by the madness and the growing bloodshed, Gandhi again turned to fasting as the best technique for affecting the conscience and actions of the two great religious communities. To save his life, interdenominational talks began and were contined practically around the clock. On January 18,

1948, a delegation of 100 Hindus, Moslems, Sikhs, and Jews appeared at Gandhi's retreat. There they agreed in writing that the life and property of Moslems in the Hindu areas and Hindus in the Moslem areas would be protected. Doubtful at first, Gandhi at last asked that hymns be sung and all join in prayer before he would break his fast.

Once he had regained enough strength, Gandhi resumed his practice of having public prayer meetings. On January 30, Gandhi wrote to various Hindu leaders urging them to work together in the task of building India. He ate a light supper, checked his nickel-plated watch (one of the few objects which he owned), and walked to the grounds where his daily meetings were held. When he appeared, most of the five hundred men and women who had been waiting for him stood up and bowed. In response, Gandhi smiled and gave the traditional Indian gesture of "greeting and blessing" by touching the palms of his hands together.

As he moved toward the little platform on which he usually sat, a 35-year old Hindu editor from Poona stepped up to the Mahatma and bowed. The editor was deeply angered at the terrible events of the last few months and blamed Gandhi for the death of so many Hindus. Taking a pistol from his pocket and standing only two feet from Gandhi, the editor fired three shots. Gandhi's arms which had been raised in general greeting sank slowly to his sides as he fell to the ground dead.

* * * * * * * * * * *

Gandhi's pattern of nonviolence and soul-force succeeded because the technique suited many of his fellow countrymen. India was ready for independence, and the British were no longer willing to fight to continue their political control. As events developed, the "nonviolence" produced much violence. Although it has very limited applications under authoritarian dictatorships, we are likely to see more of this pattern under real democracies. In fact, we are already witnessing some aspects of "nonviolent insurrection" being practiced today in the civil rights movement in the United States.

Cairo, 1956. Gamal Abdel Nasser greeted by crowd after four years as Egypt's strongman.

Wide World Photos

Petrograd (now Leningrad), Russia, 1917. Lenin speaks to the masses after his return from exile.

C. P. Cushing Photo

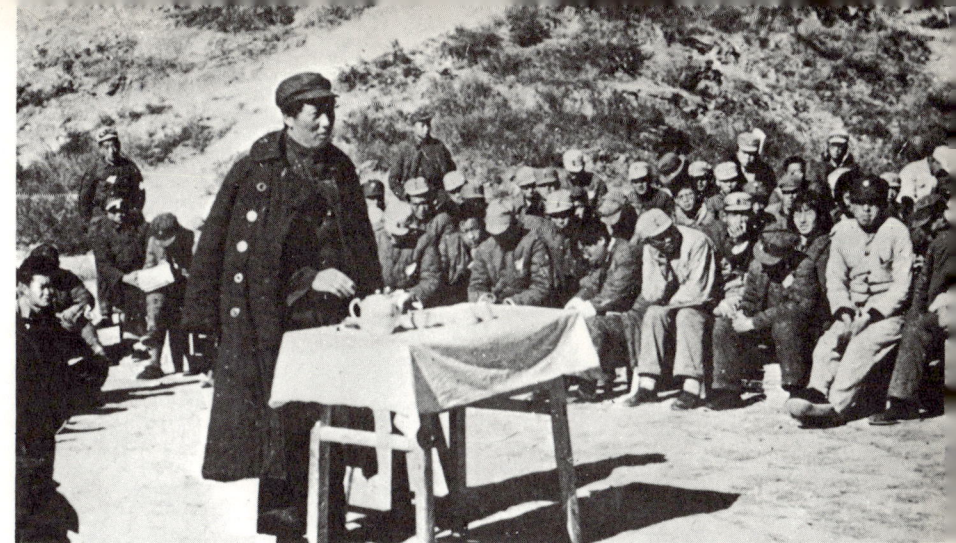

North Shensi base, Yenan, 1937. Mao Tse-Tung addresses a group of his followers at the end of the Long March.

Eastfoto

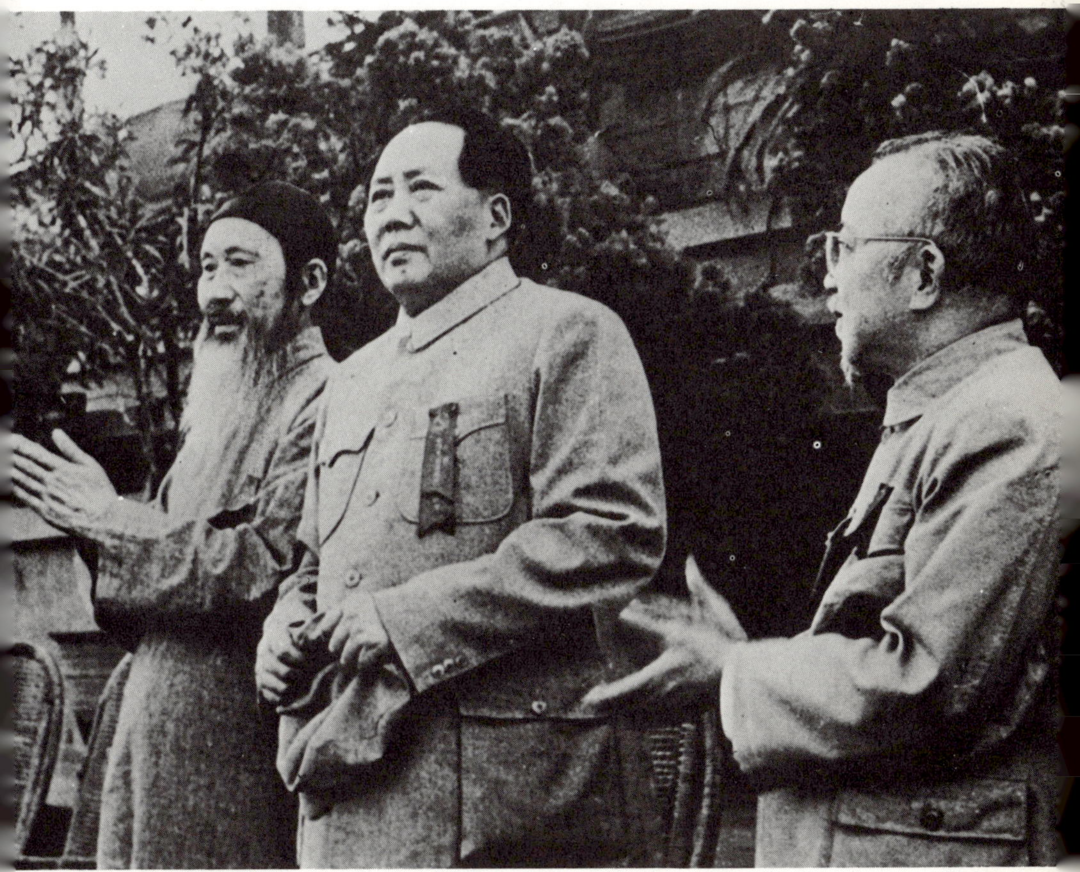

1954. Mao Tse-Tung and other leaders of the Chinese People's Republic.

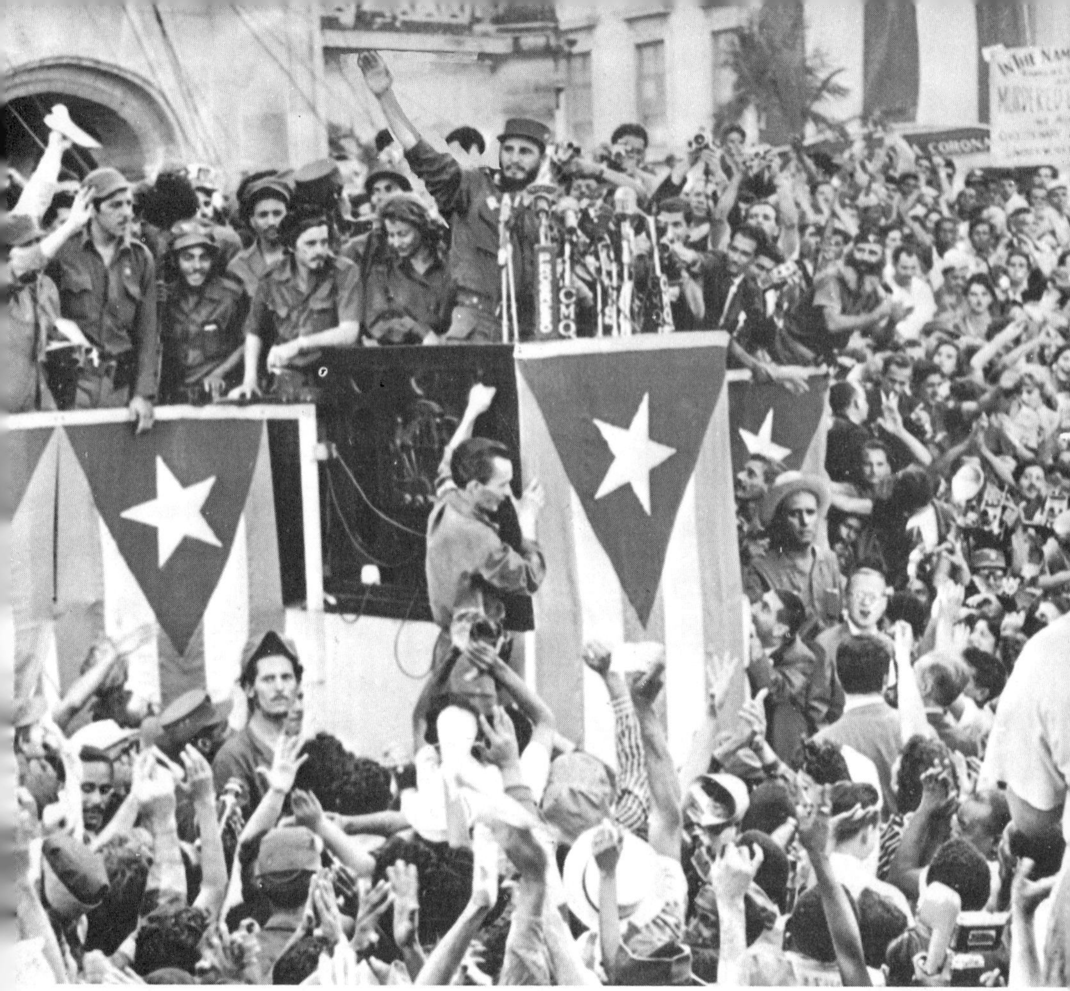

Wide World Photos

Havana, 1959. Fidel Castro, leader of Cuba's revolutionary forces, addresses crowd to defend the executions of former Batista men as war criminals.

Wide World Photos

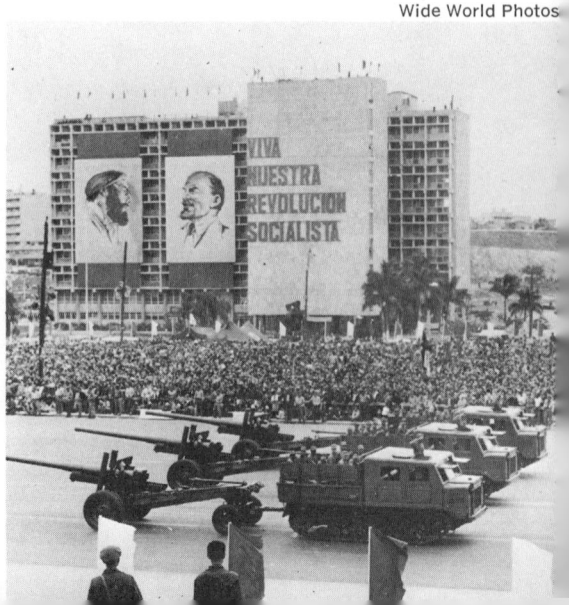

Havana, 1962. Soviet-built personnel carriers towing artillery pieces roll through Havana during a parade honoring the third anniversary of Castro's revolution.

Magnum

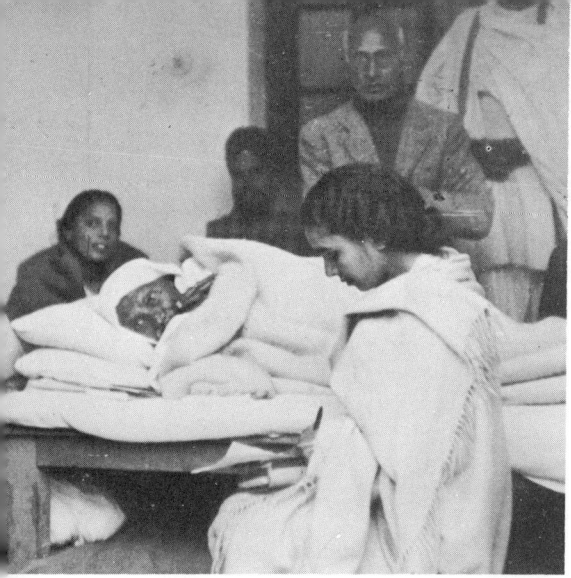

New Delhi, 1948. Gandhi, in a final dramatic act of self-denial before his death, won a promise of peace from warring religious sects with a five-day fast taken against strict orders from his doctors.

Government of India Information Services

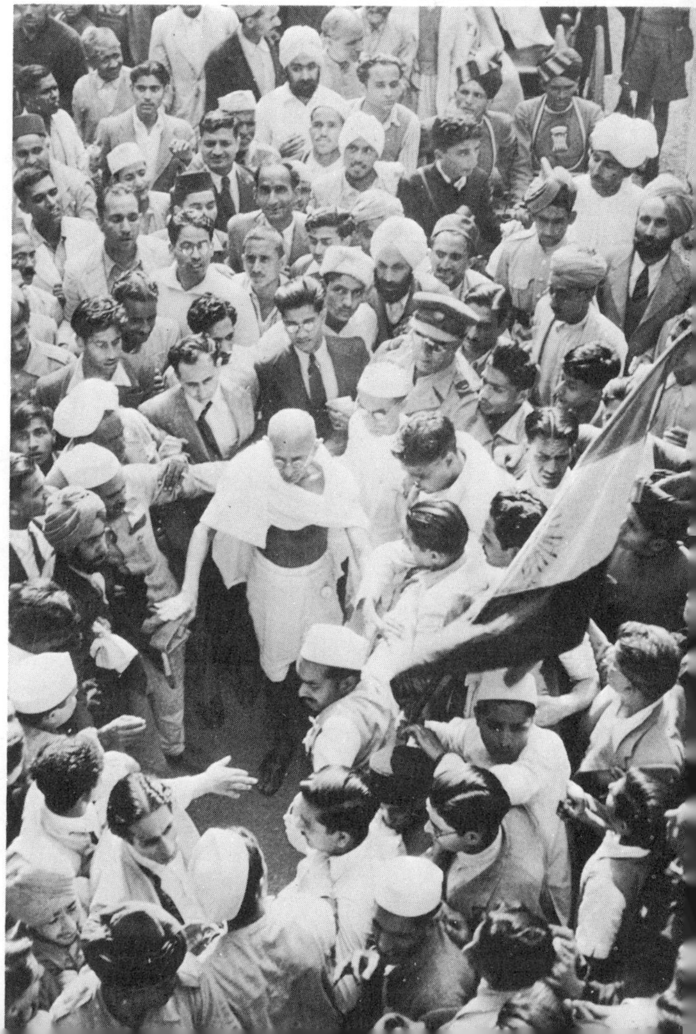

New Delhi, India, 1945. Mahatma Gandhi surrounded by followers after his interview with the British Viceroy.

Leopoldville, 1960. Soldiers from various contingents of the U.N. Force on guard.

United Nations

Leopoldville, 1960. A Ghana Police Officer of the U.N. Force stands on duty while crowds await a political demonstration in the Republic of the Congo.

United Nations

Philippines, 1957. President Ramon Magsaysay greeted upon his arrival at Cebu.

Philippines, 1954. Magsaysay discusses with the people of a *barrio* in Bataan Province a new artesian well installed since he became President.

North Viet Nam, 1954. Ho Chi Minh, Viet Minh leader, and Chinese Communist advisers.

Black Star

South Viet Nam, 1964. Two captured Communist guerillas are shown in the foreground as Republic of Viet Nam soldiers search a sugar mill for hidden Viet Cong weapons.

COLD WAR CONFLICTS

ESSENTIALLY the *cold war* is a struggle over how the developing nations can best be modernized, a test of the relative efficiency and acceptability of evolution and democracy versus violent revolution and communist dictatorship. In the slightly more than twenty years that have elapsed since its outlines took shape, the cold war has consumed much of the resources, energy, and even lifeblood of a considerable portion of mankind.

In the Congo, in spite of the primitive nature of the area and the lack of government structure and trained personnel, prompt assistance from the west has helped Africa defeat both Russian and Chinese communist domination. Sometimes, as in the Philippines, progressive local leaders have ended or mitigated the grievances of the populations on which the Communists sought to ride to power. But sometimes, as in Vietnam since 1958, failure by both sides to assess properly the intentions and capabilities of the other have led from economic and political confrontation through small scale military conflict into the deadly arena of *limited war*.

These aspects of world tension are reviewed in the next three chapters.

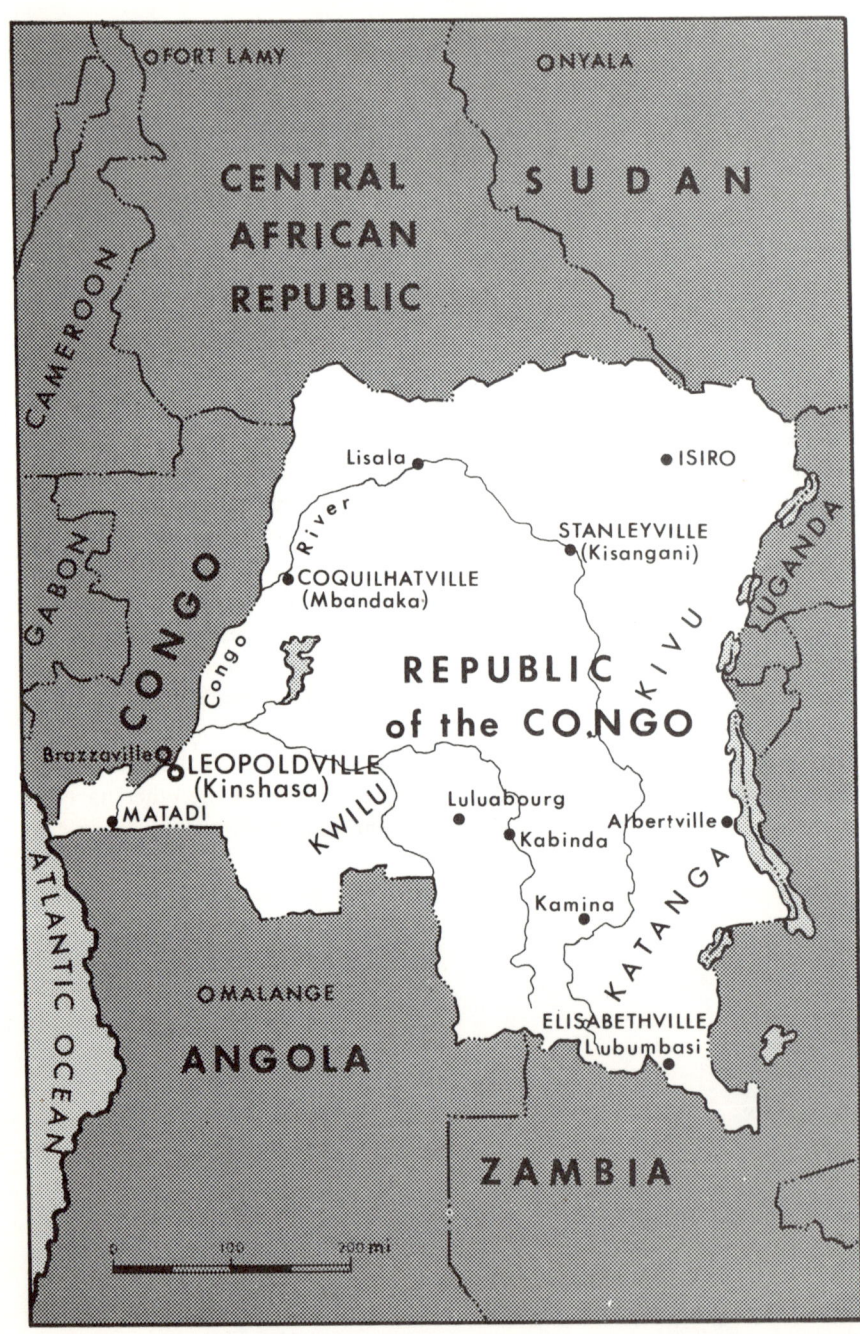

CHAPTER VII

THE CONGO: AFRICA DEFEATS THE COMMUNISTS

IN the last forty years of the 19th century and the first forty years of the 20th, a series of western colonial patterns were imposed on the diversified African scene. The French in West Africa put the emphasis on culture, educated the local elites in France, and even placed some of them in the Chamber of Deputies and the Cabinet in order to teach them the art of politics "French style". The British, largely in East Africa and Nigeria, taught law and justice, educated some of the African elite in England, and sent them back to their local capitals for experience in government.

The Portugese in Angola and in Mozambique—the oldest colonial areas on the continent—disregarded racial differences but emphasized class lines as they attempted to make over their domains in the image of Portugal itself. The Dutch in South Africa reversed this pattern, taking the position that there must be no mixing of the races or cultures since this was as harmful to Africans as it was to Europeans. They thus developed a tremendously wealthy state which was split in two by the doctrine of apartheid.

Disregarding the Spanish impact, which was negligible, and the American shadow presence in Liberia, which was without real governmental or even private direction, the other colonial power in Africa was Belgium in the Congo. This darkest part of Africa, after being the private preserve of King Leopold II of the Belgians for almost a generation, became so badly managed that it had to be taken over by the Belgian Government in 1908. In general, it may be said that the Belgians thought of the African as a good workhorse, who should therefore be kept healthy, useful, and contented. His fondness for tribal wars was arrested by stern measures, he was given a little basic education, a relatively good job, and virtually no political freedom. This resulted in a smooth-running and immensely prosperous, unified Congo, the pride of the Belgians, and the despair of politically-minded Africans.

Under the Belgians, Christianity in its Protestant and Catholic forms spread widely in the Congo. Christian practices were frequently an overlay on time-honored pagan beliefs. These included worship of a chief god under whom there were lesser gods and messengers who controlled such important aspects of life as rain, rivers, lightning, and trees. The Congolese believed spirits lived in the forests and moved about at night to influence such events as hunting, harvests, the birth of children, and the recovery or death of sick persons. In addition, many of the Congolese believed that objects such as large trees or strange-looking rocks possessed magical properties and were able to help persons who propitiated them and injure those who did not. Because the Christian missionaries tended to be contemptuous of such primitive forms of religion, the Congolese often accepted Christianity as a "passport to better things" but continued to practice their own beliefs in secret.

Given such a background with ideas and beliefs carried down from extremely early times, it is not surprising that the impact of modernization was deeply unsettling to the Congolese. The past hundred years have seen Africa travel through time at an unprecedented rate. Most of the Congolese have had to move through thousands of years of development in three generations.

Explorers passed through and spread word of rich and growing cities to which some villagers went and returned with tales of huge buildings and strange customs practiced by the white men. Others brought back western clothes and sewing machines. White traders set up local stores, and white planters cut down forests to grow new crops; for a time, rubber was king. Steamers chuffed up the Congo River. White doctors challenged the village medicine men. Troops from a distant central government appeared, led by white officers, and the African kingdoms and tribal groupings melted away. Representatives of this central government collected taxes and recruits and began telling the village chiefs what to do. Radios brought strange voices and news into the chiefs' huts. Foot trails turned into roads, buses and automobiles reached the villages, airstrips were cut from the jungle, and the outside world was not weeks but hours away. The villagers who stayed at home became restless. In the 1930's and 1940's more and more of them left their villages for the big cities.

The Impact of the City

Throughout Africa south of the Sahara, the move to the white man's cities was rapid and shattering. Leopoldville, for instance, grew from under 40,000 in 1930 to 450,000 in 1960. For the transplanted Congolese, the "structured world" of the village was left behind and a new mold had to be formed.

In the cities, the Africans found themselves forced to live in a "native quarter". Sometimes, as in Elizabethville, this area was planned by a company; sometimes, as in Leopoldville, it was carefully laid out by the state.

Most of these "native quarters" were divided into tribal areas; a man newly arrived from the village could live again with members of his own tribe. But there was no real chief, and housing was often cramped compared with that in the villages which, by African standards, were clean and not overcrowded. Used to knowing personally everyone he met, the transplanted villager saw more strangers in a morning than he would see at home in a lifetime; in fact, the impact of his first bus ride with forty complete strangers was enough to make many Africans jump from the vehicle.

Once he had a place to stay, the villager had to learn new words and new skills, such as those of the miner, the millhand, the dockworker, or the household servant, and he had to adjust to a rhythm of life built around a clock rather than the sun, moon, and seasons. Strange as it may seem to westerners, primitive men can agree to meet at a given place, *or* at a given time, but to combine exact "watch" time and "map" place is a concept which puts a new strain on their behavior patterns.

For the man from a Congo village transplanted to a city, the feared but dependable medicine man was far away, yet new spirits and hidden dangers lurked at every street corner—plus the very real dangers of robbers, false friends, confidence men, unscrupulous women, and over-zealous or brutal police officers and soldiers. In most "native quarters" there were far more men than women. Family ties were weak, prostitution was rampant, and beer parlors were everywhere. The old restraints and taboos of the village "family" were gone. Except for the priests and missionaries, who talked of salvation, and the police, who could be bribed, few knew or cared if a man did nothing all day, was drunk all night, or even committed a robbery.

The reports reaching the villages that city wages were relatively high were correct, but the cost of rent, food, clothes, transport, and amusements was even higher. Many uprooted villagers were broke long before pay day, forcing them to borrow from money-lenders at rates up to 100 percent per month. Under these circumstances the confused African sought something that would give his life meaning. One way to gain an ordered life was to join the Force Publique or the city police and let a Belgian officer become his new, all-powerful chief and medicine man. The big companies such as the OTRACO complex with its hundreds of river boats and dockers, also acted as parent and chief. Still a third solution was to get a job as a houseboy in a white home, but this required a knowledge of French or English and the learning of countless details regarding the rituals of dress, eating and drinking, and housekeeping practiced by the white men and their unpredictable women.

The white man's churches and missions offered some guidance on how to behave, but to the newly arrived villagers it seemed largely directed toward how to get into the white man's heaven or even a black heaven organized on European lines. Except for a selected few, schooling stopped at about the fourth grade. Trade unions were beginning to grow and their leaders sometimes took on the role of "city chief", but unless one was an officer or a ward organizer, unions gave only marginal security.

Thus, for the transplanted villager, city life in the 1940's and early 1950's was confusing but bearable. Then, as that period drew to a close, the world market for the raw materials of the Congo shrank sharply, wages dropped and unemployment grew. In towns like Leopoldville, Stanleyville, Luluabourg, the port of Matadi, and a half a dozen other river centers, thousands of Africans found themselves out of work and with little to do but sit in the shade. The city world of wages and clocks and action, for which they had left their villages, was melting away and the need for food and security became overwhelming.

Some went back to their villages, some turned to tribal associations, or trade unions, some found themselves caught up in "study groups" that later turned out to be communist-oriented, and some turned to crime. If they failed in crime, they were killed, beaten, or jailed. But, if, as the saying went in Leopoldville, one "hit the right street" he could become a "big man" overnight. A successful store robbery, a racket such as selling "protection" to bars, highjacking beer trucks, or "running a string of girls" in a dance hall could give man all the food, clothes, women, and prestige he needed. No father, uncle, or village council was on hand to criticize, and a man of means could even hire his own medicine man for strength against the evil spirits of the night or equally dangerous daytime competitors.

When the Congo was prosperous under the Belgians, the jump from village life to city living was hard enough at best. But when, after June of 1960, the strong hand of the Belgians in the army, the police, the government, and business weakened or disappeared, the "city villager" found himself in a world of chaos. It is not surprising, therefore, that since 1959, the former Belgian Congo has produced a series of dark and bloody events which seem far removed from the main stream of history. Actually the happenings there highlight in an extreme fashion many of the problems occurring today throughout most of the developing world. This is partly because the Congo is large—about 1,200 miles in either direction; because of its approximately 15,000,000 inhabitants who make it, after Nigeria, the most populous black state in Africa south of the Sahara; partly because of its central position; and partly because of its great mineral and agricultural wealth. The troubles of the Congo may also cast light on communist activity and thought about the cold war in Africa today.

A Look at Congolese History

The legends of many present-day tribes in the Congo suggest that they came from the north, possibly because the Sahara region has been drying up since the end of the last ice age. Some members of the Baluba tribe in the Congo can recite by memory the names of 128 chiefs who have ruled them, a succession running back to about the 5th century.

Recorded history, however, begins only with the coming of Europeans. In 1482 the Portuguese navigator Diego Cao sailed into the mouth of the Congo River, went up until he was stopped by the Matadi Rapids, and recorded the event on a rock where his inscription can still be read. In 1856, Dr. David Livingstone moved about in parts of the eastern and southern Congo, and Arab slave traders had explored the region considerably by 1860.

The first complete transit of the Congo by a westerner took place less than 90 years ago when Sir Henry Morton Stanley came down the length of the river taking 1,000 days to go from Zanzibar to the Atlantic. This was the period of the "scramble for Africa," and in 1885 King Leopold of the Belgians took over the area as his personal property under the euphemistic title of "the Congo Free State". When the forceful and bloody exploitation of the inhabitants became a scandal, the area was annexed by Belgium in 1908, though its legal entity was kept distinct from the mother country.

During the next fifty years the Belgians carried out a remarkable economic development of the Congo. They took some 70 major tribes, more than 15 million people, and welded them into a smoothly-working economic whole; they built six major and a dozen minor cities. They cleared large areas of land and developed highly successful plantations; they dug profitable mines, and they set up light industries. By 1959, more than 96,000 Belgians were working or living in the Congo.

To keep this economic machine working they opened 5,000 miles of riverways, built 3,000 miles of railroads, laid down 90,000 miles of roads, and ran the largest internal airline in Africa. By the late 1950's the Belgian Congo had more than 700,000 bicycles, and 50,000 automobiles—figures which may not overwhelm Detroit, but which are nevertheless striking for a developing area.

By African standards, wages in the Congo were high and working conditions good. In Leopoldville, for instance, a textile worker made $30 per month while workers in the Katanga mines made even more. The national product of the Belgian Congo rose over 70% from 1948 to 1958; the 8-hour day came into many industries; and real progress was made in terms of health benefits, maternity care, and retirement funds.

While the literacy rate for Africa as a whole was only 15%, elementary literacy in the Congo had reached 40%. About a million and a quarter

African children were in school, mostly in the first four grades, and two fine universities had been started. Some 250 newspapers and magazines were being published, most of them in French. Motion pictures were popular and sports were encouraged.

Some estimates suggest more than 20% of Belgium's total income came from the Congo. The Belgians were proud of what they had done, and they had much of which to be proud. They believed that their colonial pattern was the best on the continent, both for Belgians and for the Africans. And they thought that the African (whom as a rule they considered to be a child) was contented and even happy under their rule.

In spite of their realism on the economic side, the Belgians made a series of basic political miscalculations, and the small but growing number of politically-conscious Africans in the Congo had, by the mid-1950's, become increasingly discontented.

To begin with, Africans were unhappy that there were so few educational opportunities. More than a million Africans were in the lower grades of the new school system, getting just enough education to be field hands, servants, or unskilled workers. But the numbers in school dropped off very sharply in the middle grades, and there were only about two dozen African college graduates in the whole nation. In addition, the Belgians did not look with favor on Africans going to Europe to complete their schooling; they noted that nearly all the anti-colonial or pro-communist leaders in other African countries had received their higher education in Paris or London, perhaps with side trips to Moscow.

Another grievance: an African could be a farm worker, a factory worker, or a carpenter, but he could not be a superintendent or a lawyer. Among Africans there was growing bitterness over the difference between the Belgian standard of living and that of most Africans. Although wages were high in comparison to other nearby parts of Africa, only a handful of Congolese made as much as $400 per year; the average Belgian made $3,900 per year. Even more serious was the prohibition against Africans entering politics above the village or tribal level. The French were training African politicians in their Chamber of Deputies, and the British encouraged Africans to run for office and sit in Legislative Councils, which were essentially local Houses of Commons. Up until the mid-1950's, however, the Belgians were still arresting Congolese who became too politically-minded.

Equally serious was the failure of the Belgians to train an African above the lowest level in the keeping of law and order. Apart from relatively unimportant city police and rural gendarmes, order in the Congo was really maintained by the army known as the Force Publique. These forces were about 20,000 of the toughest Congolese the Belgians could enlist, headed by some 1,000 Belgian officers. Until independence, no Congolese in it had a rank higher than that of sergeant, and the responsibilities of a sergeant in the Force Publique were more limited than the title suggests.

Discipline was rough and the Force at times treated civilians with unusual brutality. Thus, if a tribe got out of hand, the army moved in, shot the evil doers, burnt or took away property, took over some of their women, and rapidly stamped out the uprising.

The Winds of Change

These grievances were serious, but they might have been rectified. What the leaders of the Congo felt was most serious of all was the lack of interest on the part of the Belgians in Congolese independence or home rule. Many Belgians, both in and out of the Congo, believed the Congolese would never be fit to govern themselves. Others thought that they might possibly be ready for self-government in a generation. The more informed thinkers on this subject took the position that independence might be possible in twenty years, when there was a reasonable number of college graduates and the gap in the educational ladder had been closed.

Perhaps because they rarely traveled in other parts of Africa, with only a few exceptions, the Belgians seemed unaware of the strength of "the winds of change". Many African states were demanding and getting independence, but the Belgians believed "their Africans were different", and that their approach to the colonial pattern was so effective it would last for years to come. They failed to see that, by 1955, some of the Congolese were stirring, holding both study groups and labor classes, and meeting with travelers and receiving new ideas from the outside world. With them also were students and workers who recognized that their fellow Africans were getting independence from the French and the British and saw no reason why the Belgians should not deal with them in like manner.

Three developments in Africa in 1958 pushed forward drastically the hour of independence:

1. General De Gaulle went to the French colonial capital of Brazzaville, across the river from Leopoldville, and made a speech offering the Africans there three political choices, one of which was independence. This had a wide impact on the Congolese who argued "if the French Congolese can be independent, why cannot we?"

2. Several hundred Belgian Congolese went or were taken to the World's Fair in Brussels in 1958. They included most of the top leaders in the field of government, education, and business, plus a small number of politicians. At the Fair, they met many persons from other parts of Africa and listened to accounts of how independence had been won or how soon it was to be achieved. Not by accident they were contacted by leftist and communist groups who expounded the idea that the Belgian Congo was over-

due for independence. Congolese who seemed receptive were taken on trips behind the Iron Curtain. Only a few became outright Communists, but a good many came back "African Neutralists" and "Nationalists" ready to break the ties with Belgium.

3. In December, 1958, an All-African Peoples' Congress was held in Accra, Ghana. This was an extremely nationalistic gathering attended by many leftists and some communists. It passed a series of resolutions regarding the future of Africa, including one which demanded immediate independence for all Africans still living under colonial rule. When Lumumba and other Congolese leaders returned from Brussels and Accra, they were ready to work aggressively for independence.

At the end of 1958, the Belgian Congo, on the surface, appeared calm and prosperous, but the pre-conditions of revolt were in evidence. By then the post-war boom in those raw commodities, which had made the Congo so wealthy and which had permitted the Belgians to develop their welfare state, had broken. Business profits were sinking, taxes to keep the program of social reform going were rising, and for almost the first time in what had been a tribal and agricultural society, there was unemployment.

The Congolese had a leader, in fact they had several leaders, and they were sufficiently good thinkers and orators to crystalize a whole series of political-social-economic grievances into a cause—the urge for immediate freedom. The leaders had outside help in the making of revolutions, including money and expertise. They had an organization of sorts; they had support from students and labor leaders, and they had some following among the sergeants of the Force Publique.

By January, tempers were running high in Leopoldville. When word came that the city government would not allow the leaders of the Abako Party to hold a meeting at the YMCA, Africans, including some 30,000 unemployed, started a demonstration. Several action groups appeared on the scene and soon the demonstration turned into a riot.

At first, cars were stoned and windows broken. Then the mob gained courage and began looting stores. As violence spread, block after block of houses in the African quarter were set afire; schools were gutted and churches and Catholic missions sacked.

The police tried to check the rioters with nightsticks and tear gas, but only succeeded in making them so angry they began using firearms. When the riots started again the next day, some of the Force Publique were brought in from Thysville and even they had to be reinforced by a battalion of Belgium paratroopers when the shooting spread. The official Belgian statement said that 49 Congolese were killed and 101 wounded, whereas a tract put out by the Bakongo Tribe reported the African dead at nearer 600.

In addition, white men were murdered, and white women attacked and killed. An era had ended in the Congo.

The riots took place on January 4 and 5, 1959. On January 13, the Belgian King issued a message which read, in part: ". . . it is our firm determination without undue procrastination but also without fatal haste to lead the Congolese population forward towards independence in prosperity and peace."

Although parts of this statement had been in preparation for some months, there seems little doubt that the Leopoldville riots had speeded its publication. It was the first time any official of importance had mentioned independence publicly, and the impact on Africans in the Congo was electric. Excitement among them increased further when the Belgian administration dissolved the Abako Party and arrested its leader, Joseph Kasavubu. On January 16, in order to get rid of some of the floating population, the provincial governor ordered 15,000 unemployed Africans to leave Leopoldville and go back to their villages. This may have reduced tension in the capital, but it spread the unrest throughout much of the lower Congo.

In February 1959, the Movement National Congolais [MNC] asked for clarification of the new Belgian policy, and two months later came out for the election of a Congolese government by January of 1961. The party's chief competitor, the Abako, then demanded that a central government be formed by March of 1960. April, 1959 saw riots in Leverville; there was fighting in Luluabourg; when the charismatic orator Lumumba spoke at an MNC meeting in Stanleyville, rioting became so violent that twenty-six Africans were killed. The Belgian authorities blamed Lumumba for the trouble and promptly arrested him, along with various other MNC leaders.

As a result of these events Belgium's Minister for the Congo, Van Hemelrijck, became convinced there would be serious trouble unless there was a rapid and effective transfer of authority. He therefore sought the setting up of an African provisional government by the end of 1959, to be followed by a four-year period for nation-building and general elections. In order to succeed in any such orderly and rapid transfer, the Belgian Government realized it needed the support of the European population in the Congo. Following the pattern developed earlier by De Gaulle in Algeria, Van Hemelrijck went to the Congo. He was given an enthusiastic reception by the Africans, but the attitude of the white settlers ranged from disinterest to hostility.

When opposition to his plans also developed in the Belgian Cabinet and the Parliament, Van Hemelrijck resigned early in September of 1959. The new minister, De Schrijver, said there would be popular elections at the commune level in December and that provincial assemblies would be elected before the end of 1960.

All this was to the good, but it was still another example of "too little and too late". In mid-September, Lumumba's MNC declared that they would not participate in the proposed elections and soon the Abako, the PSA and other minor parties followed suit. The Africans felt that these elections were a delaying tactic and they did not "wish to be ruled by elected Belgian puppets". Instead, they proposed that representatives of all Congolese parties be invited to a round table conference in Belgium.

The Belgians were faced with a difficult choice. On the one hand, they could expand their military forces and carry out a nationwide counterinsurgency operation which would be long and costly; on the other hand, they could come to terms with the leaders and play off the more conservative Africans against the extremists. Brussels had neither the money, the troops, nor the inclination to stop the spreading violence by force, so it chose the second alternative. In November, De Schrijver announced there would be "a grand conference" in January, 1960, in Brussels.

Some 96 Congolese leaders were in Brussels when the Conference opened on January 20. In this group there were a number of activists, including Lumumba and Kashamura. The Belgians were not disturbed, for the majority were relatively conservative Congolese who had worked for and with them in the past and were not talking about immediate independence. It was felt in Brussels that they could be counted on to vote "right" in the two important issues before the conference—the timing of independence and the character of the future state.

Even before the conference got underway, however, the Congolese were contacted by progressive Africans—persons from states which had already won their independence, plus a certain number of leftists, radicals, and communists. They supplied the delegation with money, legal brains, and entertainment, and convinced them that it was essential to organize and hold a common front on the important issues.

The radical parties like MNC-Lumumba, MNC-Kalonji, the Abako, the PSA, and the Parti Du Peuple voted in opposition to such matters as universal suffrage, the eligibility of Belgians for citizenship in the new state, and recognition of the King of Belgium as head of the independent Congo. On the other hand, Conakat, the PNP, and the traditional chiefs representing tribal groups supported these measures which would have strengthened the position of the Belgian authorities. A third group, including the Union Congolaise, held to a middle-of-the-road position. But all of these questions were unimportant in comparison with the granting of complete independence. When the Belgians tried to put off this point until late in the agenda, or even until some future conferences, consideration of independence was proposed at once. To the surprise of some of the Belgians, the moderate politicians and most of the "traditional chiefs" joined with the progressives in calling for immediate independence.

The Belgians pointed out the almost complete lack of high-government experience among Africans, the 12-year gap in the educational system, and other reasons for delaying independence for from ten to fifteen years. Nonetheless, the conference voted to grant complete independence on June 30, 1960. The extremists had won, but the Belgians felt they still could win, partly through influencing national elections, and partly as much-needed advisors after independence. Believing that their investments would be safe, no matter what happened, the Belgian businessmen were probably less disturbed than they appeared to be over these developments; in addition, the liberal attitude of King Baudoin was a calming factor.

The Belgian Gamble

There are those who believe that the Belgians took a calculated risk in giving the Congo independence too rapidly. They hoped to emulate Britain's gain in India, where British prestige and British business made a remarkable comeback after independence was granted. According to these observers of the African scene, the Belgians felt that the same swing of the politico-economic pendulum might happen to them in the Congo.

If this play failed, they thought they could peel off mineral-rich Katanga, the wealthiest part of the Congo, to be an "independent" country under their "friend" Tshombe. Katanga then would maintain close economic ties with its former metropole.

Many observers feel that the possibility of either of these alternatives working was smashed when, within ten days of the coming of independence, the Belgians sent back troops to try to restore order. This move not only crystallized feeling against the Belgians in all the Congo, but greatly strengthened Congolese and other African sentiment against Tshombe and the "pro-Belgian state" of Katanga.

Under arrangements worked out in Brussels, the first national elections for the Belgian area of the Congo were held in May, 1960. Some hundred parties were represented by 1,000 candidates. The Belgians backed their conservative or friendly supporters with funds and know-how, but progressive Congolese nationalists were even more active, supported by Africans from other countries which had already gained independence. Leftist and communist political organizers came or were brought into the Congo and were assigned to guide the thinking, develop the programs, and set up the organization for various parties. These included parts of Lumumba's wing of the MNC, Gizenga's and Mulele's factions of the PSA which centered in Kwilu Province, and the CEREA Party headed by Kashamura, an avowed Marxist who received money and light arms from the Belgian Communist Party. Younger elements in these parties carried on considerable violence and intimidation, scaring away voters who knew little or nothing of the democratic process.

A total of 137 seats in the national parliament were at stake. No single party received a majority, but Lumumba's MNC won 35, the largest single block, and he became the first Prime Minister. The 50-year old Kasavubu, a Catholic from the Ba-Congo tribe, won easily in the Presidential race.

The Congo became independent, June 30, 1960, and the Belgians put on an impressive ceremony for the occasion. Leaders from all of Africa and many parts of the world attended. There was dancing in the streets and unrestrained celebration by all except the most pessimistic. The Congolese leaders and people were happy at having gained independence. Nationalists and leftists were pleased because they expected to exert considerable influence on some members of the new regime.

Lumumba's extremely anti-Belgian remarks surprised and shocked many Europeans attending the ceremonies. Most of the Belgians, however, were not too unhappy, for they believed the Congo would follow the general path taken by British India. In other words, they thought that the Congolese would have to turn to more advanced countries for aid because they did not have the know-how to keep the country running at anything like its current level. Furthermore, the Belgians were convinced that, after a short period of anti-European outbursts, the leaders of the new Congo would seek advice from them because they were French-speaking, knew the Congo, and were among the few western peoples willing to live there.

For many years law and order in the Congo had been maintained by the Force Publique. The Force Publique had not escaped the liberal ideas which seeped into the Congo during the 1950's, including a small amount of communist infiltration into some units through school teachers and leaders of study groups. With the coming of independence, long-standing grievances regarding pay and the ceiling on promotion above the rank of sergeant rose to the surface. Because so many civilian Africans were being promoted fast, the sergeants in the Force Publique protested. The commanding officer of the Force, Belgian General Jansen, told his troops there would be opportunities for some noncommissioned Africans to become lieutenants and that there would be a modest pay raise. In conclusion, he said he expected his troops to go back to their barracks and "stop acting like civilians".

These were famous last words. By July 7, General Jansen was out of the Congo, and almost all of the Belgian officers were separated from their commands in the Force Publique, though some remained inside the country. The African sergeants and corporals took over jobs for which they had not been trained.

Law and order melted away. Such military units as still maintained discipline were too few to deal with the wave of demonstrations, riots, robberies, and rapes which broke out simultaneously in a large number of the cities and towns. In addition, old tribal quarrels flared up and intertribal fighting began in many forest areas.

Lumumba and the United Nations

For their penetration of the government, and for the psychological warfare to drive the Europeans out of the Congo, the leftists were fortunate in having someone like Patrice Lumumba as the top man in the government. The details of organizing and running the newly independent Congo, however, were too much for him; its political and economic problems were more than the enthusiastic ex-postal clerk could understand. He had the masses behind him and a few of the politicians, plus much support from other parts of Africa, but he lacked organizers inside the Congo and he had little executive experience. As time passed, the government bogged down, the parliament got out of hand, security forces failed to function, and in spite of outside aid, the economy ground to a halt.

The chaos reached such a point that two and a half companies of Belgian paratroopers were flown into the Congo on July 8 to be followed soon by 1,200 more Belgian troops. The Congo had been admitted to membership in the United Nations on July 7, and five days later a cable went to the Secretary-General from President Kasavubu and Prime Minister Lumumba. It stated that the Belgians had violated their treaty of friendship by sending troops into the Congo, and it asked for military aid for protection against this and other external aggression. The next day, the Congo declared that a state of war existed with Belgium.

In Kwilu province, and some other parts of the Congo, there flourishes a religious sect called Mpave, or Kimbanguist, after its founder Kimbangu, whose followers believe in the resurrection of a black Messiah. During the months before independence, leftist groups working among the Congolese in the deep bush had spread the word that the Messiah would appear when the Congo was free, and the Africans were told that on that day they would become like the whites. Some of them thought this referred to the color of their skins, while others believed it meant they would become like the Belgians in wealth, position, and power. To further these ideas, agitators had sold tin boxes to the tribesmen to be buried in graveyards. The Congolese were instructed that once they were "really free", they should dig up the tin boxes which would then be full of gold.

In some places the more primitive Congolese were even taught that the electric lights which they saw shining in the buildings of many of the Christian missions were really the headlights of automobiles. It was explained these vehicles would come out of the ground at the time of independence and be theirs if they took over the missions. There were several cases of Africans cutting roads from mission compounds to their villages so they could drive these automobiles home.

Independence day came and went but the Messiah did not appear; the believers did not become white; their tin boxes were not filled with gold; and automobiles did not come out of the ground. When they complained to their leaders they were told that the "Day of Miracles" had not occurred because the Belgians and other Europeans were still in the Congo and they, the blacks, were not really free. Discontent then turned to anger, the cars of Europeans were stoned, mission stations were attacked, plantations were burned, Belgian men were killed, and Belgian women were raped.

These incidents were bad and numerous, but not so bad or so numerous as reports on the radio or the Congolese press made them. Hour after hour, Radio Leopoldville and other Congolese stations, which were controlled by Kashamura and his followers, played up the riots, attacks, and atrocities. In addition, Africans were encouraged to look over the homes of Europeans which they wanted for their own use in the future, and Congolese groups began entering or breaking into the larger houses and scaring and sometimes attacking European wives while their husbands were at work. As a final psychological trick, in a few towns, such as Luluabourg, lottery tickets were sold on the white women.

Faced with such propaganda, plus disintegration of the government, virtual stoppage of business, widespread robbery, pillage and arson, along with some murder and rape, all over-emphasized on the government radio and in the press, the morale of many Belgians cracked. During July and August, 1960, more than 20,000 Belgian technicians and their families left the Congo; 1,500 of them crossed the river to Brazzaville in one night. With them went most of the brains that had kept government and business functioning in the Congo.

A certain number of Belgians had planned to leave at the time of independence. Still more left when they saw that things were not going well. Apparently the deliberately-organized psychological campaign speeded the departure of many more. The first stage in any Communist seizure is to put an end to the government of the colonial power; the second is to get rid of the western technicians. By the end of July, 1960, both of these goals had been largely accomplished in the Congo.

To fill the vacuum, more than 400 Communist technicians flew into the Congo in July alone. Some came as diplomats, some as advisers in the bureaus; others were transport or health experts. Most of them stayed in the cities, but a few moved out to the bigger plantations. While they took directions from Lumumba and his ministers, they undoubtedly reported also to the much-expanded Soviet Embassy.

Communist Infiltration and Political Chaos

Lumumba was an eloquent man, and the personification of a partially-educated Congolese seeking to shed colonial chains. He was also a convicted embezzler, a sometimes heavy drinker, and a speaker who changed facts to suit his purposes. Actually Lumumba had been in jail for sedition when the Belgians, who needed an advocate for a strong central government in order to balance Kasavubu, released him and sent him to the round table conference which gave the Congo its independence. It was his second trip to Brussels under Belgian auspices. Burning with a desire to help the Congolese, Lumumba's ideas on how this should be accomplished changed almost every day, and from a fairly conservative beginning, he reached a point where he could say and believe: "I am an idea. I am the Congo."

Such a man was unlikely to distinguish between socialists and communists, and with the coming of independence he was the type whom the Communists believed they could influence. Thus, although there were true African patriots in the government, Lumumba soon found himself surrounded by leftists, fellow travelers, and outright communists. The Deputy Premier was Antoine Gizenga, a Marxist who had been to Moscow and had taken a Czech-sponsored course in communism in Conakry, the capital of Guinea. Lumumba's Special Counsel was Pierre Elengesa who had studied in Moscow in the late 1950's and who supported the Soviet proposal for having the Communists develop the Congo's economy.

State Secretary Jacques Lumbala, also a graduate of the communist school in Conakry, favored the use of Russian rather than United Nations troops to restore order in the Congo. More aggressive was Pierre Mulele, another Conakry graduate, who had organized Marxist courses in Leopoldville and whose chief assistant, Elie Bouras, was a known Greek Communist.

In Lumumba's Cabinet as Minister of Information was Anicot Kashamura, who had studied Marxism in Conakry and who had been taken to both Russia and China. Politically confused, he pushed Communist material on Radio Leopoldville, occasionally interspersed with the programs of Moral Rearmament.

On the economic side, Lumumba was guided by Alphonse Nguvulu, Minister of Economic Affairs, who had been to the Belgian Communist Party Congress in Liege just before the elections of 1960, and who made violent anti-white speeches over Radio Leopoldville. Also close to Lumumba was his Press Attache, Serge Michel, who had been labelled as a Communist by the French for his activities during the Algerian Rebellion. He strengthened the leftist passages in Lumumba's speeches and urged the people of the Congo to spy on each other.

Moreover, there was the attractive Guinean half-caste, Madame Andree Blouin, who had been brought into the Congo by Mulele and who was believed by some to have been at one time the Soviet's number one agent in the Congo. On the suggestion of Vice-Premier Gizenga she was made Chief Protocol Officer, a spot from which she could be sure that communist diplomats always had easy access to Lumumba and other high officials of the government.

This chaotic situation naturally produced growing doubts about the future of Lumumba and his government at the United Nations and in various western capitals. At the same time, resistance to Lumumba's erratic policies also began to build up in the Congolese National Assembly and other parts of the Leopoldville government. Part of this feeling sprang from personal opposition to Lumumba whose actions were usually unpredictable, whose decisions were increasingly arbitrary, and who had begun to hold press conferences at odd hours to announce policies which had been discussed only with his leftwing advisers. Some of his opposition was natural tribal jealousy, and some of it was more or less normal jockeying for power in the new state. But a feeling had begun to grow among Congolese leaders, both in the government and in the military, that the Congo's independence was in name only. As one of them put it, "we have become free of the Belgians who were tough but understood us, merely to be taken over by the Russians who are tougher and understand us less."

Seeing the country dissolving beneath him, Lumumba asked for assistance from various countries including the United States. To avert a direct confrontation with Russia, however, President Eisenhower suggested that Lumumba go to the United Nations for help, and that the United States would render its share of aid through that body.

On the night of July 13, the United Nations Security Council adopted a Tunisian resolution calling on the Belgians to withdraw their troops and authorizing the Secretary-General to provide such military assistance to the Congo as might be necessary. The first United Nations troops arrived in Leopoldville from Ghana and Tunisia within twenty-four hours and the Belgian Army began its withdrawal soon afterwards.

One aspect of the chaos in the Congo was the spread of tribal revolts and the growth of regionalism. The most important disaffection of this sort developed in the southeast Congo province of Katanga. This was the center of the mining operations of the Belgian-controlled Union Miniere, whose uranium production played an important role in the making of the first atomic bomb. Convinced that the rest of the Congo was hopelessly out of control and would either sink into tribalism or end up under the domination of Moscow, Moise Tshombe announced that Katanga was independent.

When the United Nations buildup of troops in the Congo began to be substantial, Tshombe issued a warning that he did not wish them in Katanga. And as the last Belgian troops left the Leopoldville area, Tshombe stated that he wanted them to remain in Katanga for as long as eighteen months.

At the end of July, Lumumba came to the United States where he visited with high officials in Washington and New York, and received a pledge of technical and financial aid for the Congo through the United Nations. Then on his way back to Leopoldville he stopped in Guinea, and was given assurance that both Guinea and Ghana would provide armed assistance to the Congo against Belgian or any other European forces within its borders.

By August, the United Nations mission to the Congo was expanding rapidly. A race developed between the United Nations and the Communist Bloc to see which could get advisers into key positions faster. The Communists were prepared to move into the Congo, but not in numbers or at a rapid rate.

The feeling against the Belgians ran so high in the United Nations that, on August 9, the Security Council, by a vote of nine to zero, adopted a resolution calling upon the government of Belgium to withdraw its troops immediately from the province of Katanga and declared that "the entry of the United Nations Forces into the Province of Katanga is necessary for the full implementation of this resolution." On the same day Albert Kalonji, a rival of Lumumba's, proclaimed the independence of his tribal area known as Kasai.

Three days later, Secretary-General Dag Hammarskjold flew into Elizabethville, the capital of Katanga, with an advanced United Nations unit of 300 Swedish troops to replace the Belgians in that province. Brussels, however, announced that it would not fully evacuate its three big bases in the Congo. At this, Lumumba, who was falling increasingly under the influence of pro-Soviet advisers, demanded that all white United Nations troops leave the Congo and that from then on only African soldiers serve with the United Nations in that country.

On August 16, Lumumba declared that his government had lost confidence in some of the personnel sent to the Congo by the United Nations, and he asked that a 14-nation Afro-Asian Commission be set up to replace it. He also demanded the immediate dispatch of non-white United Nations troops to Katanga, the withdrawal of all non-African soldiers from that province, and the placing of the United Nations' planes at his disposal.

As the days passed, Congolese feeling against the white units of the United

Nations grew, resulting in a series of incidents such as the manhandling of eight Canadians by Congolese troops. In an effort to check the growing breach, the Secretary-General appointed Ambassador Dayal of India to serve as his personal representative in the Congo. In spite of this, disorders, housebreakings, robberies, attacks, and beatings increased in Leopoldville and other cities.

On September 2, Lumumba announced that the leader of an opposition party, Jean Bolikango, and six of its members had been arrested for plotting his assassination. Lumumba's old rival, President Kasavubu, was disturbed by this arbitrary action, and a struggle for power developed between the two leaders. Finally, September 15, the President dismissed Lumumba, accusing him of projecting discord into the government, depriving citizens of fundamental liberty, upsetting the economy of the nation, and plunging the country into civil war.

In his place Kasavubu called on Joseph Ileo, President of the Senate, to form a new government. Lumumba promptly declared that Kasavubu was no longer President of the Congo and called upon the people, the workers, and the army to rise. Lumumba was supported by many members of the Council of Ministers who officially accused Kasavubu of having committed high treason, declared him deprived of his state functions, and overrode the dismissal of Premier Lumumba. The Congolese Chamber of Representatives voted 60 to 19 to nullify the dismissal of the Prime Minister. Absent from this voting were 29 senators, including a block of anti-Lumumba representatives from Katanga who had returned to Elizabethville.

By now the government of the Congo was completely paralyzed and even greater disorder began to spread through the nation. If the state were to survive, order had to come from somewhere, and the main source of power was the Chief of Staff of the Force Publique, former sergeant, but now colonel, Joseph Mobutu. Much of the Force Publique was a shadow of its former self, but some units still had discipline and took orders from Mobutu. The Chief of Staff arrested Lumumba, but the guard put around him was not large, and the popular leader was soon rescued by Congolese soldiers who were more loyal to Lumumba. Lumumba thereupon collected some additional loyal troops whom he could trust as guards and called a joint session of Parliament, which conferred special powers on him to rule the Congo. There was almost as much confusion inside the chamber as outside, but the vote was believed to have been 88 for Lumumba versus 25 against him. Since the total membership at the time was 221, this was too few for a quorum, but Lumumba was not deterred.

Finally, Mobutu announced a temporary army take-over to neutralize both the Lumumba and the Ileo governments and sent home what was left of the National Parliament. When Kasavubu ordered the numerous Communist missions and technicians to leave the Congo, Mobutu carried out the exodus so effectively that more than a dozen planeloads of Communist sympathizers flew out of Leopoldville in less than a week. Some of them went only to Stanleyville, the leftist center, 800 miles up the Congo River, but most of them left the country entirely. Their departure marked the collapse of Moscow's plan to dominate the new government by infiltrating Communist advisers. With it ended the first phase of the assault on the new Republic of the Congo. The Communists had been stopped, partly by the United Nations, partly by the United States and the Belgians, but mostly by Africa itself. The Congolese did not want to become a Red satellite.

The Congo has suffered many growing pains since that first summer of independence and its early years have been incredibly difficult. The rebellion in Katanga had to be put down, two more attempts at take-over by Moscow and two additional tries by Peking were checked. Order had to be brought back out of economic chaos. Furthermore, after 1965, Congolese relations with Belgium took a turn for the worse, leading to claims by Mobutu that the Belgians were planning a coup, and to the forced departure of the Belgian Consul-General. Internally, the continued lack of administrative know-how, a well-organized Congo-wide party, and a really popular national government held back the democratic process.

Only time will tell whether the Congo has gained sufficient strength to stand as a nation. In 1967, no one can deny that the young country has overcome more than its share of communist-inspired insurgency. On at least five occasions, it has been the center of cold war conflicts in Africa and has preserved its independence.

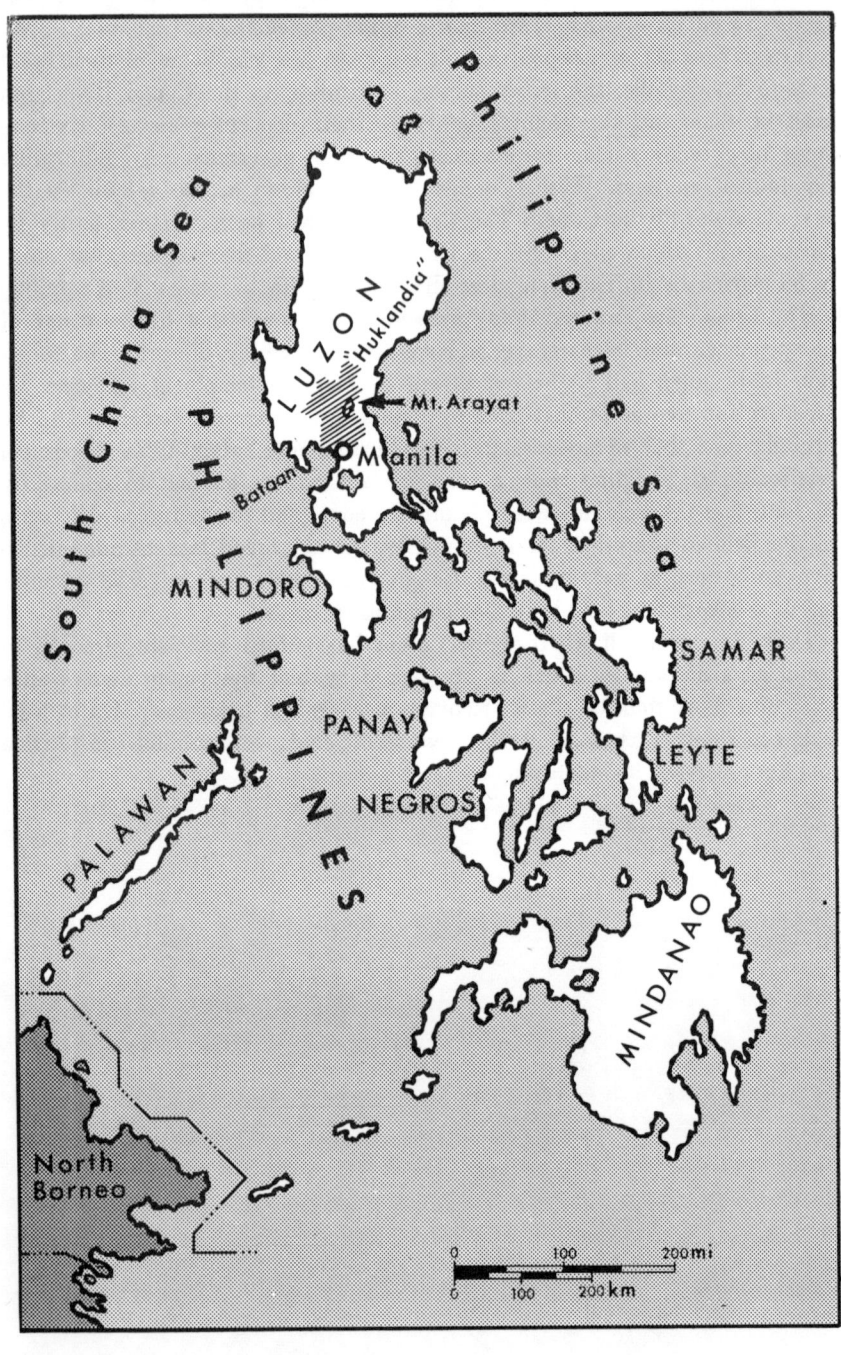

CHAPTER VIII

THE PHILIPPINES: HOW MAGSAYSAY STOPPED THE HUKS

IN midsummer of 1950, the Philippines were ripe for revolt. The government was weak, corrupt, and lacking in popular support. Unemployment was widespread, while insiders were making huge fortunes. Elections were fraudulent and the people had lost faith in democracy. Many peasants were without land, and those who had small holdings were squeezed between absentee landlords, unscrupulous moneylenders, and the growing power of the Hukbalahap guerrillas (Huks), who formed a well-armed, communist-led party of revolt. With headquarters in Manila and guerrilla forces of 100,000, they controlled wide areas of the island of Luzon, planned to take Manila by Christmas of 1950, and all of the Philippines within two years. It was clear that only a miracle could prevent a communist victory.

Historical Background

For some 350 years after Magellan reached the Philippines in 1521, the Spaniards ruled the islands. They developed large estates and took out much wealth, chiefly in the form of gold and agricultural products. The British occupied Manila briefly in 1762, but although the Moros [Moslems] rebelled occasionally, in general the islands were typical of Spanish colonial areas until the mid-19th century. Then, with nationalism developing in Latin America, the idea of independence spread in the Philippines. Revolts broke out against the Spanish, one of which was in process when the Spanish-American War began in 1898. Manila was captured by Filipino and American troops in August of that year, and four months later Spain ceded the islands to the United States. The Philippine leader, Aguinaldo, then asked that the Philippines be given its independence. When this was refused, he started a revolt against the Americans which lasted three years.

American rule continued for a generation, but thanks to governors like

William Howard Taft and Henry L. Stimson, the islands made substantial political and economic progress. Then in 1934, a bill providing for a self-governing Philippine Commonwealth passed the U. S. Congress and was signed by President Franklin D. Roosevelt. The Philippine Republic was established later that year. Its constitution was similar to that of the United States, and complete independence in 1946 was guaranteed.

Although the cities progressed under American rule, many country areas such as those in central Luzon had poor roads, primitive schools, and few hospitals or clinics. Tropical disease and illiteracy were widespread. Furthermore, most of the able and ambitious government officials sought work in the cities. Consequently, rural areas had to put up with fourth-rate officials who usually did little for the people and much for themselves.

Under these circumstances it is not surprising that there should have been agrarian unrest centered in the rice-producing areas of central Luzon. One popular leader was a labor organizer named Ramos who, in 1933, launched a political party called the Sakdal. Despite restrictive election practices, the Sakdalistes managed to elect several public officials including a provincial governor. In 1935, fearing that the new constitution would hurt their position, the Sakdals carried out a bloody uprising. The revolt was quickly put down and Ramos fled to Japan. The affair was widely publicized and set the pattern for things to come.

When the Japanese tide swept over the Philippines, its leaders expected to find the inhabitants bitterly anti-American and their policy in the islands was in part based on this fallacy. The Japanese did not understand the Filipinos who, though Asian, fought alongside the Americans against the invaders. In a mistaken effort to inspire respect and obedience, the Japanese frequently acted with arrogance and cruelty.

With much outward show, the Japanese announced that the Philippines were now independent, and they set up a government which had little support and less respect. The Filipinos soon found out that their "independent" government took orders directly from Japanese advisers.

The Japanese censored everything printed or spoken, and the audience for American broadcasts grew rapidly. Even suspicion of anti-Japanese feeling led to arrest, imprisonment, torture, and often death. Suspect villages were flattened, livestock was killed or taken away, food supplies dwindled, and the general standard of living dropped. Robbery and rape by Japanese or pro-Japanese Filipinos was condoned. And, on top of all this, Filipinos were forced to bow in respect each time they met a Japanese.

Many Filipinos left the cities and villages occupied by the Japanese and became guerrillas. The thousands of islands of the Philippines—many of them mountainous and heavily wooded, with swampy lowlands—are ideal for guerrilla activity. Operating from these remote areas, dozens of guerrilla chieftains sprang up with semi-independent bands. Their impact on the Filipino nationalists was immense. Furthermore, they were so numerous and so scattered, they were in a position to spy on Japanese actions in the greatest detail. General Douglas MacArthur called them "history's most effective fifth column". Important among the guerilla groups were the communist-oriented Huks.

The Communists and the Huks

The groundwork for communism in the Philippines had been laid in 1925 when an Indonesian Communist, Tan Malaka, visited the islands to get delegates to go to a conference in Canton run by the communist-dominated International Organization of Trade Unions. The secretary of the Philippine Labor Congress, a man named Crisanto Evangelista, not only went to Canton, but attended similar trade union conferences in Berlin and Moscow. He became a communist himself and affiliated his Philippine Labor Congress with the Red International. The next year, when the Philippine Labor Congress split, Evangelista headed the radical wing which was soon reorganized as KAT, a political party with working class membership. Its constitution, which was approved in August, 1930, followed the teachings of Marx, Lenin, and Stalin. On the 13th anniversary of the Communist Revolution in Russia, the KAT adopted the name of the Communist Party of the Philippines.

The organization was legal at first and held its small and quiet meetings openly. As time passed, however, these gatherings became larger and more disorderly. Finally, in September 1931, the Communist Party of the Philippines was declared illegal and went underground. An affiliate, the Society of the Children of Sweat, was also outlawed.

When this happened, its top leaders went to jail where they remained for many years. Then, in 1938, an important American Communist named James Allen was sent to the Philippines to help obtain their release. Once the high command of the old Party was free, negotiations took place between a newly-organized Communist Party of the Philippines and the Socialist Party, under Pedro Santos. Allen played a role in arranging a merger which was sanctioned by the Communist International. Not long after this, "democratic elections" were held among the joint membership of the Socialist and Communist parties. Evangelista, the long-time communist labor leader, became chairman; Santos became vice-chairman; and Guillermo Capadocia, one of the communist founding fathers who had been arrested in 1931, became secretary. With his work well done, James Allen returned to California, but he arranged to have the Communist Party in the Philippines responsible to a group called the "Philippine Committee of the Communist International" with its headquarters in Los Angeles. Because Evangelista's political thinking had become "a little out of date", he was sent to Moscow to study the latest revolutionary techniques.

The expulsion of the Americans from the Philippines in World War II and their replacement by the hated Japanese gave the Communists an opportunity to move into the role of on-the-spot defenders of Philippine independence. They organized a guerrilla force, "the peoples anti-Japanese army", whose long title was shortened to Hukbalahap or Huks. Although these guerrillas had firm bases in the mountains, their strength centered around the poor rice farmers of central Luzon.

Veteran Marxist leaders Evangelista and Santos, imprisoned by the Japanese, were so badly treated they died shortly after being released. The third member of the communist-socialist hierarchy, Guillermo Capadocia, was expelled from the Party for collaborating with the Japanese. Thus, in early 1942 a new generation of communists had to take over the leadership of the Huk movement. These included Jesus Lava, Mateo de Castillo, Luis Taruc, and Casto Alejandrino. Taruc became the new party leader. Peasants, many of them followers of Pedro Santos, welcomed the opportunity to take up arms. Among them also were refugees from the Japanese, and even gangsters and outlaws who had fled from the urban centers to evade the long arm of the Japanese law.

At first the Huks devoted their energies to keeping out of the way of the Japanese, getting food, and stealing, capturing, or buying arms and munitions. Then, in order to deny wealth to the landlords and supplies to the Japanese invaders, they began to destroy what they could not take away. The manor houses of particularly obnoxious landlords were burned down, if possible with their owners inside.

These activities were neither well-directed nor properly coordinated at the start. To correct this situation, the Chinese Communist Party sent four experts to the Philippines under the command of Field General Ong Kiet, who gave the guerrillas more discipline and direction. Taruc, the able and energetic communist leader, was designated operational commander. At first, the guerrillas numbered about 500 and were armed with weapons abandoned by the Americans or captured from the Japanese. Later, Taruc was able to supply his growing forces with arms smuggled into the Philippines from American sources.

The center for training Huk guerillas was in the Mount Arayat region of central Luzon. Some of the indoctrination was done by experts from the famous Eighth Route Army of Chinese revolutionary fame. Before long, Taruc had enough Chinese fighting under him to organize an all-Chinese guerrilla force which received financial support from wealthy Chinese living in the Philippines.

Using the techniques which the Communists had found successful elsewhere, the Huks organized "defense groups" at the village level headed by communists. These were supposedly to protect the villages against attack, but they were used as village shadow governments. As such, they collected taxes, ran schools and clinics, presided over courts, issued communist newspapers, performed marriages, and generally functioned as communist centers of authority.

In addition to the defense corps, the Huks set up a "struggle force" which collected supplies, highjacked convoys, and handled the distribution of weapons, food, and medicines in a way to strengthen the cause. Friendly villages were given extra quantities of food or money, whereas villages which did not cooperate were subjected to brutal reprisals. The Huk department of intelligence had its own "eyes and ears" and carried out investigations, kidnappings, and executions.

On the propaganda side, the Huks set up a Department of Culture and Information which supplied political advisers to every military unit as well as to the defense corps and the struggle force. One of their most successful techniques was organizing discussion groups among the guerrillas and the peasants. During these sessions opinion could be crystallized and persons of hostile thought recognized and later liquidated.

Within a year, the Huks had more than 10,000 guerrillas fighting for them, largely against the Japanese, but also against other guerrilla bands who threatened their control of areas such as the central Luzon rice bowl. American guerrillas operating in that area tried to form a joint command with the Huks at that time, but the American commanding officer was captured and killed by the Japanese and the plans were not carried out.

Recognizing the Huk strength, the Japanese made a strong offensive in 1944 against Huk headquarters on Mount Arayat. Many Huks were killed or captured, but the core of the movement survived. By 1945, the guerrillas were stronger than ever. According to Huk reports, they had taken part in more than 1,200 actions against Japanese forces and had killed at least 25,000 pro-Japanese Filipinos.

From the communist point of view, the years of anti-Japanese fighting had been a great boon. The war had forced the Huks to gain the confidence of thousands of peasants; they had learned the art of guerrilla warfare; and they had even been able to organize and run their own shadow government. Since the population of the Philippines was largely agrarian, this accomplishment gave them a broad base for future political power.

Thus, by the end of the war, the Huks had become a legend in the Philippines. They had created an image of a brave fighting force which kept the resistance going and which constantly attacked the Japanese, and they held a considerable area of land until the arrival of American forces under General MacArthur.

In October, 1944 the Huks took advantage of the brief hiatus between the Japanese retreat and the arrival of the Americans to dominate new areas and put in their own officials at almost every level, until they controlled six provinces. They even sent a guerrilla force to take over the city of Manila, but the U. S. Army disarmed it, and Taruc and some of his lieutenants were put under arrest for a time. The Huk guerrilla units in the countryside were then ordered to surrender their arms. They refused, and demanded to be incorporated into the Philippine Army as a unit. This powerplay was quickly rejected, and the Huks went underground. The men of the fighting units dispersed after burying their arms, and the communists started a new recruiting campaign.

Government Reestablished

President Osmena and several other Filipino leaders, who had been taken out of the islands before the fall of Bataan, had been in the United States during the War. When MacArthur returned, they were with him. Three days after they landed on Leyte, General MacArthur announced that he was restoring "government by constitutional process" as rapidly as conditions would permit. He handed over civil government on Leyte to President Osmena. When Luzon Island was liberated, President Osmena was given full civil authority to reestablish a Filipino government. The police were reconstituted, the civil service reorganized, the courts reconvened, and the legislature again went into session. In addition, a free press was encouraged, Radio Manila went on the air without censorship, schools began to reopen, and hospitals received medical supplies.

In an election held early in 1946, Manuel Roxas was elected President of the new independent Republic of the Philippines and was sworn in, July 4 of that year. Manila was a shambles, thousands of towns, villages, and farms were destroyed, and the country had lost much of its capacity to produce food or money-making exports. In spite of these conditions, however, thinking Filipinos believed that with an able, honest, and far-seeing government their future would be bright.

Although they had vanished as a fighting force, the Huks were politically active and ran their own candidates at the local and provincial level in the Philippine election of 1946. Realizing they were not strong enough to elect national candidates, they joined with the Communist-organized Democratic Alliance which supported Osmena. The Huks also were able to control part of the Congress of Labor Organizations, as well as the old Socialist Party, and to combine them into the National Peasants Union, the PKM. This was a legal party, and the Huks took care to remain behind the scenes.

The Philippines needed imports, for there was a great shortage of food, building materials, farm implements, medicines, and other important items.

UNRRA shipments helped, and, in 1946, the U. S. Congress provided war damage payments of about $400 million. Then the Reconstruction Finance Corporation advanced a $100 million loan, and other U. S. agencies followed suit until American assistance to the Philippines amounted to over $2 billion in the next eight years. The result was an inflation which pushed up the cost of living to six times the level of the last prewar year.

A small group of operators became rich, often through graft. The worst scandal grew out of the handling of war surpluses. The United States transferred $600 million worth of war materiel to the Philippines for $220 million. Some of this went directly to the Philippine Government; the rest fell into the hands of black market operators who resold the items. The government ended up by receiving only about $40 million, while private profits were many times that amount.

After less than two years in office, able and forceful President Roxas died in April, 1948. He was succeeded by his Vice-President, Elpideo Quirino. Quirino was surrounded by unscrupulous office holders, politicians, bureaucrats, and cronies. Under their influence everything in Manila was for sale: surpluses, offices, or tax exemptions. By 1950 it was said that seventy-five percent of taxes due were not being collected; but much of what was came from "the little people".

The sale of offices became so flagrant that in some cases they were auctioned off, if not on a public basis at least to "friends of friends". Import duties could be avoided for a price, public lands were being sold to insiders, and more and more legitimate businessmen found themselves hamstrung unless they crossed the proper palms with gold.

Beyond this graft, there swirled an underworld empire of racketeering, extortion, kidnapping, gambling, and white slavery, whose lurid operations became well-known throughout the islands. Thus, the insiders grew in power, and the discontent of the poor mounted week by week.

In all of this the people still had one hope. Before the War, under the United States, they had seen elections which were relatively honest. Now that they were independent, with a government based on the pattern of the United States, they believed it would be possible to have honest democracy and "kick the rascals out". President Quirino was the candidate of the Liberal Party in 1948, running against Jose Laurel of the Nacionalistas. There were many other issues, but the campaign turned on the corruption in government under Quirino.

Any hopes the masses may have had that they could get a fair hearing and put an end to their grievances were soon dispelled. The politicians of the Liberal Party in the wards and precincts picked their close supporters as voting inspectors, and the ballots were "counted" by party stalwarts. To "keep order" the Liberals organized "Peace and Security Squads", often made up of gangsters and criminals who earned their money by seeing to it that persons who might vote the Nacionalista ticket had difficulty in getting to the polls. When the Nacionalistas objected, dozens of fights broke out. More than 200 persons lost their lives on Election Day.

From early morning, there was never any doubt of the outcome, and Quirino's Liberal Party captured 68 out of the 100 seats in the House of Representatives. For hundreds of thousands of Filipinos this was the end of a dream. Quirino was reelected, but he had lost public confidence. Even more serious, great numbers had lost confidence in the idea of democracy and the possibility that their grievances could be met through the ballot or under any western-type government.

The Communists did not cause either the breakdown of the democratic process or the economic chaos. What they did do, however, was speed up the breakdown of public and private morality and to prepare for the day when disillusioned Filipinos would find the situation so intolerable they would take matters into their own hands.

The election campaign of 1948 had been bitter and the Huks made widespread use of terror. When the ballots were finally counted, it was announced that six candidates of the Democratic Alliance, including Jesus Lava and Taruc, had been elected to Parliament. They were soon thereafter unseated following charges of violent and fraudulent campaign tactics. Lava and Taruc then returned to central Luzon, where they pushed forward with the Huk-led peasant uprising.

The Huk Rebellion

This revolt had broken out first in May, 1946. Huk armed strength was then about 15,000 men. Rarely had a guerrilla force been so well-armed and trained. They were the elite elements of the Huk guerrillas who had fought the Japanese on the same terrain for three years. They began with raids on police stations to obtain more arms, and organized terror in anti-Huk farm and village areas.

To protect the villagers, the government in Manila moved in substantial numbers of constables, but these proved to be worse than useless. In order to build up rural police rapidly after the departure of the Japanese, the new government had taken in anyone who applied, including men with every form of police record. It is not surprising, therefore, that when these constabularies moved into a village they took what they wanted. In fact, their record was so bad that in some cases the Huks were invited into settlements to protect the villagers against the constabulary.

Thus the peasants were caught between corrupt and vicious police and the Marxist Huks who played fair with their supporters but liquidated their opponents. Many of the farmers thought the Huks were the lesser of two evils. The Huks promised that, once in power, they would put an end to tenant farming, break up the big estates, organize a system of low-interest loans, and insure good prices for farm crops. As a result, Huk numbers and support increased, and ambitious young men from the lower classes, as well as intellectuals, joined their cause.

It is interesting to note that, although the Huk rebellion flourished among peasants and migrant laborers, it met with little success in areas where most of the farmers owned their own land and were relatively well off. The Huks were active in the cities and gained control of some labor unions in order to use them to carry out strikes and riots. They concentrated on student groups, government workers, and, where possible, on the officers and men of the armed forces. Although the Huk strength was in the countryside, the central headquarters of the communist politburo was in the city of Manila.

Due in part to disintegration of the Philippine economy and growing corruption in government, the Huks were able to dominate the four provinces of central Luzon and to expand slowly to the other areas where there were many tenant farmers. Disturbed by the growing Huk trend, the Philippine Government, in 1947, launched a major attack on the Huk stronghold in the Mount Arayat area. It was spearheaded by a 2,000 man constabulary with artillery, but the results were pitifully small. The Huks simply melted away, slipping out to other areas or burying their arms, picking up their plows and acting the part of dumb peasants. After this fiasco, few people took the government troops seriously and the Huks carried on ambushes and attacks in the daytime, even on important roads.

In March of 1948, both the Huks and the Communist Party of the Philippines (CPP) were declared illegal, along with their affiliate, the PKM. But a month later after President Roxas' death, his successor, Quirino, started negotiations for an amnesty. Taruc went to Manila where he was given a warm welcome and for a short time allowed to take his seat in Congress. Negotiations there continued for several weeks, but little progress was made. In August, 1948, the communist leader slipped out of Manila and went back to Huklandia to head his guerrilla forces once again.

The Huks speeded up their aggressive actions. They changed their party name to HMB, and said their goal was "to liberate the people from American imperialism and neocolonialism". They mounted a series of raids on army camps, police stations, and supply centers, most of which were successful.

One of their attacks backfired badly in April, 1949. Mrs. Manuel Quezon, the widow of the great Philippine nationalist who had died in the United States during the War, was motoring with an official escort to a town in eastern Luzon to dedicate a monument to her beloved husband. The Huk intelligence organization learned of the automobile convoy and may have concluded that President Quirino was in the party. In any case, when the cars reached a narrow point in the road, a Huk patrol opened up with machine guns and Mrs. Quezon was shot and killed as were her popular daughter and several leading officials.

The Huks appeared indifferent to the public indignation and pressed forward in what they believed were the final stages of their revolution. Following standard guerrilla practice, their units became larger and they began to attack towns and small cities. Anti-communist officials were kidnapped or murdered in broad daylight and constabulary barracks were ransacked. The Huks entered hospitals where they murdered wounded government troops. They took over the provincial capital of Tarlac and killed and looted at will. The Chief of Staff of the Armed Forces of the Philippines was ambushed two miles from his own headquarters. By August, 1950, the Huks were moving freely in the outskirts of Manila and openly shooting down victims within the city limits.

Documents seized later showed that the Huks planned to capture Manila on Christmas Eve of 1950. This was to be done through a general uprising headed by students, trade union elements, and embattled farmers; plans for this coup were backed by over 100,000 well-armed communist guerrillas divided into 35 Huk divisions. The final take-over of all the Philippines was to be completed by May 1, 1952. The communist plans were detailed and well-laid. Government strength appeared to be lessening and the hour of Huk victory appeared at hand.

Magsaysay Given Control

In September, 1950, President Quirino called on 43-year-old Ramon Magsaysay and gave him a free hand to end the Huk rebellion. Magsaysay was possibly the only Filipino who combined the courage, wisdom, knowledge, and experience to succeed at such a task so late in the game.

When the Japanese invaded, he served for a time with American troops in the islands; later he was sent back to Zambales to organize underground resistance. He believed in the cause of Philippine freedom; he knew his province well; and he was a born leader. The Japanese tried in vain to capture him. Soon he came to symbolize the independence movement throughout western Luzon. After the War, the people of Zambales sent Magsaysay to the House of Representatives.

He was in no sense typical of Philippine politicians. He was not a lawyer; he had no Spanish or Chinese blood but rather was a pure Malayan. He looked and acted like a leader and above all was esteemed for his honesty. There was a saying in those days in Manila that every man had his price except Magsaysay.

THE PHILIPPINES

Magsaysay was given the portfolio of Minister of Defense. Within a matter of hours he had dismissed several high-ranking army officers who had previously been considered untouchable. Other officers were sent into field commands. Army units which had not performed well were retrained. And the pattern of maintaining large garrisons in barracks in the main towns was promptly changed. Having been a guerrilla leader himself, Magsaysay understood the requirements of anti-guerrilla units. He took the old slow-moving batallions, cut them down in size, and gave them mobility.

When a poorly-disciplined army moves against guerrillas, there is usually a problem of false claims of success. Often, government troops, who had been sent against the guerrillas, might make contacts with some of their outposts; then they would fire most of their ammunition and return boasting they had scored a great victory and had killed hundreds of guerrillas. Magsaysay gave each unit cameras, and from then on all claims of attack, casualties inflicted, and outposts overrun, had to be backed up by photographs. Without visual proof, citations and promotions were few and far between. The old-line Filipino generals laughed at the "camera boys", but the idea worked. Verbal victories changed to real victories over the Huks.

Previously, senior officers had stayed in Manila or provincial headquarters. Magsaysay ordered the commanders to get into the field and take charge themselves. He then had a machine gun mounted on a jeep, installed special headlights and spent much of his time on personal inspection trips. His itinerary was not given out beforehand, and no one could tell when or where the Minister of Defense would jump out of a jeep to inspect a unit or observe an attack. Sometimes he made promotions before he left a unit in the field; other times he dressed down or demoted inefficient officers.

Magsaysay had seen how the Japanese and the Philippine constabulary had lived off the land. He knew the impact on a civilian population when troops take over a village. The new Minister of Defense increased the rations of the army and made sure that his men lived on them and not on "borrowed" supplies. He was particularly severe against looters and had special investigators run down charges of rape. At first the populace was incredulous, but before long the word spread that under Magsaysay the Philippine Army could be trusted.

While giving the army in the field a new image, Magsaysay was also active in Manila where the communist politburo had its headquarters. In addition to its political activity, organizing strikes, and recruiting students and workers, this headquarters was the center of the Communist politico-military intelligence network for all the islands.

Magsaysay himself played an important role in its dissolution. He was asked to meet alone and unarmed with a Huk leader in a Manila slum.

The two talked for a time and Magsaysay persuaded him to act as a double agent. Information was slow in coming, but through leads supplied by this agent, Magsaysay was able to pick up the trail of some of the members of the communist politburo. He learned that communist messages were carried by a special courier—a woman selling vegetables. Every house to which this woman went was noted. Then, in a series of lightning raids in mid-October, 1950, the suspect houses were surrounded and most of the politburo was arrested.

More arrests followed, and the operations of the guerrilla bands became disunited. Government intelligence began to penetrate the operational units and was often able to learn their plans in advance. Thus Huk losses climbed steadily, arms and ammunition were not replaced, and fewer recruits joined their ranks. Perhaps most important of all, the legend of Huk invulnerability was cracked. Now it was the government troops who won skirmish after skirmish. With the Huks in retreat, the government forces were able to supply real protection to farms and villages, although guerrilla units remained in the mountains.

Hopefully, the people turned their attention further to the government. A wave of popular sentiment arose demanding honest elections. The outcry reached such a point that President Quirino had no choice but to turn to "the most honest man in the Philippines". He asked Magsaysay to supervise the election. Magsaysay agreed and two million voters went to the polls in a free and open election. Magsaysay's military guards kept watch over the ballot boxes through the final count. Of the nine Senatorial seats contested, all were won by opposition candidates. Then the results were given clearly and honestly to the press and the radio. The results of this election were less important than the fact that faith in democracy had been reestablished in the Philippines.

The Liberal Party to which Magsaysay belonged had been defeated, but the Defense Minister won a great personal victory. It was not surprising that when the next election came around, in 1953, Magsaysay ran for office. He campaigned on his war record against the Japanese, on the military defeat given the Huks, and on the promise that he would move against dishonest landlords and usurers. He won with the largest popular vote in Philippine history and took office as President, not representing a party but virtually all the people of the Philippines.

Magsaysay's Reforms

Magsaysay had won the election but the Huks were still a factor to be reckoned with. The people of the Philippines still had many grievances and Magsaysay moved to end them.

On a minor level he refused to hold the expensive, over-decorated Inaugural Ball, and he substituted a public reception for anyone who wished to come. He also ended the elaborate organization of palace guards, which in the past had kept the people far from their President.

Because graft had been so rampant, he invited anyone who wished to do so to telegraph, at government expense, their complaints. When the telegraph lines became jammed, he organized a "complaints and action committee". This move was so popular that the committee had to consider almost 60,000 complaints in the first year of its operation. Many of the matters handled were trivial, but the important thing, however, was that the people realized that at long last it was possible to get action on just grievances.

The "complaints committee" was an interesting psychological move against corruption in high places. To most poor farmers, however, particularly those in the regions where the Huks continued to operate, the problem of land-ownership was much closer and much more important.

The Huks had talked for years about giving land to the tenant farmer, but they had done little about it. Magsaysay set out to show that he really meant to keep the promises he had made as a fighter against the Huks and while he was campaigning for President.

He established a new branch of the military service called the Economic Development Corps [EDCOR] and directed that first consideration be given to resettlement on the Island of Mindanao. The Moros who inhabited that island were not particularly friendly and there were few roads through the heavy forests; but there was unoccupied land. Settlers had to be fed and sheltered, and supplied for a while. An elaborate survey had to be made to establish land titles, and these titles had to be proven in court in order to convince the new settlers that the land was really theirs.

Once reasonable progress had been made on Mindanao, a campaign was begun to win over the Huk guerrillas still fighting in the hills. Guerrillas who surrendered were given money or a chance to obtain land on Mindanao. If they brought one or more weapons with them, they received proportionately more money or more land. And, if they brought proof that they had killed their Huk commanding officer, the reward was even greater.

At first only a handful of Huks surrendered, but, as the resettled areas grew and prospered, former Huks were sent back or even volunteered to go back to talk to their comrades still fighting in Huklandia. Before long, Huks were surrendering in twos and threes, bringing machine guns with them. Then squads began to come out of the forests, and, in some cases, even larger groups appeared with their officers or their officers' heads. Every Huk still fighting in the hills knew that, if he wished, he could have a farm on Mindanao.

In order to keep a proper balance, Huks and non-Huk farmers were resettled in mixed groups. There was no important flareup of Huk sympathy in the new communities, and fewer than ten percent of the transplanted farmers left their new land holdings. More than 30,000 land patents, averaging 20 acres each, were issued during the first year Magsaysay was in office. In addition, some 3,000 families were moved to 65,000 acres of public land. Even in Philippine terms, the numbers involved were not large, but the heart of the grievance—lack of land—had been removed. As the guerrilla uprising melted away, Magsaysay was able to work toward remedying the water problems. This included a campaign of so-called "liberty wells", some of which were dug right under the noses of the few remaining Huks.

The actual economic successes in these fields were often limited, but the psychological impact was tremendous. Poor farmers saw that the government cared and was working to put an end to their just grievances. There was no need to look for help from guerrillas in the hills. The Huk rebellion collapsed basically because the grievances on which it had flourished had been ended.

After Magsaysay's untimely death in 1957, many old vices reasserted themselves. But nothing can detract from the brilliance of Magsaysay's achievement.

CHAPTER IX

VIETNAM: 1954-1967
THE ROAD TO LIMITED WAR

OVER the past generation North and South Vietnam have watched an entire spectrum of coups, revolts, and insurgencies. These have included an independence rebellion against the French, which assumed violent form (as described in Chapter V). Next came a peaceful societal revolution which ended in violent social change. An observer could have studied how Ho Chi Minh betrayed the revolution in the north; how a series of army, or national coups, took place in the south; and finally how a cold war conflict grew into limited war. These latter developments are examined here.

With the fall of the great fortress of Dienbienphu in the spring of 1954, South Vietnam was prostrate. The Japanese occupation during World War II had almost stripped it bare, and the long rebellion against the French had smashed much of what was left. Additionally, the situation was complicated by poor communication between cities and farms, by religious and regional schisms, by a flood of refugees from the north, by a dearth of trained officials, and by a controversial "First Family".

In spite of these problems, there were assets: the energy of the Vietnamese people, the natural wealth of the country, and certain patterns left over from the French colonial rule—all greatly assisted by substantial amounts of outside aid from nations who wished to see Vietnam become a democracy. Unfortunately, in the north, a communist rather than a democratic solution was sought. Use was made of the northern part of Vietnam as a convenient base for aggression. Because of the infiltration by the Communists from North Vietnam, what might have been a good example of nation-building was slowed and turned first into a cold war contest, then into guerrilla warfare, and finally into a limited war with hundreds of thousands of fighters engaged on both sides.

The future of all Vietnam was presumably settled in Switzerland during

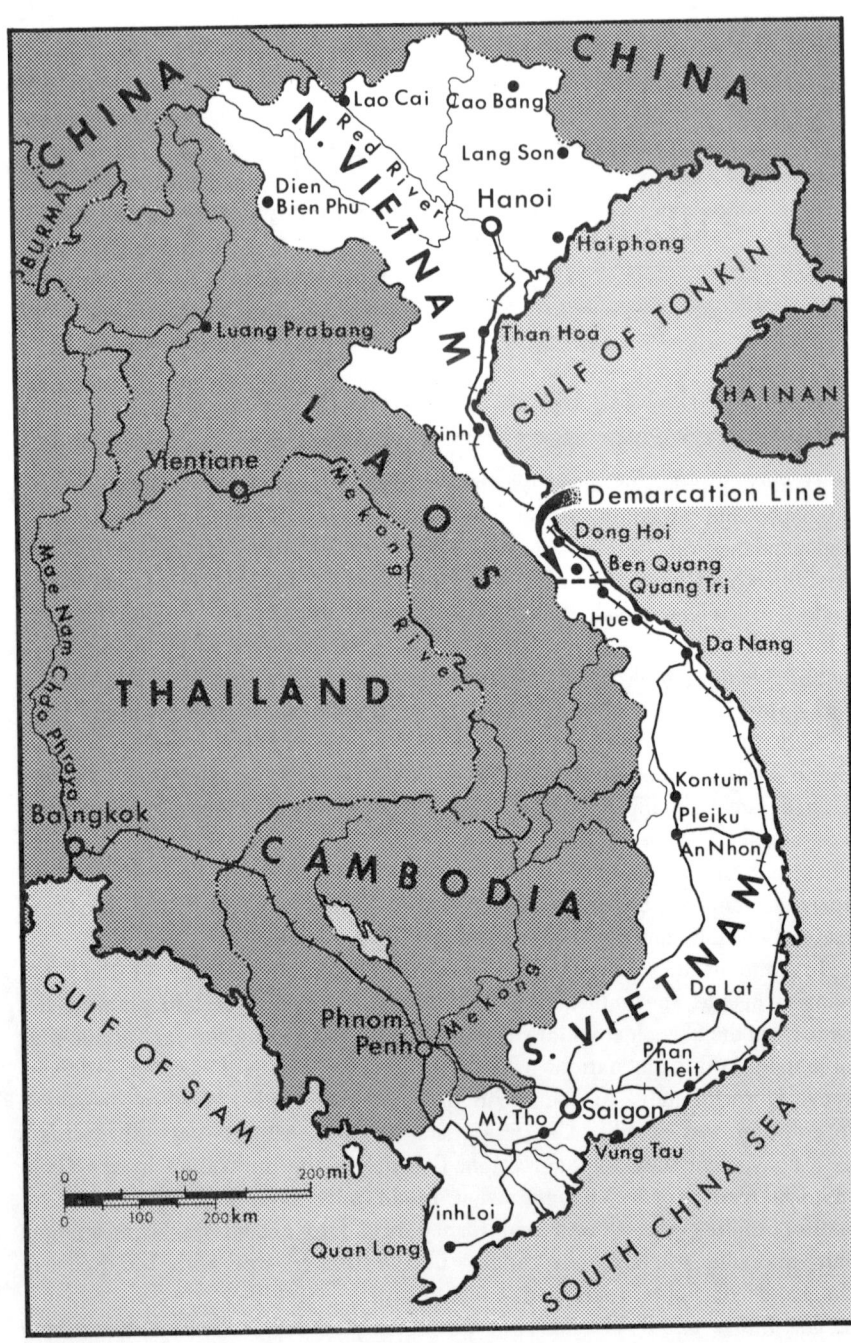

the summer of 1954. Under the terms of the accords reached in Geneva, Switzerland, Vietnam was divided at the 17th Parallel. The Viet Minh, now known as Vietcong, agreed to keep their troops north of this line and the French agreed to stay south of it. There was a prohibition on bringing new military equipment, apart from replacements, into either the northern or southern zone. The entrance of additional troops was also forbidden, as were foreign bases and participation in military alliances. The two parts of the country were to be supervised by an International Control Commission, made up of representatives from Canada, India, and Poland. It was agreed that nationwide elections would be held in July of 1956 to determine whether or not these two parts would be united.

Diem Assumes Direction of South Vietnam

Once this division had been established, the former Emperor of Vietnam, Bao Dai, looked about for a man to head the government of the South. He chose a scholar, a former civil servant and Vietnamese patriot by the name of Ngo Dinh Diem. Diem had his weaknesses, particularly from the western point of view, but he was a man of character, integrity, and ability. He was one of the six sons of a well-educated Catholic mandarin. After he graduated first in his class from the French School of Law and Administration, he became a Provincial Governor at 28, and was chosen over the heads of many older men to be Minister of the Interior of Cochin China in 1933. When he found the French would not allow him to carry out new reforms, he returned to private life. Later he declined a ministerial portfolio under the Japanese and also turned down an offer of a cabinet position from the Communist leader, Ho Chi Minh. He was subsequently active in the negotiations which brought Bao Dai back into power. But, when that ruler offered him the premiership of South Vietnam in May, 1949, he refused on the grounds that the French had not granted the country true independence.

This led to growing estrangement with Bao Dai. In the summer of 1950, Diem left Vietnam to visit Japan, the United States, Italy, and France. While in the United States, he developed useful friendships with various American leaders, including the then-Senator John F. Kennedy.

The spring of 1954 found Diem in Paris. When Bao Dai asked him to form a new government in Vietnam, he accepted, provided he was given complete military and civilian power. The Emperor agreed, and Diem returned to his homeland. From then until his death, Diem ran South Vietnam as an intelligent aristocrat, or true mandarin. His point of view was: "I know what is best for my people." Diem brought with him to his office an ardent Catholic belief, a strong feeling against colonialism and neocolonialism, violent opposition to communism, and a willingness to accept outside economic aid to make South Vietnam viable. Because he considered those who had worked with the French to be collaborators, he turned his back on most of the former political leaders of Vietnam.

On assuming office, Diem had to deal immediately with several powerful groups or sects. The first of these was the Binh Xuyen, a gang of river pirates who had recently bought the police concession for the enforcement of law and order in Saigon. Another was the Cao Dai whose million members maintained their own army and practiced a mixture of Catholicism, Buddhism, and Confucianism, with reverence for Joan of Arc, Victor Hugo, Mohammed, and Sun Yat-sen. The third group was the Hoa Hao which, under the leadership of an illiterate general, believed in faith healing, plus concepts from various Far Eastern religions. These two latter groups were so strong politically that Diem found it necessary to include representatives from them in his second Cabinet.

Early in 1955, it appeared that both the Cao Dai and the Hoa Hao would join the Binh Xuyen in opposing Diem. In spite of the fact that he could depend on only two battalions of regular troops, Diem rallied various democratic elements, got rid of his disloyal chief of staff, and moved against the Binh Xuyen. First they were pushed out of the main section of Saigon. Then, after heavy fighting, Diem forces captured the Chinese area of the city and destroyed the headquarters of the pirates, which included a menagerie of various man-eating animals, the Binh Xuyen's "execution squad".

Following these successes, Diem held a referendum so that the people could choose between himself and Bao Dai. It was not an ordinary election but, as Diem saw it, a "collective demonstration of loyalty to the ruling authority". Even after making allowances for considerable irregularities, Diem received a strong majority. A factor in Diem's success was that, beginning in October of 1954, the United States had started channeling its military and economic assistance to South Vietnam, not through the French, but directly to the government, which meant of course through Diem. This gave him strength in political, economic, and military circles, a leverage which he used most skillfully. Thus when, on October 26, 1955, the "Southern Zone" changed into the Independent Republic of Vietnam, Diem, in full control, became its first President.

According to the Geneva Agreements, general elections for both North and South Vietnam were to be held in July of 1956, elections which would decide whether or not there would be national unification. There were four million more persons in North Vietnam than in the South. Under the iron control of Ho Chi Minh's political machine, the North was expected to go communist by an overwhelming margin in spite of anti-communist feelings. Furthermore, through their control of many of its villages, the

Vietcong might well carry South Vietnam as well. It was undoubtedly because of this that the Vietnamese Communists at Geneva had agreed so readily to an armistice and to the prospect of early nationwide general elections.

After analyzing this prospect, Diem came out against general elections, his reason being that truly free voting could not take place in the communist-controlled areas of Vietnam north of the 17th Parallel. There was pressure for the election from both the Soviet Union and Great Britain, but France and the United States stood aside and the general elections were "postponed".

One of Diem's basic problems in South Vietnam was the influx of refugees from the north. At the time of partition, over 800,000 residents of North Vietnam, most of them Catholic and anti-communist, had moved across the 17th Parallel into South Vietnam. Due in part to $55 million of American aid given for this purpose, strides were made toward caring for them.

These refugees were useful in that they constituted a link with the North. Thanks to them, the people of South Vietnam received firsthand knowledge of what life in a communist state was like. Usually the Communists are able to keep the nature of a communist revolution hidden from the people they are trying to subvert. On the mainland of China, for instance, most of the people knew little about what had happened in Russia or even distant parts of China until it was too late to resist. The people of South Vietnam, however, had the facts of the brutal communist take-over in North Vietnam against which to judge the promises of the Vietcong.

How Ho Chi Minh took the Villages

The South Vietnamese were aware, too, that Ho Chi Minh had divided his take-over into various steps. The first of these was a so-called "anti-imperialist stage", which lasted from 1946 to 1949. During these years, the goal of the Communists was to promote national unity on as wide a base as possible under the slogan "The Fatherland Above All". The Indochinese Communist Party, which Ho himself had organized, "voluntarily" disbanded, turning over political leadership to a united front called "the Vietnamese Alliance". Private ownership was carefully respected, farmers were forced to pay rent to the landlords, businessmen prospered, and bourgeois leaders were given honors and good positions in and out of government.

To encourage greater participation in this united front, a political organization known as the Democratic Party was started, with its membership largely consisting of wealthy merchants and landlords. A parallel body, the Socialist Party, was organized among the intellectuals, while the Vietnamese Alliance was broadened to appeal to as many politicians and other leaders as possible. But, behind the scenes, the Communists continued to exercise the real control.

In the summer of 1950, Ho Chi Minh went secretly to China to discuss with Mao Tse-tung the best strategy for communist victory in Vietnam. Mao told him that he had been paying too much attention to the united front and that the time had come to strengthen communism in North Vietnam. Therefore, when Ho got back from Peking in March of 1951, the old Indochinese Communist Party was reactivated, this time under the name of the Vietnamese Labor Party. Its new slogan was "the anti-imperialist and anti-feudal fights are of equal importance". Progress in these "fights" was to be accomplished in several steps, including the economic leveling of the population by taxation and public trials, anti-landlord terror, a land rent reduction, a land reform program, and liquidation of the rich. All of this was to be backed by "reform of bad thinking". These steps had been carried out by Mao in China a few years previously, and Ho was provided with experts to make sure that the programs went smoothly in North Vietnam.

As a start toward economic leveling, a series of new taxes were imposed. Their levels were set at meetings where party members and others "corrected" the estimates made by non-party members regarding the amount of land they owned, the size of their harvests, and the sums they got for their crops. These corrections were always upwards, and the resulting tax pattern was hard on upper-level peasants and ruinous for the landlords, who were often forced to sell their personal possessions to make the needed payments. The same pattern of domestic tax revision was used against businessmen and traders, who soon found they were unable to continue in business and at the same time "have the honor of paying the taxes set by the people". In addition, restrictions were put on the price at which land or businesses could be sold, thus forcing the wealthier elements of the population to get rid of their property at low rates. Because the Communists fixed the overall sum to be raised by each village, it was in the interest of every man to raise other people's taxes as much as possible so he would have to pay less himself.

By February of 1953, the Communists running North Vietnam felt that the time had come to carry out the next step in communization and actually "liquidate" the landlords. They therefore organized meetings, supposedly to find out which landlords were not paying their taxes in full, but actually to bring about their destruction. In order that the good name of the Communist Party should not be damaged by excesses, the local communist leaders were told to stay away from these meetings and to send to them the most ruthless of their followers.

Once all the peasants in a village had assembled, the tough cadres took over and asked such landowners as were present if they had paid their taxes in full. If there was any question, they were told to state who had advised them not to pay. If a landowner did not answer these questions properly, he was beaten or tortured by being crushed under heavy stones, hung up by his thumbs, held under water, or having his hands burned with cloths soaked in oil. After being so mistreated, most landlords not only admitted that they were behind in their tax payments but blurted out the names of real or imagined persons who had "helped" them to evade paying. If they could be found, these persons were then brought to the meeting and tortured, in turn, until they confessed.

This organized terror continued throughout North Vietnam for about two weeks and led to the beating or death of thousands of landowners whose only crime was that they could not pay the impossibly high taxes which had been set earlier by the "People's Committees". Finally, the Central Committee of the Party sent out orders from Hanoi to stop the meetings, but to hold in jail all those landlords who had confessed to any form of wrongdoing. Although clearly this campaign had been planned by the top Communists for months in advance, the word spread that when Ho learned of its excesses he burst into tears. His real feelings came out when he purged the Communist Party of some of its weaker members by ordering that all those who had not showed the "proper spirit" regarding these meetings be sent to Reeducation Camps for three years.

The Communist Party in North Vietnam next organized public trials for the "enemies of the state" who had been uncovered by the vigilance of the people during "the heroic days of the political struggle". In preparation for these trials, members of the Communist Party and their followers were made to memorize slogans to be shouted at the right time. The general spirit of the proceedings was set by an old Chinese saying of the third century B.C. to the effect: "Better betray others than be betrayed yourself." In the circumstances it was not surprising that most of the landlords tried were convicted of tax evasion or other counter-revolutionary acts and executed.

The excesses of this wave of terror disillusioned many intellectuals and other thinking people in North Vietnam, who, until February of 1953, had been willing to go along with the Communists. Ho Chi Minh and his followers, therefore, set out to put an end to "bad thoughts" such as admiration of free enterprise, western parliamentary and legal systems, and freedom of the press. A nationwide educational campaign was started, called "controlled discussion". During this campaign, everyone had to attend meetings organized by the Communists at which wealthier persons were put on the platform, told to think out loud, and prodded by mass pressure until the errors of their thinking were exposed. These "discussions" sometimes lasted continuously for three days and nights until the people on the platform were so weak that they would agree to anything. As a result, many unsuspected "wrong thinking" enemies of the state were uncovered. Those who disclosed "little errors" were given correctional training, but those who were guilty of "grave errors" were sent to jail or killed. After this "national brain-washing", the people of North Vietnam realized the danger of talking in public, and saw that it was unwise to express any opinions other than those laid down by the Communist Party.

With the landlords out of the way and the people forced to accept the idea that the Communist Party was "always right", Ho Chi Minh then proceeded to move against the richer peasants, the next highest branches on the tree. More public meetings were held, at which the villagers were forced to declare their incomes and be classified as rich, above average, average, below middle, poor, or landless peasants. Any person who understated his income was promptly "corrected" by his pro-communist neighbors, and the same process was set in motion among businessmen in the towns.

Once everyone had been classified, another wave of public trials was held to "bring to justice" the richer or above-average peasants on the theory that "private property is public theft". The people were taught to shout proper slogans, such as "Long live Ho Chi Minh—death to rich and traitorous peasants." Special meetings of party members were held, at which they were instructed in the type of crimes to be expected from wealthy traitors. Trials were then held on soccer fields or other places where large numbers could gather and listen to communist speeches against enemies of the state. Then the richer peasants were brought in, often forced to crawl on their hands and knees, and members of the crowd came forward and denounced them. When a sufficient number of denunciations had taken place, a "People's Tribunal of Party Activists" came to the village to impose sentences. Some of the richer peasants, who had confessed the error of their ways and had denounced other peasants, were let off with sentences of from one to five years of hard labor. But most of them were condemned to be shot and the sentences were often carried out on-the-spot, with the children beating tin cans and the crowd chanting revolutionary slogans as the "enemies of the people" fell. Then the lands of these richer peasants were, in turn, given to the village or to "deserving comrades".

A particularly inhuman aspect of this type of "people's justice" was that, once a man had been publicly convicted of being a landlord or a rich peasant, no one was allowed to talk to him, his wife, or children; nor to give them work, food, shelter, or help in any way. Thus not only the man himself was killed, but frequently his entire family died of starvation.

With the landlords and richer peasants out of the way, the remaining hard-working farmers of average wealth in North Vietnam thought they could relax. But acting under orders from Hanoi, local communists then proceeded with another round of accusations, public trials and executions, this time directed at above-average or average peasants and other persons who were not practicing "good thoughts". Thus, thousands more men, women, and children were liquidated and still more acres became available for distribution.

By now the peasants realized that no one was safe and a wave of anti-communist feeling spread through North Vietnam. The party then declared that land reform was completed and admitted to serious mistakes. A campaign called the "Rectification of Errors" was started which enabled the top Communists to purge the party once again, liquidate unruly cadres, and take in new party members.

According to theory, with the landlords and rich farmers liquidated and their lands distributed to the poorest peasants, the masses in North Vietnam should have been pleased at what had happened. This was especially true since the Communists had stopped such evils as the forced sale of alcohol, prostitution, and the collection of certain taxes heavily imposed by the French. Illiteracy was largely ended, and most villages had schools, while the brighter older children were being sent to regional centers or to Hanoi for higher education. Furthermore, clinics and hospitals were opened in many villages and hamlets which had never had medical facilities before.

But as the farmers soon found out, some of the lands taken from the landlords or the rich went to state farms on which peasants had to work for wages set by the government. Other confiscated holdings, although in theory privately owned, were lumped into collective farms where the "owners" were in no sense their own masters. Even the peasants who received holdings of their own were told what to grow, how to grow it, and were forced to sell at fixed prices. This was bad enough, but everyone had to buy all supplies from government-owned stores where prices were high and desirable goods were scarce. Constant efforts were made to increase production, which meant that men, women, and children found themselves working much longer hours.

Angered by all these developments, the peasants rebelled in many parts of North Vietnam. In Nghe-An Province, for instance, some 20,000 peasants, armed only with sticks and stones, created such a disturbance that a whole division of regular troops was required to quiet them. These revolts were put down with the greatest ruthlessness, and thousands of poor peasants were shot. Gradually the armed forces of the Communists restored order, and it became clear that the members of the Communist Party, and not the people themselves, were the masters of North Vietnam.

The communist dream turned out to be a nightmare, not only for the landlords, the rich or above-average citizens, but for the poor as well. A possible escape was to join the Communist Party, but its members had to work harder than anyone else, were constantly checked for "errors of thought", and were blamed for failures of production or distribution, failures for which they frequently were in no way responsible. Such blame involved public trials, popular denunciation, complete loss of face, and either execution or sentences which took them to forced labor camps where the death rate was extremely high.

In spite of constant meetings and other forms of urging by Communist Party members, the press and radio, and other propaganda devices, production lagged as peasants and workers found that added work bore little or no relation to better earnings. Thus, the standard of living in North Vietnam fell, a development which the Communists blamed on "saboteurs and counter-revolutionaries". This, in turn, led to more reprisals.

It was evident to the people of North Vietnam that the communist solution was no solution at all, and that most people were as badly off as they had been before. The communist argument that their children would live better, once socialism had been built, offered little encouragement. The people of South Vietnam, however, were quite convinced that they did not want to be taken over by the Vietcong. They did not like the war and in various degrees they did not like the Chinese, the French, or the Americans. In fact, many of them did not like the autocratic government in Saigon and its regional and provincial representatives. But the alternative was, such that they were willing to fight to escape the fate of their cousins and friends north of the 17th Parallel.

The Communists Infiltrate South Vietnam

As U. S. money, know-how, and materiel moved into South Vietnam, the economy of that country began to undergo substantial improvement. But the best-informed observers there were convinced that the Vietcong would not let this progress continue long unhindered. They noted that arms and munitions hidden by the Vietcong were being discovered in considerable numbers, and that communist strength was beginning to make itself felt in the more remote areas. Diem recognized the danger and organized a Self-Defense Corps, whose purpose was to defend the villages. He also started to build roads into the mountains and canals into the swamps where the Communists were likely to hide. But he found little American support for such an anti-guerrilla program even after he had made a trip to the United States with this object in mind. Thus, the village-based Defense Corps, and the somewhat more mobile Civil Guard, had to make do with poor equipment and little pay.

Most westerners continued to feel that the danger would come from an organized attack from North Vietnam and not through guerrilla-type insurgency. Thus, for some years after 1954, U.S. military assistance went largely into building a conventional 150,000-man Vietnamese Army, plus a 50,000-man Civil Guard, rather than into developing a counter-guerrilla organization based in the villages. The United States provided equipment for the troops, along with funds for their recruitment, maintenance, and pay. In addition, it supplied a military training mission, all at a cost of $235,000,000 for the year 1955 alone.

This military approach had a certain logic, particularly in the light of Korea, but it turned out to be one-sided and too early. Since 1954, South Vietnam had been faced with a powerful but hidden foe in the form of enemy infiltrators, party members, or sympathizers who had gone underground. After the Geneva Accords were signed, most of the troops of communist General Giap who were in the South had marched north beyond the 17th Parallel. But they had left many guerrillas south of the line, who promptly hid their weapons and returned to farming. These men and other communist sympathizers continued to be influential in village committees and local government throughout much of South Vietnam. Furthermore, they not only had power themselves, but they were backed up by a secret network of strong-arm men and assassins ready to beat or liquidate anyone known to oppose a communist regime or its representatives.

Thanks to outside aid, plus hard work and savings by the people themselves, by 1959, South Vietnam had made real progress. The resources of the country had been restored and, above all, rice surpluses were beginning to appear.

The Communists came to the conclusion that South Vietnam would not collapse economically but was, in fact, on the road to viability. They also decided that the Diem regime was never going to permit the holding of the general election, a factor which they had been counting on to take over the South. Therefore, they decided that the time had come to step up the infiltration from North Vietnam and to begin to make active use of their supporters who had been "sleeping inside the country".

Throughout 1959 and 1960, a growing number of guerrillas slipped along infiltration routes into South Vietnam. Most of them were natives of that part of the country, communists, or recruits whom Ho Chi Minh had ordered to move north in 1954 across the 17th Parallel in order to continue their training, and to be ready for "the Day of Liberation" when they would return to South Vietnam. Ho Chi Minh had encouraged these men to get married and have children before they moved to North Vietnam so that "their hearts would remain in their southern villages". Their instructions were to pretend to take up normal life again but actually to recruit the most militant villagers into the "liberation movement". Once a young man had taken rice to a group of communists or had helped them transport supplies, particularly weapons, he had involved himself so much on the communist side that he had no alternative but to continue for fear of being betrayed to the government. The techniques of this gradual recruitment were both tricky and ruthless. Any evidence of wavering or betrayal was punished immediately, whereas supporting actions were properly rewarded. Thus many villagers began to hate the Vietcong guerrillas, but they feared them more than they did the representatives of the government of South Vietnam.

After starting secretly, this move against South Vietnam was brought into the open in the autumn of 1960 at the Third Congress of the Communist Party of Vietnam in Hanoi. At that gathering the Communists were given two tasks by Ho Chi Minh: (a) to carry on the Socialist Revolution in North Vietnam, and (b) to liberate South Vietnam from the "atrocious rule of the U.S. imperialists and their henchmen". In December of 1960, the Communists announced the creation of the National Liberation Front of South Vietnam. It, of course, took its orders from the Communist Party of North Vietnam and was the political arm of the Vietcong guerrillas. Thus, having consolidated their position, the guerrillas were able to begin their attacks on small outposts.

As a result, the security situation in South Vietnam took a sharp turn for the worse. In the next fifteen months, about 4,000 persons, many of them government officials, village headmen, policemen, and school teachers were assassinated. These killings were often done in particularly cruel ways, such as disemboweling, or the cutting off of hands and feet. The bodies were then left in public places as a warning to other supporters of the government. In addition, about two and a half thousand persons were kidnapped. Some of them were killed, while others were forced to be guerrilla fighters, porters, or spies. By autumn of 1960, around ten government officials were being killed and five more kidnapped by the Communists each day.

By this time, also, it was estimated that over 4,500 communist guerrillas were hiding in the jungles of South Vietnam, or living secretly in its many villages, while the lowest estimate on guerrillas infiltrating from the north was one hundred a week. In addition, ambushes against small government columns and surprise attacks on government outposts were happening daily. As the months passed, the size of the attacking groups increased steadily. In September, 1961, a band of over twelve hundred guerrillas took a provincial capital only sixty miles from Saigon and held it long enough to kill the provincial chief, his deputy, various pro-government civilians, and a good many soldiers as well.

In order to combat the new threat, the army of South Vietnam had to be retrained for jungle warfare. To solve the problem of security in the villages, the planners in Saigon studied the successful counter-guerrilla campaign which had been carried out a few years earlier by the British in Malaya. One important aspect of that struggle had involved taking farmers from scattered houses and small villages and bringing them together into settlements surrounded by stockades and ditches. There they could organize their own defense units, keep tight security control at the village gate, and so make kidnapping, murder, or hit-and-run attacks difficult or even impossible. These settlements became known as *strategic hamlets* and they worked well in Malaya, where the insurgents for the most part were of a different race from the villagers, where food was so scarce that one could not live in the forest, and where the Malayans did not mind being moved from their homes. A large number of strategic hamlets were put together in South Vietnam, but they were successful only in a limited number of cases, for the villagers did not take readily to the idea of being separated from their old homes and from the graves and spirits of their ancestors.

The weaknesses of the strategic hamlet program, and the continued expansion of communist-controlled areas in South Vietnam, made it clear that in many respects the battle for Vietnam was the battle for its villages. In this struggle, as was the case earlier in China itself and against the French in Indochina, the communist guerrillas showed great persistence and skill. Because this kind of take-over happened so frequently, as Denis Warner and others have described, it is worth examining in some detail how the Communists went about taking a village in South Vietnam.

The village in question, which is located in the western part of the Mekong River Delta, has almost six thousand inhabitants. It was previously the property of one very rich, and about fifty moderately rich landlords, but they had all left during the rebellion against the French. In the mid-1950's the place had been well-treated by the Diem government, which maintained an administrative office, a police detail, and a group of militia in the village. Because of this relatively good treatment, the villagers were somewhat pro-government.

Communist Party members from outside the area came into this village in 1960. Pro-Saigon elements were so strong that these cadres had to hide in the daytime, often lying underwater in the rice fields and breathing through straws. With the coming of night, they would return to the village to push contacts among farmers who wanted land. After a while, one farmer was converted and his house became the local headquarters.

The Communists meanwhile made good use of front organizations to bring together persons who were broadly sympathetic, but not yet ready to be real communists. Thus, a farmers' association, a youth group, and a women's group all came into existence and quickly expanded. With the government proving hostile or uninterested and the party backing its campaign to end grievances, within two years more than half of the villagers were taking part in some kind of communist-sponsored activity.

But government officials and persons loyal to the regime in Saigon continued in the village, and the party pushed its campaign of terror against these "enemies of the people". One of the techniques it used was to say that the "village notables" and the security agents of the Diem regime were preparing for the permanent return of the grasping landlords, who would not only take over their land but insist on obtaining back rent. Thus the villagers were told that if they wanted to protect their newly-acquired lands they must get rid of the notables and the government agents. Since this could not be done by elections or other peaceful means, the only possibility was murder. Gradually the people of the village began to feel that the killing of a government official was in their interests.

After these killings had gone on for some time, the government could find no more notables to represent it, and security agents refused to stay in the village overnight. Finally, the central government gave up the attempt to govern the village and fell back on a detachment of soldiers in a military post not far away.

Once it had control in the village, the party opened several clinics, conducted schools, and organized farmers' cooperatives. As the months passed, the Communists were so successful that a festival was held, and 600 flags were flown, to celebrate the open organization of a branch of the National Liberation Front. From then on, the village was publicly stamped as pro-communist and so marked on government maps.

As a result, the villagers realized they must protect themselves, and made some simple weapons and booby traps of bamboo spikes and nail-studded, wooden boards. A half-hearted attack by the Army of South Vietnam was turned back; the people of the village then took new heart and strengthened their defenses, including building walls and gates. Thus "the masses were agitated towards revolution" and learned that the more the government brought pressure on them the more they should resist. But, although the villagers now opposed the government, most of them did so for their own purposes, principally to protect their land. They were not ready to accept Marxist doctrine or to act aggressively. Relatively few of them became Communist Party members. In this, and hundreds of similar villages, the Vietcong looked strong because the government was weak.

By 1962 it became clear that the safe havens in North Vietnam were working well, that the infiltration routes of the Ho Chi Minh Trails were capable of much greater use, and that firm bases in isolated areas in South Vietnam could be set up and maintained. Under these circumstances, General Giap and his officers moved into Phase II of Mao's schedule for an insurgent take-over. This is the guerrilla "hit-and-run" period. Sabotage and terror increased, attacks were made by guerrilla groups on hostile villages on police posts, and on military garrisons. There was also a steady increase in the number and size of ambushes against moving columns, attacks which by now were carried out by bands of two to six hundred, aimed at obtaining arms and other supplies.

Most of the captured materiel went to the newly-organized "Peoples Militia". This was the backup force at the village provincial level which worked with the regular guerrillas, whether they were local or infiltrated from the north, and served as vigilantes, fund-raisers, guards, and sources of intelligence. Its primary purpose was to protect pro-Vietcong villages.

At the same time, the Communists expanded their circle of propaganda, sending agents into nearby villages to neutralize them and eventually bring them over to the communist side. Along with this infiltration, the Communists moved in on political and religious organizations, youth groups, and the press. Furthermore, the communist economic network, which had been so effective against the French, was revised to discredit and subvert the economy of South Vietnam.

In spite of greatly expanded armament and increased training by American advisers, the forces of South Vietnam did not fare well under this increased pressure. The strategic hamlet program had been pushed too fast. Many hamlets were overrun and their military defenders killed. Small outposts were wiped out. Mobile forces ran into the same troubles which had been experienced by the French. They were trapped in ambush after ambush until troop morale became very low. In spite of the fact that more guerrillas were being killed, their overall numbers and their efficiency continued to improve. They began to attack stronger hamlets, larger armored columns, and towns of greater importance.

Aware of these developments, the planners in Saigon remembered that an important aspect of the victory won by Magsaysay against the Huk guerrillas in the Philippines had been his campaign to induce Huks to surrender in exchange for safety, for money and for allocations of farm land. The government of South Vietnam, in April, 1963, proclaimed a campaign of "open arms to guerrillas" to encourage them to surrender through promises of personal security, economic assistance, family reunion, and jobs or land. The offer was extended to "all persons who had been flattered, deceived, exploited or forcibly enrolled by the Communists". Although a certain number of Vietcong took advantage of this offer, the policy was not nearly so successful as it had been in the Philippines. In fact, intelligence showed that the Vietcong were getting new recruits both from North Vietnam and locally faster than they were losing them in battle or through surrender. South Vietnam was still losing the guerrilla war.

Politics and Buddhists in Saigon

While these dark and bloody events were happening in the villages, rice paddies, jungles, and hills of South Vietnam, events in the bigger cities were of a far different nature. Western, and particularly American, aid was pouring into the country, and the cities showed all the signs of a wartime economy. The cost of food and living skyrocketed, new millionaires were made overnight and proved themselves willing to pay almost any price for western luxury goods. A building boom took place with expensive new apartments springing up, often side-by-side with refugee hovels. Hue and other cities, with their tree-shaded streets, their many temples and churches, and their leisurely flow of traffic, changed under the impact of war and inflation, changes that ranged from western dress and new automobiles to wide-open bars and nightclubs.

It was a time of economic instability, a time when the Vietnamese intellectuals, politicians, and soldiers gathered at the sidewalk cafes and in the salons of political chiefs and would-be leaders. To a high percentage of educated city-dwelling Vietnamese—whether Catholic, Buddhist, pro-French, pro-American, or pro-Communist—intrigue became a major occupation.

In March of 1956, elections had been held to pick a Constituent Assembly which, in turn, would develop a constitution for South Vietnam. There was heavy voting and the supporters of Diem won handily. Among the victors was his sister-in-law, Madame Nhu, who ran in a "safe constituency" made up largely of Catholic refugees from the North. The Assembly thus elected approved a draft constitution for South Vietnam. It required a strong President with a five-year term of office. He was to be an executive who had veto power over all legislation and could rule by decree when the National Assembly was not in session. This assembly, a body of 123 seats, was elected soon thereafter and showed a large majority for Diem and his supporters.

Over the next two years, however, opposition to the Diem regime, growing out of both political and economic grievances, increased both in and out of Saigon. In May, 1958, therefore, the government announced a program of land reform, limiting farms in most cases to 245 acres and holding down land rents. It was a step in the right direction, but at best it did not go far enough, while in many parts of the country it was not implemented at all. Various other reforms—farm loans, education from the village to the university level, medical care, better housing particularly for the refugees, and more jobs for all—were advocated, debated, and sometimes made law. All of this might have led to a societal revolution "from the top". But in most cases the implementation was weak or even nonexistent. When elections were held in April, 1960, the Diem regime won again. There were, however, widespread stories of falsification, intimidation, and corruption in the counting of the ballots.

As criticism of his regime mounted in the city, and guerrilla successes expanded in the countryside, Diem became more and more angry over attacks in both the Vietnamese and European press. Censorship was therefore tightened. Diem gave fewer interviews, and the reporters who did see him came away with the impression that he and his supporters were "alone in knowing what was best for South Vietnam" and felt that any criticism must be the work of an enemy or a communist. Conviction grew among the liberal and progressive Vietnamese that the Diem clan was becoming too powerful, that graft and corruption were spreading, and that the hoped-for benefits of independence from the French were not being realized.

This feeling finally came into the open, November 11, 1960, in the form of an attempted military coup undertaken by a group of army officers on the grounds that President Diem had to give up his office. Through his nepotism and his autocratic regime he had shown himself "incapable of saving the country". Although shut up in his palace, Diem was able to rally his strongest military units. The rebels were overcome with the loss of about 300 lives.

The popularity of the Diem family was not increased by these developments; so in order to improve his position, President Diem announced a new reform program. In elections held in March, 1961, he reportedly polled sixty-five percent of the vote in Saigon and ninety percent in the provinces. It is probable that Diem was only partially aware of the irregularities, to use a mild word, which accompanied these "elections". To him they were a demonstration of national loyalty for his anti-communist regime. If, to produce such a "demonstration", there had to be intimidation, violence, bribery, miscounting of votes, and even the barring from office of duly-elected persons, Diem felt that the end justified the means.

Opposition to the Diems continued to grow during 1961. On February 27, 1962, the Presidential palace in Saigon was again attacked, this time by two fighter planes. Several bombs were dropped, but Diem, his family, and his staff escaped without serious injury. The arrest of twenty officers and several civilians during the next two weeks brought out that the bombing had been intended as the signal for a coup which would overthrow the Diem regime. The government made widespread arrests to stamp out the insurgents, who were anti-communist but more liberal than the Diem oligarchy.

Even after this, Diem's mandarin-type integrity might have overcome the city-based dislike of his autocratic methods had he not had to fight the Communists and at the same time counter popular resentment toward his large family, including his brother, Ngo Dinh Nhu, and the latter's sharp-tongued wife, Madame Nhu. Ngo was brilliant, impulsive, strongly anti-communist, and the organizer of a Catholic trade union movement which had helped Diem come to power.

Madame Nhu, who feared no one, was attractive, ruthless, vain, and a political power in her own right. She had never been at all fond of Americans, but growing criticism of the Diem regime in the American press caused her to become even more bitter. This feeling was strengthened by the recent unsuccessful coup when the palace was bombed and Madame Nhu was slightly injured. She and her husband believed that the Americans were involved in this revolt. Because Ngo Dinh Nhu directed the "special forces" and used them and the police in part to strengthen the family regime, he became steadily more unpopular, and Diem's enemies increased proportionately. Even the Catholics in Vietnam split, not only on the Diems but on the future of their country, as criticism of "police state" methods grew.

Such outspoken mistrust led the Diem regime, in May, 1962, to put a stop to unauthorized public meetings. While this made sense to an autocrat like Diem, it angered many Vietnamese. Arrests increased, until it has been estimated that by 1963 some 20,000 "enemies" of the regime were in jail. Included among them were well-known newspaper editors, able civil servants, loyal soldiers, and much-needed doctors. In spite of this crackdown, the criticism went on in private.

As opposition to Diem and his family and government spread, various new groups became involved. The most powerful of these were the Buddhists, whose political activities became a highly controversial aspect of the Diem years. On the one hand, there are many informed observers who believe that Diem and his over-zealous Catholic followers were discriminating against, and even persecuting, the Buddhists and other non-Catholic groups. These persons feel that the situation had gone so far that the Buddhist leaders had to fight back in order to preserve and strengthen Buddhism in South Vietnam. This is essentially the version of the controversy which was given to the outside world, and the one accepted by a substantial number of observers and participants in the struggle. It influenced policy makers in Washington and other capitals. On the other hand, there was evidence—some factual and some circumstantial—to support the assessment made by the Diem regime itself. This was the conclusion that a segment of the Buddhists had been penetrated and captured by extremists. Some of these were aggressively pro-Buddhist, some were neutrals in the fight against the Communists, while others were communist sympathizers or communist agents. In addition to many politicians and army officers in South Vietnam, this view of the situation was shared by a number of high American officials and some of the American press.

The population of South Vietnam at that time included about 6,000,000 practicing Buddhists, 1,500,000 Catholics, 500,000 other Christians, 1,500,000 members of the Cao Dai sect, 1,000,000 supporters of the Hoa Hao sect, 500,000 Hindus and Moslems, 1,000,000 Animists, and about 4,000,000 Confucians. This meant that only about thirty-five per cent of the population was Buddhist in the proper sense of the word, and these were divided among fourteen different sects. Although Diem was a Catholic, there were, in 1963, only six Catholics out of seventeen in his Cabinet, three Catholic Generals out of seventeen in his army, whereas more than one-half of the forty-two province chiefs in South Vietnam were Buddhists.

During the years Diem was in office, over 1,300 new Buddhist pagodas were built and about an equal number of old pagodas were restored. It is true that many of the Catholics were better educated than the non-Catholics and so were more vocal. It is also true that in Vietnam, before the coming of the French, the Buddhists had little power, while the country was run for the Emperor by his Mandarins, most of whom were Confucians. But until 1963 there was little serious religious friction in South Vietnam. When it did come to the surface, it was dramatic and violent, and so skillfully carried out that the techniques used are worthy of study.

The Buddhist "Command Post" for the summer and autumn of 1963 was the Xa Loi Pagoda in Saigon, and the brains behind the movement were those of a clever, ambitious, and wily Buddhist monk called Thich (Venerable) Tri Quang. Not too much is known about his background, but he had been arrested at least twice by the French for "dealings with the Communists", and his brother was Minister of the Interior under Ho Chi Minh in North Vietnam.

In contrast to the calm religious atmosphere in most Buddhist shrines, the Xa Loi Pagoda resembled a political headquarters. Telephones there rang constantly. Mimeograph machines were busy turning out leaflets, and banners for parades were being painted, frequently carrying slogans which followed the communist line. Furthermore, a series of persons attended meetings in the pagoda who later appeared as mob agitators and leaders.

Early in May, 1963, the Diem government issued a decree that religious flags should not have precedence over the national flag of South Vietnam. An unfortunate dispute developed over this point in the town of Hue on Buddha's birthday, a dispute in which Thich Tri Quang became involved, breaking into a Buddhist service and reading slogans into a microphone as part of a violent anti-Diem speech. When Tri Quang tried to have the tape of this address replayed over the Hue government radio station, an argument ensued, the police were called in, and eight persons were killed in the violence which followed. Both sides blamed the other for the casualties. Thich Tri Quang and his followers lost no time in organizing a series of demonstrations to play up the incident.

The Buddhists wanted publicity. They got it in a terrible way. On June 11, a small automobile drove up to the front of the Cambodian Embassy in Saigon. Out of it came a 78-year-old Buddhist monk named Thich Quang Duc. Just at this time, a group of Buddhist monks also arrived at the Embassy and made a circle around their aged companion, who sat down in the traditional lotus position. Gasoline was then poured over the praying man, who tried to ignite his robes with a pocket lighter. When it did not flare up, a monk set him ablaze with matches, and the scene was recorded by press photographers who had been tipped off beforehand from the Xa Loi Pagoda. Over the next few days most of the world press carried vivid photographs of the immolation.

A series of demonstrations followed to emphasize the fact that the venerable Duc had killed himself in protest against the anti-Buddhist cruelty of the Diem government. And the Xa Loi Pagoda blossomed with banners like the one reading: "Youth of Vietnam follow resolutely in the steps of Thich Quang Duc." When questioned by reporter Marguerite Higgins about the burning, Tri Quang told her: "It would be most unwise for President Kennedy to appear to be associated with Diem's actions. There will be, for example, many more self-immolations. Not just one, or two, but ten, twenty, maybe fifty. President Kennedy should think about these things."

There were six more self-burnings that summer. Evidence developed by the government of South Vietnam, by a United Nations investigating committee, and by various members of the foreign press, brought to light that these immolations were far from self-inspired. Some of the monks at the Xa Loi Pagoda had come there recently. It does not require much time or training to become a Buddhist monk of the lowest order. Thus, it was easy for anyone who so desired to take on the guise. Among these new arrivals were said to be a group of agitators who recruited impressionable Buddhists and then stirred them deeply with a series of atrocity stories regarding the torture and killing of Buddhists by the Diem Government.

Once the selected victim had reached a point where he believed that the best way to help Buddhism was by burning himself to death in public, he became a hero in Xa Loi circles. Other monks were eager to write last statements and death letters for him. He was supplied with new robes and gasoline. If he wished, he was given pills to reduce the pain, although police who tested the pills reported they had little more effect than aspirin. Then the place for the burning was chosen where it would have the greatest publicity value. The press, particularly the European correspondents, were tipped off that something important was about to happen. Finally the victim was driven to the site of the burning. Other monks appeared on the spot and they or the victim started the fire. Once the man was dead, highly colored stories were given to the press regarding new atrocities committed against the Buddhists by the Diem regime. The monk's body was then collected, if possible by the monks rather than by his family, an elaborate funeral was held, and there was oratory, tears, and growing hatred for the Diems.

The majority of Vietnam's Buddhists looked with disfavor on the political agitation, violence, and suicide coming out of the Xa Loi Pogoda. But Thich Tri Quang and his followers dominated the streets of Saigon and, through them, the headlines of the world press. The result was a widely-held belief that Diem, his family, and his followers were persecuting the Buddhists so cruelly that the monks were being driven into extreme action. Although time after time Diem met Buddhists' demands, his gestures of conciliation were usually ignored by the press, while cases of police brutality and mob demonstrations or burnings by Buddhists were given front-page play. Unfortunately the beautiful but acid-tongued Madame Ngo Dinh Nhu, the wife of Diem's brother, involved herself in the controversy. Even though she may sincerely have believed that the Communists had infiltrated the Xa Loi Pagoda, her remark that the Buddhists "have barbecued one of their monks whom they had intoxicated" did the Diem cause incalculable harm.

By the end of August, 1963, most of the top Vietnamese generals agreed with Diem that action against the Buddhist extremists was necessary. A carefully worked out and brutal police-plus-special-forces operation was undertaken. Xa Loi and other centers of extremism were raided, leftist documents seized and many arrests made. But pressure from many sources, including the Buddhists and liberals, reached such a point that the Government retreated, and Tri Quang and the others who had been arrested were freed the next day. This was the turning point in the Buddhist-Diem controversy. After it, neither the military nor the police dared take strong steps against Tri Quang and his supporters.

Under the impact of these events a split developed within the Kennedy Administration in Washington, and, when those who favored moderation towards the Buddhists gained the upper hand, Diem was informed that his regime must become more democratic and more ready to meet Buddhist demands. This amounted to a green light for those who opposed the Diem regime.

Up to this time the students of South Vietnam, in general, had taken no part in this struggle. Late in August, however, elements among them began to hold anti-government rallies. Stirred up by Buddhists and other activists, these meetings led to demonstrations; the demonstrations became violent; casualties ensued; and over 1,000 arrests resulted. Most of the detainees were released within three days, but the President's brother said he had proof that not only the Buddhists, but the students also, had now been infiltrated by communist agents. Pressure, such as the arrival in Saigon of a new U. S. Ambassador, Henry Cabot Lodge, and even a television interview by President

Kennedy on the subject, left the position of the Diem Government unchanged.

Washington decided to put still heavier pressure on the Diem Government through various new channels. By the second week in September it was estimated there were 12,000 Vietnamese troops in the city of Saigon, thus reducing the number of soldiers available for use against the Communists. Because it was felt in Washington that the government should devote more effort to fighting the Communists and less to quarrelling with internal enemies, a resolution was introduced into the U. S. Senate calling for the end of all U. S. economic and military aid to South Vietnam and the withdrawal of U. S. advisers unless the Diem Government abandoned its policy of "cruel repressions".

In mid-September President Diem announced that he was ending martial law and would soon hold new elections for the National Assembly, but the United States kept pushing. In October, Washington disclosed that it would withhold further financial aid to the Vietnamese Special Forces unless they were deployed against the Vietcong. Since these were specially trained anti-guerrilla units, holding them in Saigon and other cities made little sense in terms of the war effort. They were, however, under the command of the President's brother, Ngo Dinh Nhu, so their departure from Saigon clearly weakened the Diem regime.

During October of 1963, Saigon buzzed with rumors of coups and counter-coups. There is evidence that at least two groups of officers were planning moves against Diem and his family, and that the rulers learned of these plots and decided to turn them to their own benefit. Apparently, the palace planned to have some military units loyal to the Diems stage a pseudo-coup which would be joined by enemies of the regime. Once such opponents had been identified, Diem and his supporters would carry out a counter-coup and do away with their chief political enemies.

Thus, when troops moved into the streets of Saigon during the siesta hour, November 1, 1963, the Diems and their friends were not disturbed. Before long, however, they realized that the incoming troops were not the detachments they had expected to see in action. Diem telephoned to supposedly loyal commanders, but no help came and fighting began around the palace. When, during the night, it became clear that the palace would be overrun, Diem and Nhu escaped by secret tunnel and hid in the house of a wealthy Chinese friend. Madame Nhu was out of Vietnam at that time.

At about dawn the next morning, the attacking forces commanded by a Colonel Thao entered the palace and found that Diem and his brother had gone. They were soon located in a Catholic church, where they agreed to surrender on promise of safe conduct out of the country. But after being put in an armored personnel carrier, Diem was shot and Nhu was stabbed to death under circumstances which are far from clear.

Once order had been restored in the cities, direction of the government was taken over by a "Military Revolutionary Council" of twelve generals headed by Dong Van Minh, generally known as Big Minh, and with Nguyen Mgoc as Prime Minister. This coup by the military put an end to the autocratic rule of the family of Ngo. But it produced about as many problems as it solved, for nine years of suppressed unrest came to the surface.

Although many political elements in South Vietnam could unite against the Diems, they could not agree on the policies to be carried out after their removal. Under the government of Big Minh and Prime Minister Tho, many effective officers and civilians were shunted aside and replaced by persons often less capable and certainly less experienced. But most of the local officials stayed on in the villages, more bureaucrats were added in the provincial centers, and neither the Buddhists, the Catholics, the middle-rank military, nor the intellectuals appeared happy with the developments. Furthermore, the price of rice rose sharply and the state of the economy worsened. General Minh was urged to travel about and use the techniques that served Magsaysay so well in the Phillipines. But he was not an orator or a glad-hander and the role did not fit him. General Minh was pushed out three months later.

In the less than thirty months that followed, South Vietnam had eleven violent or unconstitutional changes of government. A measure of political stability descended on the political scene only when, in March, 1965, Nguyen Cao Ky, the Commander of the Air Force of South Vietnam, took control.

Escalation into Limited War

Much more important to the world in general was the growing involvement by the Communists, on the one hand, and the United States and six of its allies, on the other, in the fighting in Vietnam. From words of support to massive economic assistance, from military advice to combat instruction, and from garrison duty to actual fighting, America moved slowly but steadily into the center of the Vietnamese conflict.

As early as October 23, 1954, President Eisenhower had made clear American support of the independence of South Vietnam. Vice-President Nixon, visiting Saigon in July, 1956, gave President Diem another letter of support from Eisenhower, and personally observed "the militant march of Communism had been halted". Then the next spring, when Diem was in Washington, the two Presidents issued a communique stressing peace, independence, and national unity.

In October of 1960, on the fifth anniversary of the independence of South Vietnam, the American President again pledged continued assistance "in the difficult yet hopeful struggle ahead". After this, for the first time, Americans became targets for Vietcong terrorists. Within a month, a U. S.

Public Safety Adviser and his driver were ambushed and killed by the Communists in full daylight.

The then-Vice-President, Lyndon B. Johnson, spent two days in Vietnam in May of 1961. After talking with President Diem, he told the National Assembly of that country that the United States would support an expansion of Vietnam's fighting forces. At that date, economic assistance from the United States to Vietnam since 1955 had totalled more than $1,250,000,000.

President Kennedy mentioned the expanding battles there in an address to the General Assembly of the United Nations on September 25, 1961. A week later President Diem told the National Assembly of South Vietnam that "it is no longer a guerrilla war we have to face but a real war, waged by an enemy who attacks us with regular units, fully and heavily equipped, and who seeks a strategic decision in Southeast Asia in conformity with the orders of the Communist International." As an example of how much the situation had deteriorated and of the contempt which the Communists held for law and order, the mutilated body of the Chief Liaison Officer of the International Control Commission was recovered from the Saigon River about two weeks later.

After hearing a personal report from General Maxwell Taylor, President Kennedy, November 16, 1961, stated that "the United States plans . . . call for sending several hundred specialists in guerrilla warfare, logistics, communications, engineering and intelligence to train the forces of President Ngo Dinh Diem. The plans also call for fairly largescale shipments of aircraft and other special equipment."

Following this statement, ten U. S. fighter-bomber trainers and four transport planes were added to the Air Force of South Vietnam. Then, December 11, 1961, some 400 uniformed U. S. Army personnel arrived to operate two companies of helicopters on reconnaissance and supply missions against the Vietcong guerrillas. It was the first substantial commitment of U. S. military personnel in the expanding struggle. But it was clearly necessary in view of the trend of the conflict. For in mid-January, 1962, Radio Hanoi broadcast the formation of a communist political unit known as "the People's Revolutionary Party" inside South Vietnam. The fact that this was announced by the communist government of North Vietnam refuted the contention, previously put forth, that the guerrillas in South Vietnam were purely local and had no connection with the Communists in the northern part of the country.

Although Americans were not yet fighting, the first U. S. military casualties of the growing conflict occurred in early April, 1962, when two U. S. soldiers were killed and two others were reported missing after an attack by communist guerrillas on a small village in the north.

Meanwhile intelligence reports indicated that increasing numbers of communist guerrillas were slipping into South Vietnam and the size of the Vietcong units continued to increase, as did their fire power, strengthened in many cases by newly-acquired mortars and heavy machine guns. Guerrilla morale was also high, whereas the troops of South Vietnam often showed weak discipline and sometimes little will to fight. Desertions increased, too, as some soldiers went over to the Vietcong with or without their arms, while others simply buried their guns and went back to their villages. Throughout the summer and fall of 1962 the Army of the Republic of South Vietnam, known as ARVN, tried several attacks in strength. But almost without exception they were ambushed or beaten off, suffered heavy casualties, and lost much equipment to the guerrillas during hurried retreats.

The start of 1963 saw some of Diem's best troops badly routed at a place called Ap Bac in the Mekong Delta, a defeat in which three American advisers were killed and five U. S. helicopters were shot down. At the end of that January, there were approximately 12,000 American advisers in uniform in Vietnam with another 4,000 arriving before the year was over. But in spite of an estimated 21,000 Vietcong killed and 4,500 captured, the guerrillas ended the year stronger than ever, while the South Vietnamese continued to be ineffective.

By 1964, the Communists boasted with considerable justification that they controlled some two-thirds of South Vietnam in the daytime and more at night. They also claimed that many military units of the Saigon government were at least twenty-five percent below normal strength, that the South Vietnamese casualties were running at the rate of 8,000-a-year killed and 16,000-a-year wounded—with desertions probably totalling at least four times the latter number. Furthermore, new recruitment was slowing down on the southern side, while the Communists claimed that citizens of South Vietnam were "flocking to the guerrilla units".

Although the U. S. by now had advisers down to the battalion level on the ground and in many South Vietnamese aircraft and ships as well, American know-how and advice were not being followed. Ho Chi Minh and his top commanders such as General Giap came to the conclusion that it was time to move from Mao's *Phase II* of guerrilla warfare into Phase III, which is essentially limited warfare. Its goal is to attack and destroy important enemy units and key positions, to fight back when attacked, and thus ultimately to wear down the will of the enemy resistance until negotiations can be entered into successfully on terms that are favorable to the Communists. With the escalation into *Phase III*, the Vietcong began concentrating their guerrilla bands into units of a thousand or more men, equipped with newer and heavier arms and prepared to fight side-by-side with regular North Vietnamese battalions brought down intact over the Ho Chi Minh Trail.

The Communist plan was that by such tactics they would be able to control the Central Highlands of South Vietnam, to capture and hold a series of beachheads, and to develop a stranglehold on the Mekong Delta. These plans were put into effect so successfully that, by the end of 1964, at least one district capital had been overrun, several key highways had been taken over or blocked, and attacks on camps and moving units of the South Vietnamese forces had resulted in substantial victories. Moreover, desertions from the ARVN were now estimated at more than one thousand a week. The guerrillas were capturing or acquiring arms faster than they were losing them, and the realization began to spread in the civilian, government, and military circles of South Vietnam that the Communists were winning the war.

Because most of the firmness at this time came from the Americans, in February, 1965, the Vietcong set out to show them up as "paper tigers". They attacked American installations, shelled barracks, damaged planes, and blew up supply dumps. During a raid, eight Americans were killed and twenty-six wounded. Furthermore, terrorist attacks on American-occupied buildings in Saigon and other southern cities became so frequent that the 2,000 American wives, children, and dependents were evacuated from the country. If the United States had permitted such tactics to continue, its position would have steadily weakened, and the will of the South Vietnamese to fight would have crumbled.

Therefore, on February 7, 1965, forty-nine U. S. carrier-based planes, for the first time, bombed and strafed military installations in North Vietnam. This raid was followed by even larger ones which penetrated further into North Vietnam. Jets of the U. S. Air Force, on February 18, made their first direct attacks on Vietcong guerrillas in South Vietnam. Then, in the second week of March, 3,500 U. S. Marines arrived to guard the U. S. airfield at Danang. These additions to the 23,000 U. S. advisers and technicians already in the country were given a strictly "limited defensive role", but the move was clearly necessary because the army of South Vietnam either could not or would not supply adequate protection to U. S air and other installations.

In order to strengthen that army in its task of ferreting out guerrillas hidden in dense jungles or tunnels, the U. S. announced, before the end of March, that it was supplying nonlethal tear gas. At the same time, the U. S. Air Force, in its stepped-up raids, began using napalm fire bombs against communist strongpoints. Partly in retaliation for these acts communist terrorists bombed the U. S. Embassy in Saigon, killing two and injuring 183 persons, about a third of whom were American citizens. In addition, the tempo of guerilla attacks increased and it became apparent that if South Vietnam was to be denied to the Communists there was no alternative to even further U. S. involvement.

On April 7, 1965, President Johnson, speaking at the Johns Hopkins University in Baltimore, declared he was going to ask Congress for one billion dollars for an American economic aid program for Southeast Asia, centering on the delta of the Mekong River. But he also emphasized that the United States was ready at any time, anywhere, to engage in unconditional discussions regarding peace. When the Communists rejected President Johnson's offer to begin peace talks, the U. S. stepped up its air raids.

The Soviet Union and Red China then renewed their previously-made threats to send troops to South Vietnam, while the U. S. estimated that armed infiltrators from North Vietnam now numbered almost 40,000, including several battalions of North Vietnamese regulars. Before the end of April, 1965, total U. S. strength in South Vietnam had reached 42,000, the Koreans had committed a division, and Australia agreed to send a combat battalion. These reinforcements were clearly needed, for, in the first week in May, the Vietcong had scored more victories. In one of these, which occurred only sixty miles northeast of Saigon, a U. S airlift could not prevent the death of more than 900 government troops.

As a partial answer, in mid-June, 1965, the United States staged the first of a series of air raids by B-52 heavy jet bombers, flying all the way from the Pacific island of Guam on a 4,300-mile round trip. Ten days later, at the request of the Vietnamese military, U. S. Army troops made their first major attack of the war. With Australians and units of the Saigon government fighting beside them, U. S. infantry forces overran the Vietcong positions in what was known as Zone D, about twenty miles north of Saigon—an area which had been the exclusive preserve of the Vietcong for many years.

In spite of such advances, the Communists continued to hold or control so much of South Vietnam that an airlift had to be established between five of its major cities whose road connections had been cut by the Vietcong in the autumn of 1964. Following his sixth factfinding trip to South Vietnam, Secretary of Defense McNamara declared, in mid-July, 1965, that in many respects the military situation there had deteriorated in the past fifteen months. Furthermore, he noted that Soviet-type ground-to-air missile sites similar to some of those established in Cuba during the missile crisis were being set up in North Vietnam.

As U. S. involvement grew into limited war, President Johnson, in a television address on July 28, 1965, said: "Most of the non-Communist nations in Asia cannot by themselves resist the growing might. . . of Asian Communism."

The limited war in Vietnam in which the United States and its six allies— South Vietnam, Thailand, South Korea, Australia, New Zealand, and the Philippines—were now engaged, had grown out of several serious miscalculations by the Communists. They signed the Geneva Accords in the belief they could "pick up" South Vietnam within two years through nationwide elections. When President Diem refused to hold such elections, the Communists believed they could bring South Vietnam to its knees through economic subversion, terrorist activity, and political pressure. When, due to U. S. aid, it became clear that this collapse was not going to happen, they thought they could take over South Vietnam through guerrilla action. U. S. assistance on the economic front and extensive use of American military advisers prevented this from happening.

The Communists then took the big gamble and moved into limited war. At first this decision proved to be a correct one for Hanoi. The army of South Vietnam, in spite of having large amounts of U. S. equipment and guidance from several thousand U. S. advisers, lost battle after battle. Casualties mounted on both sides, but morale in the South sank, while more defections of South Vietnamese, and increased infiltration—first of guerrillas and then of army units from the north—kept communist morale high. By the end of 1964, South Vietnam was tottering on the edge of defeat.

Reluctantly and sadly, the U. S. government came to the conclusion that it had no choice but to resist force with force and to move into limited warfare itself. By the autumn of 1965, the U. S. buildup of troops including Army, Navy, Air Force, and Marines totalled 165,000 men. The communist answer to this was still greater escalation, with approximately 4,000 combat troops in organized units infiltrating South Vietnam each month. To meet them, the United States sent in more than 100,000 additional troops in the first six months of 1966. The Communists on their part replied by increasing the infiltration rate to over 5,000 a month and greatly expanding their armament to include more machine guns, bazookas, larger mortars, and 75-mm artillery. In spite of such increased enemy strength, the United States and its allies were no longer losing the war, but they were not winning it either. Still more troops were needed.

Early 1967 saw their number pass the 400,000 mark. It is possible that this figure may go even higher before the tide of battle turns. Would the American people support such an effort? The Communists believed they would not and that, wearied by protracted conflict, saddened by mounting casualties, which, by February, 1967, had passed 6,000 killed and 35,000 wounded, and confused by communist propaganda, America would be willing to accept communist terms in exchange for a cease-fire.

Again the Communists had miscalculated. Although there was some inevitable anti-war feeling in the United States, the election of November 8, 1966 showed that, for the most part, the American people stood behind their President on this issue. There was a growing recognition that the communist effort to take over South Vietnam had to be regarded as a challenge extending far beyond Southeast Asia. At terrible cost, the United States and her allies were learning that, in such a situation, they have no choice.

WHAT LIES AHEAD

In general, evolution through the ballot or by the enlightened regime is more appealing to the average man than is violent revolution. However, few of the developing countries have "built-in" political mechanisms that make rapid or basic change possible, and the result is that thinking people in a growing number of developing nations are seeking to achieve immediate freedom and "instant modernization" by non-constitutional or violent means.

This is a process which is gathering speed. In round numbers, there were six coups, insurrections, rebellions, or revolutions somewhere in the world each year from 1900 to 1940. From 1941 to 1955 the average yearly number rose to twelve; and since 1956, various types of political insurgency have increased to more than fifteen in every twelve months. What lies ahead? It would be quieting to think that we are near the end of this cycle; but there is no reason to think that its termination is in sight.

There are only a few colonial areas left in the world today, and most of them will be or already are the scenes of independence rebellions. In theory, there is much to be said for a short transitional period of tutelage by representatives of an advanced power. But, in practice, such neo-colonialist control often becomes very irritating to people who thought they had achieved independence but find they are still being run from the outside. This is often a grievance which the Communists can exploit successfully.

Because so many nations are governed by regimes which tend to block advancement by able citizens, the most important revolts over the next decade will take the form of revolutions seeking societal change. Only rarely will such insurgencies follow the orderly Egyptian pattern, and thus a growing number of anti-colonial, neo-colonial, or societal insurgencies over the next decade will have communist encouragement, support, or leadership. The number of cold war conflicts can therefore be expected to increase.

The United States must meet the challenge that lies ahead. We must gain a better understanding of the background, causes, and nature of the political violence now sweeping the world, and realize that the sooner the legitimate grievances of a people are ended, the less likely it is that violence will erupt. We need to realize, too, that not all revolutions are bad, and that a revolt may, in fact, be the only way in which a nation can modernize rapidly in the growing complexity of the technological world in which we live.

In spite of the unprecedented military and economic strength of the United States and her allies, we must not think that we can become involved in every insurgency or cold war conflict. We must choose with great wisdom and care the countries and causes to which we commit our political, moral, economic, or military strength.

However, we should also recognize that if we do not commit ourselves in certain revolts, the Communists will do so. If we act promptly and firmly in such cases, the Communists may not escalate through the various phases of guerrilla activity or even move to limited war; but if we do not act, the not-so-limited warfare of Vietnam will be repeated in other countries and other parts of the world. Total victory is not always attainable, and that fact will have to be accepted by the United States. Often, we will have to settle for what is possible rather than for what is ideal.

One of the outstanding features of our times is widespread desire for change. The United States can be a useful and influential force in the direction of that change. Lest more and more developing countries suffer the growing pains of violent revolution, we must now expand our efforts for more effective support and a greater understanding of peaceful evolution.

APPENDIX

Author's Note

In the three years that have passed since the first edition of this book the incidence of political violence has risen to approximately 26 per year. (*See* pages 213-217 for *Political Violence, 1967-1970.*) Anti-colonial rebellions, as anticipated, have lessened in number, but revolutions, or insurrections against oppressive, corrupt or outmoded regimes have increased.

It is evident that a number of thinking persons, young and old alike, have come to the conclusion that the organization of society, whether Capitalist or Communist, is not as it should be, that change is possible, that a few people can bring about such change, and that the sooner it happens the better. The years ahead are certain to see more rather than less political violence. They may not be pleasant to live through; but historians will rate them among the major turning points of history.

POLITICAL VIOLENCE
1945-1966

This listing includes the more significant revolutions, rebellions, insurrections, coups, assassinations, violent protests, riots, and other efforts, successful, unsuccessful, or continuing, to bring about political, economic, or social change by violence or unconstitutional means from the end of World War II until December 1966. Exact dates for start and finish of many insurgencies are difficult to determine, and so are based on the author's interpretation of available evidence.

In addition to violence of worldwide or continental importance, the list, which is not intended to be all-inclusive, contains incidents of national, and, in some cases, regional significance.

ADEN
1963-66: Continuing anti-British rebellion by local Arab nationalists with some outside support involving terror and assassination.

ALBANIA
1945-66: Communist leader Enver Hoxha takes over government, adheres voluntarily to Soviet Bloc, and remains in power by force despite Titoist efforts to oust him.

ALGERIA
1945: Violent insurrection against French authorities and civilians by Kabylian mountaineers, Berber tribesmen, and Arab agitators. Repressive measures so severe they stimulate strong anti-French feeling.
1954-63: Protracted successful independence rebellion against French colonial rule and presence of French settlers, by Berber and Arab nationalists. They utilize terror, assassination, mass demonstrations, and extensive guerrilla warfare to support political demands and gain eventual victory.
1963 (April): Foreign minister Mohammed Khemisti shot by Moslem assailant.
1965: Successful bloodless coup against President Ben Bella by army Colonel Houari Boumedienne.

ANGOLA
1960-66: Continuing independence rebellion against Portuguese authorities, settlers, as well as pro-Portuguese Africans, by Angolan nationalists, led by Holden Roberto, involving atrocities and guerrilla warfare.

ARGENTINA
1945-46: Temporarily successful army coup against politically powerful Colonel Juan Peron. Conservative elements force him to resign all government posts until he is recalled by popular acclaim and elected President of Argentina in 1946.

1953: Widespread but unsuccessful violent protest against Peron dictatorship by conservatives.

1955 (September): Successful insurrection against government of Juan Peron by radicals and some religious elements following Peron's break with Catholic church. Peron is ousted and a coalition government committed to a program of social and economic reform takes control.

1955 (November): Successful and bloodless coup against rebel coalition, by army general Aramburu, brings military junta to power.

1962-63: Successful army coup against President Frondizi puts caretaker government in power, which annuls Peronist gains made in 1962 elections. Moderate regime under President A. Illia is then elected, July, 1963.

1966: Successful army coup against President Illia by General Ongania with support of some religious and nationalist groups.

AUSTRIA—See TYROL

BHUTAN
1964: Temporarily successful army coup results in assassination by soldier of Prime Minister Jigme Dorji, leading to caretaker government headed by brother of former Premier and then to assumption of all power by King Wangchuk.

BOLIVIA
1946: Successful revolt against President Villarroel Gualberto by his military and political opponents leads to ousting and assassination of former President and the coming to power of Dr. T. Monjo Gutierrez, who governs through a junta.

1952: Successful societal revolution against conservative regime of General H. Ballivian by popular leader Paz Estenssoro. Involving military and mob action, it leads to improved conditions for tin miners and peasants.

1953: Unsuccessful conservative counter-coup against Paz Estenssoro involves tin barons and absentee landlords.

1961: Unsuccessful plot against newly re-elected President Paz Estenssoro by extremists results in declaration of state of siege and widespread arrests.

1964: Successful political-military coup against President Paz Estenssoro by Vice President Barriontos puts an end to civil disorder and brings to power a military junta which promises free elections.

1965: Continuing protests against the Barrientos regime by tin miners and other labor groups result in violent clashes between the miners and the troops sent to pacify them. Finally General Candia is installed as co-President and the insurrection is put down by force.

BRAZIL

1954: Popular protest and military pressure against President Vargas force his resignation. This leads to his suicide and the formation of a caretaker regime.

1955: Violence and in-fighting among groups dissatisfied with 1955 elections keep new President and Vice President from taking office until January, 1956 when the Army supports their election.

1964: Widespread popular protests, plus pressure by military, force President Goulart to resign in April, giving way to assumption of power by General Castelo Branco, who suppresses extremists and attempts to solve Brazil's pressing economic programs.

BRITISH GUIANA—See GUYANA

BRUNEI *(British North Borneo)*

1962-63: Unsuccessful independence rebellion against British rule by nationalists and extremists, with support from Indonesia and Communist China, grows into guerrilla warfare, forcing British to move in troops to suppress the terrorists. See MALAYSIA.

BULGARIA

1946-49: Successful revolution against Bulgarian nationalists carried out by Communist Party under direction of Georgi Dimitrov. Using combination of parliamentary maneuvers and terror, the opposition is eliminated and its leaders jailed or killed.

BURMA

1948-65: Unsuccessful rebellion against government, primarily by Karen tribesmen with some Communist support, continues until largely suppressed by government in 1965.

1962: Successful bloodless coup by General Ne Win, against leftwing elements which had taken over the ruling Union Party, results in coming to power of seventeen-man Revolutionary Council.

BURUNDI

1965-66: Following murder of two previous Prime Ministers, Premier Leopold Biha is severely wounded in October, 1965. Extremists among

Bahutu tribesmen oppose power of Batutsi minority, while Batutsi "activists", who are accused of receiving help from Chinese Communists, move against government as too moderate. Clash leads to terror and guerrilla warfare between opposing factions.

1966 (July): King Mwami Mwambutsa IV, who has ruled Burundi since it became independent in 1962, deposed by his son, Prince Charles. Prime Minister Leopold Biha also ousted and supplanted by Michael Michombero, as Batutsis return to power. Prince Charles becomes King Mwame Ntare V and diplomatic relations are resumed with Communist China.

1966: Successful bloodless political-military coup against government of King Mwame Ntare V carried out by Prime Minister Michael Michombero, who replaces leftist officials with army officers.

CAMBODIA
1950-53: Independence rebellion against the French authorities by nationalist elements calling themselves the Free Cambodia Movement takes the form of terror and limited guerrilla action, and hastens the granting of full independence to Cambodia by the French in November, 1953.

CAMEROON
1958-60: Communist-guided "war of national liberation", against African authorities under Premier M'bida and French trusteeship, leads to violence and guerrilla warfare on part of Cameroon's People's Union until put down by French and African troops. France confers internal autonomy on Territory in December, 1958, as step toward complete independence which becomes effective January, 1960.

1962-64: Violence breaks out again in form of civil war as dissident tribal elements, with some aid from Chinese Communists, carry out a campaign of terror and guerrilla action before being suppressed by government forces from capital city, Yaounde.

CANADA
1945-66: Continuing insurrection against government by French-speaking Canadians in eastern part of country leading to agitation and sporadic violence in support of a movement for local autonomy.

CENTRAL AFRICAN REPUBLIC
1965-66: Successful national coup against President Dacko, involving arrests and little bloodshed, is carried out, January 1, 1966, by army strongman Colonel Bokassa. It leads to ousting of President and departure of all Chinese Communists whose activities had been centered there.

CEYLON
1953: Violent demonstrations against government stirred up by local Communist Party of about 2,000, plus Indian and Chinese Communists.

1958-63: Continuing violent protests over language and ethnic differences between the Tamils and the Sinhalese majority comes to head when the government declares Sinhalese the official language and moves to curb the resulting campaign of Tamil civil disobedience. Communist involvement in the affair gives crisis political overtones.

1959 (September): Prime Minister W. R. D. Bandaranaike assassinated by Buddhist monk.

CHILE

1949: Violent protests against policies of central government include rioting and sabotage provoked largely by Communist elements and lead to the Communist Party being outlawed, individual Chilean Communists being disenfranchised, and some non-Chilean Communists deported.

CHINA *(Subject of Chapter II)*

1945-49: Successful Communist Revolution (which actually began in 1921) makes extensive use of Mao Tse-tung's tactics of utilizing peasants organized into guerrilla bands. They conquer much territory, help throw out Japanese invaders, and then force conservative Chinese Nationalists under Chiang Kai-shek to leave mainland and retire to the island of Formosa.

1966: Continuing insurrection and protests by large number of peasants, workers, and middle-level Party cadres stirs up opposition in many areas of China against the extremist Proletarian Cultural Revolution sparked by Mao Tse-tung and his youthful fanatical Red Guards.

COLOMBIA

1948: Extensive mob action and violence in the city of Bogota against the central government and the Inter-American Conference then being held in that city. The riots are backed by local and international Communists.

1949-53: Continuing conflict between members of the Liberal and Conservative parties lead to thousands of deaths as the central government is unable to preserve law and order in many parts of the country. In January, 1953, Lt. General Rojas Pimilla ousts President Gomez in a bloodless coup and is then elected by Constituent Assembly.

1957: President Rojas is removed by a five-man military junta. Realizing that widespread insecurity has reached a point where it threatens not only life and property but the future of the country as well, and, fearful of growing communist influence in some parts of the land, the Liberals and Conservatives finally agree on a bi-partisan candidate, Lleras Camargo, who is elected President of Colombia.

CONGO, Democratic Republic of *(former Belgian Congo) (Subject of Chapter VII)*

1959-60: Successful anti-colonial rebellion against Belgians by African nationalists starts as rioting among unemployed in Leopoldville, and spreads so widely that Belgian government speeds up timetable and grants independence to the area, June 30, 1960.

1960 (July): Mutiny by the Congolese Force Publique against its Belgian officers leads to almost complete breakdown of law and order. The arrival of United Nations and Communist advisors only partially fill the vacuum of skills left by the departure of the Belgians.

1960 (September): A successful army coup against Prime Minister Lumumba and his numerous leftist advisors is carried out by a group of Congolese officers, headed by Colonel Mobutu, who then dismisses the National Parliament and takes control of the country.

1960-63: Unsuccessful secessionist rebellion of mineral-rich Katanga Province in southeast Congo, led by Moise Tshombe, begins July, 1960, and is ended after considerable fighting, by U. N. military action, January, 1963.

1960-62: Unsuccessful secessionist rebellion by small, diamond-rich state of Kasai.

1961 (February): Former Prime Minister Lumumba, ex-Youth Minister Mpolo, and Senate Vice President Okito killed in Katanga Province. Motivation political but details not clear.

1961-63: Unsuccessful independence rebellion against central government in Leopoldville, involving guerrilla action based from Stanleyville, by Vice Premier Antoine Gizenga with Lumumbist and Communist support, is put down by troops from Leopoldville.

1963 (August): Unsuccessful coup against government of Prime Minister Adoula and President Kasavubu.

1963-64: Unsuccessful coup in November, in Leopoldville, against the Kasavubu-Adoula government, led by former Cabinet minister Christophe Gbenye. It involves a general strike and violence, and is crushed by Adoula, acting on basis of incriminating evidence found in briefcase of Russian Embassy officials. Gbenye escapes.

1963-64: Unsuccessful rebellion in southern province of Kwilu against national government of President Kasavubu, led by former minister Pierre Mulele, with Chinese Communist support.

1964 (March): Unsuccessful attempt at revolution against government of President Kasavubu and Prime Minister Adoula involving terror and guerrilla activity by leftist members of a "Congo government-in-exile", operating out of Brazzaville in former French Congo. Movement is under direction of Gaston-Emile Soumialot and centers in Kivu province on eastern border of Congo. Revolt spreads to Stanleyville and then southward, until put down.

1964 (September): Unsuccessful independence rebellion by leftist rebels, who establish a "People's Republic" in Stanleyville with Christophe

Gbenye as President. Dozens of white hostages and hundreds of Congolese killed by fanatical soldiers of People's Republic before remainder are saved by airdrop of Belgian paratroopers, and column of pro-Leopoldville Congolese. They are led in part by white mercenaries acting under orders from Moise Tshombe, who had become Prime Minister of Congo.

1965 (October): In a successful "palace coup", President Kasavubu ousts his rival, Premier Moise Tshombe, who is then succeeded as Prime Minister by Evariste Kimba.

1965 (November): Successful bloodless coup in Leopoldville, against President Kasavubu and newly-elected Prime Minister Evariste Kimba, by General Joseph Mobutu, who declares himself President for five-year term and calls on Colonel Leonard Mulamba to form new government.

1966 (March): President Joseph Mobutu dismisses Parliament, assumes all legislative powers, and replaces Belgian with African city names.

1966 (June): Ex-Premier Evariste Kimba, along with three other former Cabinet ministers, are tried, convicted, and hanged on charges that they were plotting to kill President Mobutu.

CONGO, Republic of, Brazzaville *(former French Congo)*

1963 (August): Successful revolution by workers and leftist students. After three days of violence in the streets, they depose President Fulbert Youlou and his entire government. Leftist civilian government of young socialists installed under leadership of Alphonse Massamba-Debat.

COSTA RICA

1948: Military coup by General J. Figueres against President Ulate leads to mob violence. Ulate remains as President, but military junta under Figueres wields real power.

1955: Long-standing dispute over Costa Rican intervention in affairs of Nicaragua mediated by Organization of American States.

CUBA *(Subject of Chapter IV)*

1952 (March): Successful military coup drives opposition candidate Carlos Prio from Cuba. Former President Fulgencio Batista takes control of island.

1953 (July): Unsuccessful coup against Batista government, led by Fidel Castro, involves attack on military headquarters in seaport of Santiago. Casualties high on both sides, but Castro uninjured and sentenced to long term in prison on Isle of Pines until amnestied, 1954.

1956 (April): Military coup against Batista government by group of army officers fails when Batista learns of plot through informers.

1957 (March): Unsuccessful assassination attempt against Batista by students.

1957 (September): Attempted anti-Batista coup, by officers of Cuban Navy, put down after bloody fighting in town of Cienfuegos.

1956-59: Successful revolution, involving guerrilla action, terror, and violence by Cuban Nationalists, headed by Fidel Castro, drives Batista from country and eventually results in establishment of Communist regime.

1961 (April): Unsuccessful attempt at revolution, against Castro's pro-Communist regime, involves abortive underground revolt, and disastrous landing on beach at Bay of Pigs by anti-Communist Cuban Nationalists with U. S. backing.

CYPRUS

1945-60: Secessionist rebellion by Greek Cypriots against Turkish minority leads to violent demonstrations and terror by underground organization EOKA, culminating in 1955-56. Greek leader Archbishop Makarios temporarily exiled. Conflict brought to halt for a time when island granted independence by British in 1960.

1963-66: Continuing armed hostilities between Greeks and Turks in spite of presence of United Nations peacekeeping force.

CZECHOSLOVAKIA

1946-48: Successful revolution against Czechoslovakian nationalists who are led by President Benes. Communists and Socialists, backed by Moscow, gradually take power and elect Klement Gottwald as President.

DAHOMEY

1963 (October): Successful military coup by Army Chief-of-Staff, Colonel Soglo, ousts ex-President Hubert Maga, who had been named head of Provisional Government following dissolution of Parliament. In January, 1964, Maga becomes Foreign Minister under newly-elected President, Sourou Migan Apithy.

1964 (March): Unsuccessful insurrection by Bariba tribesmen from north against central government put down, and many followers of former President Maga arrested.

1965-66: After successful military coup, Colonel Soglo takes over as Chief of State, ends rioting, suspends constitution, and bans political parties as "incapable of governing".

DOMINICAN REPUBLIC

1961 (May): Longtime dictator Rafael Trujillo murdered. Dr. Joachim Balaguer attempts to run government through a six-man Coalition Council with the aid of one of Trujillo's sons, who is Chief-of-Staff. After six months of rioting and general strikes, all members of Trujillo family leave country.

1962 (January): Successful coup against Balaguer's Coalition Council by military junta. Other elements in armed forces overthrow junta two days later and proclaim Vice President Bonnelly new President. Balaguer goes into exile. On platform of broad reform, Juan Bosch then elected President by a large majority.

1963 (September): Successful coup by military overthrows Juan Bosch, who is accused of moving too far to the left in his reforms, and of utilizing Communist support. Army then installs three-man civilian junta, but plots and violence continue. Meanwhile, during 1964, Juan Bosch and Balaguer organize two groups, a Revolutionary and a Reformist Party in exile.

1965 (April): Attempt by Colonel Francisco Deno to overthrow three-man civilian junta and restore Juan Bosch to Presidency meets with determined resistance from army, headed by General Wessin y Wessin. Colonel Deno then installed as President, but reports of extensive Communist support for him, which might make Dominican Republic into another Cuba, caused President Lyndon Johnson to send a substantial U. S. military force to the island. After several military clashes, as well as mob violence, the Organization of American States restores order. At the end of August, Hector Garcia-Godoy, formerly Foreign Minister under President Juan Bosch, becomes interim President, pending new elections.

1965 (November): Rightist civilian coup in Santiago prevented by troops loyal to President Garcia-Godoy. Violence continues through December, but troops of Inter-American peace force eventually disperse rioters.

ECUADOR

1947: President Jose Maria Velasco Ibarra put out of office as military quells revolts, including two reportedly Communist efforts at revolution.

1961: Velasco Ibarra, who had been re-elected President in 1960, is again overthrown in an Air Force coup and replaced by Vice President Carlos Arosemena.

1963 (July): Successful coup by four-man military junta, led by Navy Captain Ramon Castro Jijon, forces President Carlos Arosemena to resign on grounds of being too soft on Communists, plus repeated public drunkenness. Social reforms promised.

1965-66: Extensive demonstrations demanding the end of Captain Jijon's military government cannot be controlled. He is ousted by brother officers who appoint a civilian government.

EGYPT *(Subject of Chapter III)*

1952: Successful and almost bloodless societal revolution against King Farouk by "Free Officers Society", ostensibly led by General Naguib but directed by Gamal Nasser. Movement has popular support.

1954: General Naguib forced from office by Vice President Nasser who, after period of demonstrations and riots, emerges as head of Revolutionary Command Council and new ruler of Egypt.

EL SALVADOR
1948: Successful coup by army deposes Castanedo Castro because of his dictatorial methods and leads to military rule of country.

1949: Leader of junta ousted by more liberal Major Osorio.

1960: Successful military coup overthrows President Jose Maria Lemus and results in rule by six-man junta.

1961 (January): Six-man junta ousted in another military coup, and replaced by group of "anti-Communist" officers under Colonel Castillo Navarette.

ETHIOPIA
1960: Unsuccessful coup by part of Palace Guard, other Army units, and some middle-class elements, in order to overthrow absent Emperor Haile Selassie, with ill-defined participation of Crown Prince Asfa-Wossen. Emperor returns to Ethiopia and revolt is crushed by loyal troops after period of brief but violent fighting. Crown Prince is reportedly forgiven.

1963-64: Continuing independence rebellion against Ethiopian rule by nomadic Somali tribesmen in Ogadan Province along Somali border. Sporadic violence and guerrilla warfare largely contained by superior power of Ethiopian Regulars.

FRANCE
1963 (February): Unsuccessful assassination attempt against President Charles de Gaulle by opponents of program to settle Algerian problem.

GABON
1964 (February): Temporarily successful bloodless army coup by four Lieutenants forces resignation of President Leon Mba because of his ban on opposition candidates in upcoming Assembly election. One day later, Leon Mba calls in French troops under terms of 1961 treaty, and is restored to presidency over opposition from liberals.

GERMAN DEMOCRATIC REPUBLIC (East Germany)
1953: Unsuccessful rebellion against Communist rule by some 40,000 East German workers who storm police headquarters and other key buildings and seize government machinery until Soviet Union moves in troops and restores Moscow-directed regime.

GHANA
1962-65: Unsuccessful violent protests by various groups opposing personal and dictatorial regime of President Kwame Nkrumah. Nkrumah suppresses opposition by use of police and military, but unrest smolders during next three years.

1966 (March): Successful military coup against President Kwame

Nkrumah, who is absent on state visit to Far East, carried out by Major General Ankrah. Country then ruled by seven-man National Liberation Council of army and police officers.

GREECE

1946-50: Unsuccessful Communist revolution against pro-Western government. When British support of Athens government weakens, President Truman, in May, 1947, begins supplying anti-Communist forces with money, arms, and supplies. Turning point in long-drawn and destructive Civil War comes in 1949, when President Tito quarrels with Stalin and closes Yugoslavia's frontier with Greece, thus cutting off Communist guerrillas from their source of supply.

1965: A prolonged government crisis precipitated July, 1965, when Premier Papandreou resigns; at issue is his plan to purge Army of rightwing officers. King Constantine opposes on grounds it would open armed forces to Communist influence. Leftists and backers of Papandreou stage riots in Athens as King seeks new premier who can win parliamentary majority over Papandreou bloc and extreme leftists. Constantine is finally successful when Stephanos Stephanopoulos is sworn in, September, 1965.

GUATEMALA

1951: Violence and street rioting breaks out over appointments by President Jacobo Arbenz Guzman, his drastic reform program, and his organization of a worker-peasant militia. Unrest put down, but opposition to President's "softness towards Communism" increases over next two years.

1954: Successful revolution against Arbenz government carried out by Colonel Castillo Armas, who mounts an invasion from exile in Honduras. U. S. government supports Armas after receiving conclusive evidence that Communist arms were being shipped into Guatemala.

1956: Violent protests by student and leftist groups against policies of Armas government, but government forces suppress demonstrators.

1957 (July): Anti-communist Colonel Castillo Armas assassinated by a Palace Guard and Vice President Gonzales takes over as provisional President. Subsequent elections declared fraudulent and military junta rules briefly until Vice President Flores is named provisional-President by Congress.

1958: Violent demonstrations against Flores government. Conservative General Miguel Ydigores Fuentes is elected President.

1960: Violence in streets. The government declares a state of siege after which open revolt breaks out against exceptionally corrupt Fuentes regime. Fuentes government moves against guerrilla insurgents as U. S. Navy patrols the coast to prevent a rumored Communist-led invasion.

1962 (March): Violent protests by students and workers cause army to put down disorders with considerable force.

1962 (November): Attempted military coup by Air Force against Fuentes government leads to strafing of Presidential Palace before revolt is crushed.

1963 (March): Successful military coup overthrows government of President Fuentes. Officers suspend constitution and dissolve legislature.

1964-66: Smoldering civil war against military junta by Marxist guerrillas necessitates retaliation by government, which combines military pressure with civic action programs until insurgency is contained in 1966.

GUYANA *(former British Guiana)*

1963-64: Racial violence and general strikes against British-backed government, encouraged by leftist Prime Minister Cheddi Jagan, continue until moderate leader Forbes Burnham becomes Prime Minister shortly before independence.

HAITI

1945-46: Following widespread anti-government demonstrations against President Lescot, he is ousted and six-man military junta takes control, paving way for election of Estime at end of year.

1950 (May): Successful military coup ousts President Estime and army takes control of country until elections in the autumn. However, unrest continues.

1950-56: Paul Magloire elected President and makes himself dictator, but is ousted in peaceful palace coup in 1956.

1957: Following two years of crisis Dr. Francois Duvalier elected President, September, 1957, eventually taking over as complete dictator by 1961. He is aided by People's Militia and ruthless Secret Police, which together are stronger than regular army.

1958 (June): Unsuccessful coup by rebel group fails to oust Duvalier.

1963: Another unsuccessful revolution against dictatorship of Duvalier attempted by political exiles and rebels who invade Haiti from Dominican Republic, which occupies eastern half of island. Legislature is suspended by Duvalier, constitution is set aside, widespread and often arbitrary arrests are made, and attempted revolution is crushed.

1964-65: Anti-Duvalier rebel bands roam mountains of Haiti, attacking police posts and killing Duvalier supporters. Government obtains old fighter-bomber airplanes by smuggling them out of the U. S. for use against the guerrillas. In spite of such counter-insurgency efforts, rebel groups continue activities in southwest Haiti.

HONDURAS

1956: Following unsuccessful army revolt, exiled liberal leader Jose

Ramon Villeda Morales returns to Honduras, ousts President Lozano Diaz and, with support from the military, takes power in a bloodless coup.

1957: Attempted revolution from Nicaragua by Honduran exiles causes crisis which is mediated by Organization of American States; President Morales remains in power.

1963 (October): Successful military coup led by Air Force Colonel Lopez Arellano overthrows President Morales. Colonel Arellano dissolves legislature and politically-oriented civil guard, and announces elections which are subsequently cancelled. Resulting violent anti-government demonstrations, December, 1963, put down by military.

HUNGARY

1947-49: Successful multi-step Communist revolution begins when Communist-controlled press warns of rightist attempt to overthrow government. This leads to purge of moderate Smallholder's Party. Anti-Communist Prime Minister Imre Nagy resigns and he is forced into exile. Communists win most of seats in August election and take over important positions in government. Continuing Communist pressure then ends Smallholder's Party, and drives most middle-of-the-road leaders into exile, permitting formation of Communist-dominated People's Republic in February, 1949.

1956 (October): Unsuccessful rebellion by liberal intellectuals, workers, students, and parts of Army, against Moscow-dominated party bureaucracy and ruthless actions of State Security Police. Open fighting breaks out in several major cities but western powers, involved in Suez crisis, do not act, and Soviet troops, backed by tanks, crush the revolt and liquidate many of its leaders. A slightly more liberal and Hungarian-minded regime finally emerges, but anti-Moscow bitterness remains widespread.

INDIA *(Subject of Chapter VI)*

1945-47: "Non-violent" rebellion against British rule, led by Mohandas K. Gandhi and a large number of other Hindu and Moslem Indians, which began shortly after World War I, ends, and August 15, 1947 is designated Indian Independence Day.

1947-48: Widespread violent and bloody rioting, by both Hindu and Moslem religious extremists over problem of vast and mixed religious groups, gradually subsides with delineation of frontier and exchange of religious population, after establishment of independent countries of India and Pakistan.

1948 (January): Mohandas K. Gandhi shot by bitter Hindu journalist.

1955: Successful independence rebellion against Portuguese rule in Goa, followed by domination of that colonial enclave by India.

1959: Successful protest movement against Communist government of the

South Indian state of Kerala, by Socialist parties and members of Moslem League, leads to temporary change in government.
See KASHMIR.

INDOCHINA *(Subject of Chapter V)*
1945-54: Protracted successful independence rebellion, which actually began in 1929, against French rule in what is now North and South Vietnam, Laos, and Cambodia. Communist assistance results in fall of French fortress of Dienbienphu in May, 1954. France grants complete independence to Cambodia, Laos, and South Vietnam, while North Vietnam, led by Ho Chi Minh, falls under Communist domination.
For current conflict see VIETNAM.

INDONESIA
1945-49: Widespread independence rebellion by Indonesian nationalists led by Ahmed Sukarno finally leads to conference at The Hague, December 1949, with Dutch Government's transferral of sovereignty to United States of Indonesia.
1949-66: A series of unsuccessful local independence rebellions keep various islands of Indonesia in prolonged turmoil.
1965-66: Unsuccessful Communist coup in October led by Lt. Colonel Untung of the Palace Guard. Several anti-Communist senior military officers kidnapped and brutally murdered after which Radio Djarkarta announces the formation of a 45-man Cabinet which includes Communists and leftwing Air Force officers. Several top ranking non-Communist Army officers escape massacre, rally their troops, subdue rebel elements in main cities, and move against Air Force dissidents and the Indonesian Communist Party (PKI). This organization, which had the backing of Chinese Communists, reportedly numbered nearly three million. Following widespread mob violence and considerable military action, some half million Communists are reported slain and rebellious elements are controlled. Sukarno remains as head of government but faces widespread and bitter opposition from organized student demonstrations and Moslem groups. Real power gradually transferred to anti-Communists, Suharto, and General Nasution.

IRAN
1945-46: Unsuccessful Soviet-sponsored independence rebellion in northern province of Azerbaijan and Kurdish tribal areas. Civil war breaks out as Communists support rebels, and central government strikes back with troops, tanks, and airplanes. Strong stand by U. S. government eventually tips the scales and insurgency is put down.
1947: Unsuccessful political intrigue and coup by Prime Minister Ghavan ended by army.

1948-52: Nationalist insurrection against interference of other countries in Iranian affairs, particularly British ownership of oil industry, leads to violent protests and mob action. Movement reaches peak in 1951 when, under strongman Mohammed Mossadegh, the Iranian Majlis vote to place refinery at Abadan and oil wells under Iranian government ownership and control. British are forced to withdraw their oil technicians, and fail to recover property through suit before Permanent Court of International Justice.

1953-54: Prime Minister Mossadegh fails in attempt to oust Shah Mohammed Riza Pahlevi through prolonged campaign of organized demonstrations and riots supported by pro-Communist Tudeh Party. Conflict finally resolved after pitched battle, when pro-Shah mobs and Royalist troops take over Teheran. Mossadegh is arrested and sentenced to three years in jail as Shah, who had left the country, returns to capital.

1961: Violent demonstrations, led by Iranian teachers demanding higher pay, force Prime Minister Sharif-Imami and his cabinet to resign.

1963: Modified societal revolution, inherent in Shah Pahlevi's program of political, social, and economic reform, produces violent protests and mob demonstrations on part of religious groups, as well as landowners and some wealthier elements, including relatives of Shah. He "takes the issue to the country", wins sweeping election victory, and calm is restored.

1965 (January): Premier Hassan Ali Mansour killed by assassin opposed to his policies.

IRAQ

1948: Successful and widespread protest movement against treaty giving British use of Iraqi air bases, led by nationalists and supported by students, forces Prime Minister Jabr to flee from the country and causes Regent Prince Abdul-Ilah not to ratify the treaty.

1952: Nationalist extremists and Communists provoke widespread rioting and mob action which force Prime Minister Umari and his Cabinet to resign. He is succeeded as Premier by General Mahmoud.

1958 (July): Violent nationalist and anti-monarchist revolution sweeps Iraq, then controlled by strongminded and pro-British Prime Minister Nuri as-Said, who signs pact uniting Iraq with Western-oriented Jordan. Under leadership of pro-Nasser General Abdul Karim el-Kassem, King Faisal II, Prince Abdul-Ilah, Premier Nuri as-Said and two hundred other Royalists are killed when there is resistance to occupation of palace. Pact with Jordan is then abrogated, and General el-Kassem becomes Premier.

1959 (October): Premier el-Kassem wounded in unsuccessful assassination attempt to overthrow his regime and a second attempt is also thwarted.

1959: Unsuccessful revolt by army units in northern Iraq, as el-Kassem balances Communist and Nationalist elements in government. When Communists become too strong, el-Kassem moves against them.

1962-66: Long smoldering independence rebellion by Kurdish nationalists in Iraq, under leadership of Mullah Mustafa al-Barzani, becomes full-scale guerrilla war with assistance to rebels by Soviet Union. Lack of roads in mountainous Kurdish areas render decisive action against rebels impossible, and guerrilla action continues on and off until June, 1966, when Kurds are granted local autonomy.

1963 (February): Military coup ousts Premier Abdul Karim el-Kassem, who is promptly executed. Colonel Abdul Salam Muhammad Arif becomes Provisional President of newly-established National Revolutionary Council, with Ahmed Hassan al-Bakr as Prime Minister. Friction between pro- and anti-Nasser elements in government continues.

1963 (November): Government of Premier Ahmed Hassan al-Bakr overthrown by army coup engineered by President Abdul Salam Arif, who had found himself largely a figurehead. Arif remains President with Lt. General Taher Yahya as Premier. Latter announces government will work for previously planned merger with Syria and Egypt.

1965 (September): Prime Minister Taher Yahya and his Cabinet resign in face of growing anti-Nasser influence, and he is succeeded by Chief of Air Force Arif Razzak, who obtains enough power to block a Communist plot to seize power.

1965 (September): Unsuccessful effort to seize complete power by General Arif Razzak, and Razzak, who is a Nasserite, flees to Cairo. Foreign Minister Abdul Rahman al-Bazzaz then becomes Prime Minister.

IRELAND

1956-57: Unsuccessful efforts at independence rebellion by Irish nationalists through sporadic attacks on British government installations to force Britain to give up North Ireland.

ISRAEL *(former Palestine)*

1947-49: Successful independence rebellion speeds ending of British mandate in Palestine by use of violence and terror on the part of Israeli nationalists. Problem turned over to the United Nations. General Assembly then overrides wishes of Arabs and votes for partition. British mandate over Palestine ends, May 14, 1948, and that day Jewish Nationalists declare their independence under the name of Israel. Many Arab refugees leave country.

1948-55: Unsuccessful rebellion by Arabs against newly-created Jewish state of Israel leads to invasion attempt by troops of Syria, Egypt, Lebanon, and Transjordan. Although short of arms, Israeli forces hold part of new

Jerusalem and drive Arabs out of Galilee and Negev. The United Nations brings most of fighting to an end before end of 1948, and, early the next year, Israel signs armistice agreement with four Arab neighbors. Arabs, however, never accept idea of Zionist nation and infiltration by commando or guerrilla units, plus terror and violence, continues for next eight years.

1956 (October): To put an end to continuing border clashes, terrorist infiltration, and sporadic violence, Israel sends troops across Sinai Peninsula and conquers the Gaza Strip, while French and British troops move into Egypt. Under pressure from the U.S. and the USSR, Israel and two European allies agree to United Nations request to withdraw from Egypt by March, 1957.

1957-66: Border clashes continue between Israel and Syria, Jordan and Egypt, with each side blaming the other for starting violations. Arabs refuse to accept existence of State of Israel, and large number of Arab refugees continue to live in "temporary camps" in preparation for day when they will return to "Arab homeland" in Palestine.

ITALY—See TYROL

IVORY COAST

1963-65: Unsuccessful attempted coups and assassination plot by several cabinet ministers are put down by strong action of police and military loyal to President Houphouet-Boigny. Sixty accused persons tried secretly in 1964, and sentenced in early 1965, leading to execution of six with prison terms for about thirty others.

JORDAN

1951: Assassination of King Abdullah by Palistinean Arabs who want to change Jordan's policy regarding Israel, and seek creation of Palistinean Arab State. After brief reign by ailing Talal, Hussein ibn Talal becomes King.

1955-56: Widespread violent protest against Jordan's joining pro-Western Bagdad Pact leads to mob violence, and forces resignation of Prime Minister Majali. After several Cabinet crises, an anti-Western government is elected and Parliament forces abrogation of Bagdad Pact. Pressure builds up against British personnel in Arab Legion and on British bases located in Jordan.

1957 (April): Successful political-military coup staged by King Hussein against pro-United Arab Republic elements, Syrian extremists, and some Communists within government and army. In face of violent nationwide demonstrations and riots, Hussein ousts National Socialist Prime Minister Nabulsi, names elder statesman Ibraham Hashem as Prime Minister and pro-Western Samir Rifai as Foreign Minister.

1958: U.A.R. plot to overthrow pro-Western regime of King Hussein prevented by forceful action on the part of pro-Hashemite army units backed by landing of British paratroopers.

1960 (August): Prime Minister Hazza Majali and ten others killed by terrorist time bomb planted in his office.

1963 (February): Plot to assassinate King Hussein is thwarted, but a series of Cabinet crises ensue while riots break out between troops loyal to the King, and demonstrators demanding that Jordan join federation with the U.A.R., Syria, and Iraq. Relative calm restored in July, following elections and formation of new cabinet, but resentment continues among some Palestineans and refugee extremists.

KASHMIR

1947-66: Protracted independence rebellion by Moslem majority against Hindus. Following division of sub-continent into Pakistan and India in 1947, Pakistani Moslems invade northern Kashmir to bring country into Pakistan. When the Hindu Maharajah attempts to solve problems by making Kashmir a part of India, religious civil war breaks out, United Nations intervenes, brings about a cease fire, and establishes a truce line. This division is not recognized by Moslem-sponsored Free Kashmir Movement and unrest continues.

1959: After stirring up leftist elements, Chinese Communists take over part of Kashmir province of Ladakh.

1965: Religious-political rebellion of Moslems in Kashmir leads to limited war between Pakistan and India until hostilities are quieted by good offices of the United States and the Soviet Union.

KENYA

1952-59: State of emergency arises from bloody rebellion by members of Mau Mau Society within Kikuyu tribe, whose leader was Jomo Kenyatta. Revolt involves evil oaths and unspeakable atrocities largely against non-sympathetic Africans but also some Europeans. Faced with growing violence, aimed at driving Europeans from Kenya and restoring tribal lands to Kikuyu, British fly in substantial numbers of troops, relocate Africans from exposed settlements in defensible strategic hamlets, and place thousands of Mau Mau suspects in concentration camps. These moves, plus successful anti-guerrilla sweeps through rebel-held mountain areas, break back of resistance.

1963 (December): Kenya granted independence within British Commonwealth, with Kenyatta as Prime Minister.

1964 (January): Unsuccessful army mutiny, protesting low pay and continuing presence of numerous British officers in armed forces of Kenya. At request of Prime Minister Jomo Kenyatta, the British fly 700 troops into country.

1964-66: Long smoldering independence rebellion by Somali tribesmen, demanding that Kenya's Northern Frontier District be annexed by neighboring Somalia, forces declaration of state of emergency before fighting is brought under control.

KOREA

1950-53: Armed forces of North Korea pour south across the 38th Parallel in June, 1950, invading Republic of Korea in "war of national liberation". In accordance with terms of Charter, United Nations carries out first collective defense action as sixteen members send troops to resist aggression. Insurgency escalates into limited war as Chinese Communists enter conflict, October, 1950. After bloody fighting, armistice agreement signed, July, 1953.

1960: Insurrection against reported irregularities in elections of March, 1960, which give President Syngman Rhee a fourth term. Protest takes form of widespread demonstrations and riots and is suppressed by police and military after considerable bloodshed. When opposition proves to be nationwide, President Rhee resigns his office, and leaves country in April. Constitution revised and new elections are held.

1961 (May): Military coup, led by Lt. General Chang Do Young against recently elected government, forces President Posun Yun and Prime Minister John M. Chang from office on grounds of widespread corruption.

1961 (July): Successful military coup overthrows recently installed government of General Chang Do Young and brings to power General Chung Hee Park, who promises to return control to civilians in 1963. Following fair elections, third Republic of Korea proclaimed in December, with General Park as President.

1964 (March and June): Unsuccessful violent protest over government's external and internal policies, largely by student groups, fails to topple government of President Chung Hee Park, as police and military move against rioters with force and efficiency. However, Colonel Kim Chong Pil, number two man in government, is forced to resign, as President Hee Park imposes martial law and suspends almost 600 government officials on charges of corruption.

1965 (May): Riots and violent protest demonstrations require police and military counter-action but fail to prevent signing of treaty, which establishes normal diplomatic relations with Japan.

LAOS

1946-54: Protracted, successful anti-colonial rebellion against French rule in Indochina. From 1950 on, Communist Pathet Lao, an anti-government military force, play growing role in struggle. In 1953 and 1954, nationalist and leftist elements from North Vietnam also take part in conflict. Laos finally granted independent status within French community in summer, 1954.

1960-62: Civil war breaks out in August, as Army Captain Kong Le pushes out anti-Communist government and calls for neutralist regime to include both Communist and pro-Western politicians. Effort at coalition fails and fighting spreads, as Communist Pathet Lao take over much of north Laos. Ceasefire arranged in May, 1961, by an International Control Commission, but Pathet Lao frequently violate agreement and expand territory under their control. In July, 1962, an international conference at Geneva, which includes representatives of United States, Russia, and Communist China, agree to coalition government under three royal princes: Boun Oum (pro-Western), Souvanna Phouma (neutralist), and Souphanouvong (pro-Communist). Fourteen nations at conference sign agreement making Laos a neutral nation.

1963 (April): Foreign Minister Quinim Pholesena assassinated by neutralist soldier.

1963-64: Pathet Lao work to subvert neutralist forces by assassinating important officers and politicians. Terror brings renewal of fighting and, on request from various major powers, the fourteen-nation Geneva Conference is reconvened. In spite of growing guerrilla action and Pathet Lao demands for neutralization of the Laotian capital of Vientiane, the coalition government continues to exist, although the area it controls shrinks steadily. By the end of 1964, Pathet Lao guerrillas control about three-fourths of the country. Forces loyal to neutralist Premier Souvanna Phouma continue to shrink in number and power.

1965-66: Following unsuccessful rightist coup early in 1965, neutralist elements join forces with remaining rightists and carry out successful joint offensive, clearing Pathet Lao from many areas. U.S. increases supplies reaching Meo tribes of northern Laos, thus strengthening their resistance to Pathet Lao in that mountainous area. These developments tip the balance, and, by the end of the year, royal government in Vientiane expands its control to approximately two-thirds of the nation under increasingly dominant role of Premier Prince Souvanna Phouma and growing support from King Savang Vathana. U.S. financial and economic aid proves increasingly effective in strengthening government and villages against Communist infiltrators. Following these reverses, Pathet Lao are reinforced from outside and mount new offensive in June, 1966.

LEBANON

1952: Demonstrations and violent protests, plus widespread political pressure, force resignation of President Bechara el-Khoury on charges of corruption.

1958: Insurrection in May against Christian President Camille Chamoun, whose pro-Western policies clashed with those of Moslem supporters of the United Arab Republic. Violence spreads, and, when, in July, the Western-oriented government of Iraq is overthrown and members of royal family are killed, future of independent Lebanon appears in doubt. As a result of appeal by President Chamoun, U.S. lands 6,000 Marines who help Lebanese police and military restore order. U.S. troops leave in October after election of Fouad Chehab as President.

1961-62: Government forces put down attempted revolution by a group of Lebanese Army officers and members of Syrian Nationalist Party, but unrest continues until summer, 1962, largely taking form of frontier clashes with Syria.

MACAO

1966: Chinese Communists push independence rebellion against Portuguese administration and settlers who form small minority of population. Rioting and political pressure backed by Chinese gunboats force authorities to accede to most insurgent demands for lessened Portuguese role in government of island.

MALAGASY *(former Madagascar)*

1947: Unsuccessful nationalist rebellion against French rule leads to much bloodshed, and landing of French paratroopers before revolt is put down.

1958-60: Madagascar proclaimed autonomous Republic of Malagasy, October, 1958, and becomes completely independent in 1960, though still a part of the French community.

MALAWI *(former Nyasaland)*

1959-64: Independence rebellion, against inclusion of Nyasaland in British-controlled Federation of Rhodesia and Nyasaland, results in violent protests and extensive rioting in 1959. Leader of nationalists, Dr. Hastings Banda, is put in prison for a short time before British release him, give self-government to area, and, in July, 1964, grant independence, under African name of Malawi.

1964 (October): Revolt against prime minister Banda by group of cabinet ministers is suppressed.

MALAYA *(Federation of)*

1948-57: Unsuccessful independence rebellion, sparked largely by dissatisfaction of Chinese Communists, against newly-established Federation of Malaya under British domination. Insurgent forces successful at first, but British move in additional troops, relocate many non-Communists from exposed settlements to defensible strategic hamlets, cut off distribution of food to hostile jungle areas, and encourage non-Communist Chinese to participate in political affairs, to join labor organizations, and to fight against insurgents.

Federation of Malaya becomes an independent member of British Commonwealth in August, 1957, under rule of King Tuanku Abdul Rahman. Constructive political-social developments, plus improved methods of counter-guerrilla warfare by British and non-Communists, cut ground from under appeal of insurgents and lead to collapse of Communist rebellion by 1957.

MALAYSIA *(Federation of)*
1963-65: A federation is formed in September, 1963 out of the former Federation of Malaya and former British colonies of Singapore, Sarawak, and Sabah (North Borneo). Smoldering independence rebellion in Sabah, stirred up by President Sukarno of Indonesia is suppressed with assistance of British forces.

1964 (July and September): Racial violence, reportedly stirred by Indonesian agents seeking to break up Federation, erupts in Singapore, leading to sporadic fighting, substantial casualties, and considerable property damage.

1965 (August): Following political pressures and violent protests, Singapore secedes from the Federation of Malaysia and becomes an independent nation under Prime Minister Tanku Abdul Rahman.

MOROCCO
1947-56: Prolonged anti-colonial rebellion against French rule. Sultan Sidi Mohammed ben Youssef, Mohammed V, takes a strong position supporting drive of the Istiqlal Party for national independence. After extensive riots and the death of several hundred demonstrators in 1952, the Sultan is kidnapped from his palace and sent by French into exile. Paris installs new ruler, Sidi Mohammed ben Moulay Arafa, who is viewed as a French puppet. Terrorism and assassination flare up again, continuing until 1955 when Sultan ben Youssef is allowed to return, and France grants independence to Morocco, March, 1956.

1965: Following rioting against monarchy, and demands for political and economic reforms, King Hassan II, who succeeded to the throne following death of Mohammed V in 1961, declares state of emergency and assumes all legislative and executive powers.

MOZAMBIQUE *(Portuguese)*
1965-66: Independence rebellion breaks out against Portuguese authorities and settlers in this province, with main support from nationalist and progressive elements, using neighboring Tanzania (Tanganyika) as safe haven. In spite of reforms, terror and guerrilla fighting continue to present day, partly contained by presence of Portuguese troops.

MUSCAT AND OMAN
1957-59: Independence rebellion by tribesmen led by Imam Ghalib bin Ali from interior plateau, with some financial aid from Arab League, is temporarily successful until quieted by troops of Sultan Sayyid Sa'id bin Taymur with support of British forces.

NEPAL
1950: In struggle between modernizers versus conservatives, Prime Minister Rana forces abdication of King Tribhubana Bir Bikram, who had the support of the Nepali Congress Party, the country's major progressive political force.

1951: Soon after Nepal obtains independence, a popular revolution involving demonstrations and riots overthrows the entrenched Ranan family, who had acted as hereditary Prime Ministers of Nepal for over one hundred years and whose policy was built around isolationism and opposition to change. King Tribhubana Bir Bikram, on return to power, attempts to establish a constitutional monarchy and forms a coalition cabinet, headed by M. P. Koirala as Prime Minister. Political-economic conditions remain unsettled, preventing King from carrying out any substantial reforms.

1952: Unsuccessful attempt at revolution against King and his supporters by Nepalese Communists put down by police and army. However, influence of Congress Party is reduced and Prime Minister Koirala is forced to resign and leave country.

1953-55: Communist opposition to government continues, taking form of guerrilla activity in areas of Nepal nearest Communist China. King Tribhubana Bir Bikram dies, early in 1955, and is succeeded by his son, Mahendra Bir Bikram.

1959-61: Following first parliamentary elections, M. P. Koirala returns from India to become Prime Minister. As political pressure and unrest grows, King Mahendra Bir Bikram has him arrested in December, 1960, dismisses Cabinet, dissolves Parliament, and after banning political parties early in 1961, takes all governmental powers to himself.

1962-65: Political violence over modernization continues, fanned by border raids into Nepal from political exiles using India as safe haven.

NICARAGUA
1947: Although elected with blessing of strongman General Anastasio Somoza, Dr. L. Arguello is overthrown by a military coup. Congress of Nicaragua, taking its guidance from Somoza dynasty, then names Lacayo Sacasa as Provisional President. Violent opposition to him develops, as high army officers, with support from Costa Rica, carry out raids.

1955: Growing unrest against Somoza dictatorship, encouraged by Costa

Rica, leads to guerrilla warfare and terror aimed at undermining regime. When government of Costa Rica accuses infiltrators from Nicaragua of attempting to foment revolution there, dispute is mediated by Organization of American States.

1956 (September): Assassination of General Anastasio Somoza, longtime Nicaraguan strongman. He is promptly succeeded by his son, Luis Anastasio Somoza, who becomes President, and moves with great firmness against plotters who come from almost all groups in the political spectrum.

1957: Unsuccessful efforts on part of opponents to Somoza regime to carry out revolution based on safe haven in neighboring Honduras, leads to friction with that country until mediation by Organization of American States.

1963: Violent protest against reportedly "farcical" election of Somoza henchman, Dr. Rene Schick Gutierrez, until put down by strong action on part of Samozan security forces.

NIGER

1964: Unsuccessful revolution, led by former Prime Minister Dgibe Bakary, who had been living in exile since his organization, the Sawaba (Freedom) Party, an outgrowth of the Marxist UDN, had been outlawed in 1959.

NIGERIA

1964-66: Violence breaks out following charges of illegal procedures in parliamentary election of December, 1964. Ensuing tensions increase rivalry between Hausa Moslems in the Northern Region, the Ibo in the East, and Yoruba tribesmen in Western Nigeria, and friction extends into political parties and upsets relations between regional leaders. More extensive violence occurs following elections of October, 1965, particularly in Western Region.

In belief that federal government in Lagos was losing control of country, the military leaders carry out a national coup in January, 1966. In addition to making widespread arrests, several top governmental leaders are murdered by insurgents, including Nigerian Prime Minister Sir Abubakar Tafawa Balewa and the Premier of the predominantly Moslem Northern Region. National President Nnamdi Azikiwe is then deposed, and that office taken over by Major General Johnson Aguiyi-Ironsi, representing the army. A newly organized Supreme Military Council makes substantial changes in the pattern and personnel of both federal and regional governments.

1966 (May): Anti-government and inter-racial demonstrations continue. In Northern Region, riots grow into massacres as local Hausa seek out and kill thousands of Ibo tribesmen who had come up from Eastern

Region. In another military coup, General Ironsi is ousted and replaced by Lt. Colonel Yakubu Gowon as head of central government.

NORTHERN RHODESIA—See ZAMBIA

NYASALAND—See MALAWI

PAKISTAN

1946-47: Successful Indian independence rebellion against British. Religious strife leads to creation of Dominion of Pakistan, August, 1947.

1947: Widespread massacres take place, growing out of partition of India on religious lines and movement of some seven million Moslems from India to Pakistan.

1948-49: Violence, due to Moslem-Hindu friction in Kashmir, leads to armed clashes between Pakistan and India until United Nations temporarily settles the dispute.

1951: Unsuccessful Communist revolution crushed by Karachi government.

1956-58: Pakistan becomes a Republic in 1956, but electoral processes, patterned somewhat on those of the United States, do not function smoothly, government corruption is widespread, and economic modernization lags. This leads to political-social unrest, forcing Major General Iskander Mirza, who had been elected country's first President, to abolish the constitution, dismiss the national and provisional governments, and declare martial law, October 7, 1958. Violence and rioting continue.

1958-60: Bloodless military coup by General Ayub Khan forces resignation of President Mirza, October 27, 1958 and establishes "benign martial law". Ayub, backed by local councils becomes President, February, 1960.

See KASHMIR.

PALESTINE—See ISRAEL

PANAMA

1949: President A. Arias Chanis, forced to resign after being beseiged in his palace by police and mobs, is succeeded by Vice President Chiari. Supreme Court rules in favor of Chanis, who is re-installed as President.

1955 (January): President Jose Remon, former Chief of National Police, is assassinated and succeeded by Vice President Jose Ramon Guizado. Following political unrest, Guizado is impeached by National Assembly, and convicted for taking a part in Presidential assassination, from which he is later cleared.

1963-65: Violent opposition to continuing U.S. rights in country and in Panama Canal Zone comes mostly from the Nationalists, and other elements opposed to the United States. Destructive riots break out in January, 1964, over flying of Panamanian and United States flags in Zone, and terms of 1903 treaty. Conservative Panamanian President Roberto Francisco Chiari breaks off diplomatic relations with the United States. Tension continues, the Organization of American States mediates the dispute. President Lyndon Johnson agrees to negotiate a new treaty regarding the Canal Zone and the rest of Panama, which is mutually accepted in September, 1965.

PARAGUAY

1947 (March): Unsuccessful revolution breaks out against President Higinio Morinigo, who has ruled as Dictator since 1940. After bitter fighting, in which heavily armed regulars see action against a Communist international brigade, the revolt is quelled. Supporters of President Morinigo, however, split into two rival groups.

1947 (November): Successful coup, by faction among army officers opposing Morinigo, forces him to leave the country. He is succeeded by a duly-elected President, Natalicio Gonzales, in 1948.

1948 (October): Unsuccessful coup, centering around discontented elements in Paraguay's Military Academy, put down.

1949 (January): Bloodless coup deposes President Natalicio Gonzales. General Rolan then acts as provisional President.

1949 (February): Another successful coup by civilian and military groups ousts General Rolan as provisional President. He is replaced by Molas Lopez, who is elected President in May.

1950: Coup against President Molas Lopez results in seizure of power by supporters of Frederico Chavez, who rules country as Dictator until elected President in 1953.

1954: Successful army coup ousts President Chavez. He is succeeded by General Alfredo Stroessner, who is then elected President without opposition.

1959: Unsuccessful attempt at revolution by liberal elements, who are frustrated by harsh nature of General Stroessner's regime. In spite of support for insurgents from friendly groups in Argentina and Cuba, the army of Paraguay wins conflict and President Stroessner, who had been re-elected in 1958, remains in power.

PERU

1948 (April): Following a series of political disturbances, believed supported by a secret army society known as the Aprista, two army garrisons revolt against the regime of President Jose Luis Bustamente Rivero, but are suppressed.

1948 (October): In another military coup, President Bustamente is ousted and control of country passes to a military junta, under General Manuel A. Odira, who imprisons many members of powerful APRA Party and moves against the Aprista society as a Communist front.

1962-63: Successful military coup by army officers, claiming that recent elections were fraudulent, leads to arrest of President Manuel Prado, July, 1962, and seizure of power by junta under Major General Perez Godoy. After considerable political in-fighting, Belaunde Terry becomes President in July, 1963, and constitutional government is restored.

PHILIPPINES *(Subject of Chapter VIII)*

1945-53: Unsuccessful Communist revolution, based in Central Luzon and backed by as many as one hundred thousand well-armed guerrillas, almost takes over country, capitalizing on grievances against widespread corruption in government, profiteering in business, and inequitable land distribution. Tide turns in September, 1950, when Ramon Magsaysay is appointed Minister of Defense and given a free hand to reorganize armed forces. He instills morale in Army, develops effective counter-guerrilla campaign, ends many of people's grievances, offers money and land to Communist deserters, and revives support for democracy. These reforms lead to holding of honest elections, and eventually to Magsaysay becoming President.

POLAND

1945: Widespread anti-Communist revolution crushed by tanks and infantry on instructions from Soviet Premier Stalin.

1947 (January): "Free elections", which had been called for in Yalta Agreement, turn out to be controlled by Communist Party, which establishes a completely pro-Moscow regime. Many non-Communists arrested or forced to flee from country. Pro-Polish Communists relegated to minor roles.

1956: Growing dissatisfaction with Moscow-dominated Communist government leads to serious "bread and freedom" riots in Poznan and other cities, June, 1956. Moscow shakes up Communist regime and returns to power, October, 1956, former head of Polish Communist Party, Wladyslaw Gomulka, who had been ousted in 1948. This leads to somewhat greater independence from Moscow, and slightly more liberalized way of life.

PORTUGUESE GUINEA

1963-66: Prolonged anti-colonial independence rebellion against Portuguese regime and Portuguese settlers. Counter-guerrilla actions by substantial number of Portuguese troops bring rebellion under control by 1966, but African discontent continues. In belief that insurgents are using neighboring Senegal as a safe haven, Portugal bombs at least one village in that country, leading to break in diplomatic relations and discussion of dispute at the United Nations.

RHODESIA *(former Southern Rhodesia)*

1960-64: Tension and some violence between Africans and white settlers, growing out of position favoring white supremacy taken by European minority, eventually leads to break-up of the Federation of Rhodesia and Nyasaland. Northern Rhodesia gains independence and becomes Zambia; Nyasaland becomes Malawi. Racial tension unrelieved in Southern Rhodesia.

1965-66: Continuation of racist attitude on part of white minority in Southern Rhodesia (now called Rhodesia) leads to growing conflict between Salisbury and London. Following 1965 elections, the Rhodesian government, under Prime Minister Ian Smith, begins negotiations with the British Labor government, but refuses to make any compromise that would lead to rule by African majority. In November, 1965, Prime Minister Smith declares Rhodesia independent, whereupon the British government, backed by most of the United Nations, inaugurates economic sanctions against the rebels.

RHODESIA, NORTHERN—See ZAMBIA

RUMANIA

1946-48: Communist-dominated government which had been forced on King Michael in March, 1946, consolidates its power through pressure and a rigged election. King Michael is compelled to abdicate and go into exile in December, 1947. Establishment of the Rumanian People's Republic is declared, with a constitution based on that of the Soviet Union.

RWANDA

1960-62: Successful bloody revolution by Bahutu tribesmen overthrows longstanding monarchy of Batutsi tribe. 160,000 of the Batutsi tribe flee to neighboring countries, including Uganda, Tanzania, the Congo, and Burundi. After winning overwhelming victory in U.N.-supervised elections of September, 1961, the Bahutu-controlled government obtains full independence for Rwanda effective July 1, 1962, as the Republic of Rwanda, while Urundi, the southern half of the former U.N. trust territory, becomes the independent kingdom of Burundi.

1964: Tribal warfare pushed by members of Inyenzi, a terrorist group seeking to restore the Batutsi monarchy, leads to further massacre of many hundreds of Batutsi while thousands more flee to neighboring countries.

SAUDI ARABIA

1964: In bloodless palace coup in March, Prince Faisal becomes regent for his elder brother, King Saud II. Faisal proclaimed King in November, and pushes program to modernize country.

SENEGAL

1962-63: Attempted coup, in December, 1962, by Prime Minister Mamadou Dia, against President Leopold Sedar Senghor, over vote of censure in National Assembly, is put down without bloodshed, but leads to arrest and imprisonment of Dia. Following adoption of new constitution, based on Presidential system of government, elections are held in December, 1963. Although voting is marred by rioting and bloodshed, President Senghor is returned to office.

SINGAPORE—See MALAYSIA (Federation of)

SOMALIA
1961-66: Continuing independence rebellion against Ethiopian rule and taxation, by nomadic Somali tribesmen in Ogadan Province of Ethiopia. Sporadic violence and some guerrilla fighting is dominated by superior power of Ethiopian troops. Conflict leads to arbitration between two governments, but discontent continues.

1964-66: Somali irredentist movement leads to friction with Kenya. See KENYA.

SOMALILAND *(French)*
1960-66: Continuing desire by Somalis for independence from French rule and union with "Greater Somalia" leads to sporadic violence.

SOUTH AFRICA
1959-66: Long smoldering insurrection against apartheid program of National Party, which continues to carry out forceful policy of white supremacy against large non-white majority. Most bloody single incident occurs at town of Sharpsville in March, 1960, when 56 Africans are killed by the police. Faced with organized underground movement, the government of South Africa continues to deal harshly with any violators of its apartheid laws.

1966: Following unsuccessful attempt to kill him in April 1960, Prime Minister Hendrik F. Verwoerd assassinated, September, 1966, by white South African.

SUDAN
1955: Independence rebellion on part of pagan and Christian tribes of Southern Sudan, who object to domination of Moslems from Northern Sudan and Egypt, comes to surface in troop mutiny against leaders. Grievances are smoothed temporarily by representatives of Britain and Egypt. Anglo-Egyptian Sudan obtains independence in January, 1956, as Republic of the Sudan.

1958: Encouraged in part by local population, Egyptian troops occupy portion of northeastern Sudan along border with Egypt. They withdraw as pro-Egyptian elements prove weak and international pressures build up.

1958 (November): Successful bloodless coup by Lt. General Ibrahim Abboud, Commander of the Armed Forces, against what he terms inefficiency and corruption of the civilian government. Deposed Prime Minister Abdulah Khalil of Uma Party later admits that he knew of and approved action by military because of threat to continued independence of Sudan posed by agitation from Egypt.

1959 (March): General Abboud dismisses the Supreme Council, which had shared power with him, and appoints new council, which he dominates.

1964 (October): Bloody rioting by civilians, including workers and students in Khartoum, forces President Abboud to resign and turn over control of Sudan to a 24-man coalition cabinet of civilians headed by Sir-el Khatim el-Khalifa.

1963-66: Continuing independence rebellion by Nilotic tribes against rule of northerners from Khartoum flares again, and three hundred Christian missionaries are expelled from the Sudan on charges of supporting the insurgency. Violence continues throughout 1965, and, by 1966, grows into limited civil war.

SYRIA

1948: Successful army coup, brought about by general strikes and three days of rioting, causes Prime Minister Mardam and his cabinet to resign. Commander-in-Chief Colonel Husni al-Zaim imposes martial law and installs a new Cabinet. This government, however, is soon succeeded by another group of Ministers headed by ambitious politician Khalid al-Azam.

1949 (March): In an army coup, President al-Kuwatli and Prime Minister Khalid al-Azam are forced out of office by Colonel Husni al-Zaim. Akram al-Hawrani becomes Prime Minister although Colonel al-Zaim holds real power.

1949 (August): Colonel al-Zaim is deposed and executed in military coup led by Colonel Sami al-Hinnawi who takes power and conducts elections which lead to new Parliament.

1949 (December): In successful army revolt, Colonel al-Hinnawi, who has shown close sympathy for Iraq, is deposed by pro-Egyptian elements led by Colonel Adib Shishekly.

1951 (November): When quarrels among politicians regarding policies and personalities became too violent, Colonel Shishekly calls out his troops again and takes control of Syria, exercising authority through the post of Chief of the Military Council.

1954 (February): After adoption of new constitution, Adib Shishekly is elected President of Syria in July, 1953, but is forced into exile through quick army coup.

1958-61: In February, 1958, the Syrians vote to end their political independence and form the United Arab Republic with Egypt under Presidency of Gamal Abdel Nasser. He disbands Syrian political parties and abolishes Syrian citizenship. In 1961, however, a successful military revolt against the United Arab Republic forces Nasser to give up his claims to Syria as part of the U.A.R., and leads to election of Nazam el-Koudsi as President of Syria.

1962 (March): Revolt by army officers, who had led 1961 breakaway from Egypt, ousts government of President Nazam el-Koudsi. This leads to political-military strife and el-Koudsi is finally restored as President in a compromise between military, civilian, and leftist elements.

1963 (March): For the eighth time in fourteen years, a successful coup occurs; this time by Lt. General Amim el-Hafez and pro-Nasser officers under Lt. General Hashem el-Atassi, who overthrow Premier el-Azam. Atassi becomes President of Revolutionary council, but support for pro-Nasser government weakens, and Nasserites are unable to form a government without support of leftist Baathists.

1963 (July): Unsuccessful pro-Nasser revolt put down by government after heavy fighting. Twenty-seven Nasserite leaders executed, strength of socialist Baathists grows, leading to replacement of Lt. General Hashem el-Atassi by strongman el-Hafez as head of Revolutionary Council with Baathist Party leader, Salah el-Bitar, as new Prime Minister.

1964: Revolt in April by disgruntled landowners, against Agrarian Reform Law limiting individual holdings to one hundred acres, spreads across Syria and is backed by shopkeepers, who resent socialist policies of government. Troops restore order, but dissatisfaction continues. In May, Major General Amim el-Hafez is named head of five-man Presidential Council.

1964: Unsuccessful revolt against Baathist government of Premier Salah el-Bitar by extremist Moslem Brotherhood is crushed with considerable loss of life, strengthening anti-Nasser feeling in Syria.

1965 (January): Plot to assassinate President Amim el-Hafez, growing out of resentment among conservative businessmen and landowners against pro-socialist policies of ruling party, is blocked.

1966 (February): Following riots and clashes between army units, in which over 400 are killed, President el-Hafez is deposed. Dr. Atassi is named President, with Dr. Zayen as Premier, backed by the strength of Baathist and leftist military junta.

TANZANIA *(formerly Tanganyika and Zanzibar)*

1964 (January): Unsuccessful mutiny by two battalions of Tanganyikan army, demanding higher pay and total Africanization of partly-British Officer Corps. Various Cabinet members are arrested by mutineers, and President Julius Nyerere escapes by going into hiding. Revolt suppressed with aid from British troops flown into country on request of Nyerere. Following outbreak, 1350-man army is disbanded, and new army formed, but strength of regime is weakened.

1964 (January): After obtaining independence from Great Britain, African rebels overthrow the Sultan of Zanzibar and predominantly Arab government, utilizing African guerrillas, some of whom had been trained in Cuba. Extensive violence and massacres result in brutal death of many Arab officials and Indian businessmen. An internal power struggle then breaks out between President Abeid Amani Karume and self-styled Field Marshal Okello, a pro-Communist extremist, leading to defeat and exile of the latter.

1964 (April): Tanganyika and Zanzibar agree to merge into a single united republic. Julius Nyerere of Tanganyika becomes President, while President Abeid Amani Karume of Zanzibar becomes first Vice President of the new union.

THAILAND *(former Siam)*

1946 (June): King Ananda Mahidol is assassinated and legislature names his American-born brother, Phumiphon Aduldet to succeed him.

1947 (November): A bloodless military revolution, led by wartime Premier Field Marshal Pibul-Songgram, overthrows government and he becomes Premier to counteract danger of Communism.

1949-50: Following period of considerable pressure, political parties are outlawed, and Prince Phumiphon Aduldet is crowned King Rama IX, May, 1950.

1951: In a short-lived palace revolution, Pibul-Songgram is ousted for a few hours, but then comes back as Prime Minister at the head of an anti-Communist government.

1951-57: In one of several bloodless military coups, September, 1957, Field Marshal Sarit Thanarat overthrows government of Pibul-Songgram.

1959 (February): Sarit Thanarat takes all power, annuls the constitution, outlaws political parties, and then proceeds to carry out policy of cooperation with the western-oriented Southeast Asia Treaty Organization.

1963: Death of Sarit Thanarat. He is succeeded as Prime Minister by Field Marshal Thanom Kittikachorn.

1963-66: Revolutionary activity, fanned by pro-Communist elements based in Laos and Cambodia, leads to guerrilla action and counter-revolutionary operations by Thai patrols which are equipped with improved weapons and vehicles, largely U.S. supplied. Fighting along northeastern border contained.

TIBET

1950-56: Using internal discontent and previous Chinese rule as pretexts, Chinese Communist forces invade Tibet in late 1950, forcing the Dalai Lama, generally regarded as ruler of the country and one of its two Grand Lamas, to flee. The Dalai Lama returns in 1951 and establishes temporary Tibetan capital near border with India, after receiving Communist assurances he would have control of Tibet's internal affairs. In May, 1951, Tibetan Communists sign an agreement surrendering sovereignity of that country to the Chinese People's Republic. Tibetans, in theory, allowed regional self-government, including freedom of religion. Slow and complicated negotiations drag on, while Chinese Communists build roads into Tibet and generally strengthen their control of country.

1956-58: Growing opposition by Tibetan religious leaders and wealthier people to Communist efforts at socialization breaks into riots in 1956, causing Peking temporarily to slow down its infiltration into the religious, political, business, and social life of Tibet.

1959-66: Independence rebellion by many elements of Tibetan population leads to large-scale fighting. But Communist troops show superior strength, the Dalai Lama flees to India, and the Chinese establish a Tibetan People's Government under the Panchen Lama, in the past regarded as the country's spiritual leader. Even after ruthless liquidation of Tibetan Nationalists, including replacement of Panchen Lama by more pro-Peking official, anti-Communist feeling continues into mid-1960's.

TOGO

1963 (January): Successful army coup by small group of disgruntled soldiers, motivated largely by complaints of low pay and restricted job opportunities, overthrows government of President Sylvanus Olympio, who had led the struggle for independence of the Republic of Togo and had become its first Prime Minister. Olympio is assassinated on the same day. Nine-man insurrectionary committee assumes power, and invites former Prime Minister Nicolas Grunitzky to return from exile and become provisional President.

1963 (April): Unsuccessful plot to overthrow Grunitzky government is suppressed, leading to arrest of various prominent politicians.

1964 (May and July): Two additional plots against regime of President Grunitzky lead to further arrests, imprisonment, and expulsion of opposition politicians from country.

1965 (January): President Grunitzky assumes direct control of army as he ousts Chief-of-Staff, the acknowledged leader of group that assassinated former President Olympio.

1966 (December): Successful army coup ends rule of President Grunitzky, and leads to assumption of power by Lieutenant Colonel Eyadema in order to end the "confused political situation".

TRUCIAL STATES—SHARJA

1965 (June): Successful palace coup ousts Sheikh Saqr, who had been developing closer ties with the United Arab Republic. He is replaced by his cousin, Khalid.

TUNISIA
1952-57: Successful independence rebellion, under nationalist leader Habib Bourguiba, begins with street rioting and develops into well-organized and widespread violence and terror until French grant Tunisia its independence in March, 1957.

1958-61: In effort to stop what is claimed to be Tunisian support for rebellious Algerian nationalists, in February, 1958, the French bomb the border village of Sidi Sakiet, producing extensive casualties and increasing bitterness against French position in North Africa.

1961 (July): Series of incidents finally culminate in violent protest over continued French presence in military base at Bizerte. Anti-French rioting grows, and Tunisian troops lay seige to the town until French tanks and paratroopers break through Tunisian lines. After over thirteen hundred lives are lost, the United Nations mediates the dispute, and France hands over control of base at Bizerte, retaining only limited rights of access.

1962 (December): Unsuccessful plot to assassinate President Habib Bourguiba is thwarted, with arrest and execution of several dozen conspirators. Trials and unrest continue into 1963.

TURKEY
1959-61: Following violent demonstrations, largely by university students, against the increasing repressiveness of the government of President Celal Bayar and Premier Adnan Menderes, a successful bloodless army coup in May, 1960, leads to formation of provisional government by group of military officers known as the Turkish National Union Committee, under leadership of Lieutenant General Cemal Gursel.

After approval of a new constitution, and lengthy trials, Bayar is sentenced to life imprisonment, Menderes is hanged for treason, September, 1961, and Gursel is elected Turkey's fourth President, with Ismet Inonu as Premier.

1961: Unsuccessful counter-coup against Gursel regime by followers of former Premier Menderes.

1963 (May): Unsuccessful military coup, by cadets from Turkish War College and disgruntled former army officers, smashed by government; many participants are arrested and the leaders sentenced to death.

TYROL
1946-66: Smoldering independence rebellion by German-speaking South Tyroleans, angered by fact that Southern Tyrol was not given back to Austria after World War II, is quieted when Italy promises regional autonomy. Discontent comes to surface, particularly in late 1950's, in form of violent demonstrations, terror, and small-scale guerrilla action along border between Italian and German-speaking areas. The problem goes to

the United Nations in 1961, but unrest, violence, and raids by Tyrolean Nationalists continue.

UGANDA
1964 (January): Unsuccessful mutiny of army troops at Camp Jinga on Lake Victoria flares over demand for pay increase. Prime Minister Milton Obote calls for emergency airlift of 450 British troops and revolt is suppressed.

1966: Faced with growing internal opposition in February, Prime Minister Obote seizes all power, suspends the constitution, and arrests five cabinet ministers who had challenged his authority. On March 2, Prime Minister Obote ousts President Edward Mutesa, who is also king of separatist Buganda. Violence erupts and, on May 24, the army shells and destroys the King's palace. The King escapes and flees country.

UNITED ARAB REPUBLIC—See EGYPT

UNITED STATES
1950 (November): Unsuccessful assassination attempt against President Harry S. Truman, by two Puerto Rican nationalists.

1955-65: Increasing civil rights agitation in several states of the south, largely over school, restaurant, job, and housing segregation, leads to demonstrations, violence, and terror.

1963 (November): President John F. Kennedy assassinated. Warren Commission Report concludes attack was non-political.

1964-66: Growing racial unrest in urban areas, particularly New York, Chicago, and Los Angeles, breaks into violent protests. Most serious rioting occurs in Watts district of Los Angeles, August, 1965, resulting in more than thirty deaths and substantial property damage.

UPPER VOLTA
1966 (January): During demonstrations against austerity program of President Yameogo, Army Chief of Staff, Lieutenant Colonel Sangoule Lamizana, seizes presidency and takes control of state.

VENEZUELA
1945 (October): President Medina Angarita removed from office by a group of younger officers and civilians, and a seven-man junta, headed by Romulo Betancourt, takes over and expands constitutional rights of the people.

1946 (December): Unsuccessful military coup fails to seize Venezuelan government and, in 1947, Romulo Gallegos is elected President.

1948: Successful army coup by rightist elements ousts President Romulo Gallegos, who is succeeded by Lieutenant General Carlos Delgado Chalbaud.

1950: President Chalbaud assassinated and German Suarez Flamerich succeeds to Presidency.

1958: Unsuccessful revolt against regime of President Marcos Perez Jimenez, who had been elected to office in April, 1953, is put down in spite of attacks by jet aircraft on capital city of Caracas. Later, in January, mass demonstrations and a general strike aimed at ousting President take place. After several days of mob violence, Perez Jimenez is removed by group of military officers and civilians calling themselves the "Patriotic Junta". Violent protests continue, including an unsuccessful military coup in July, and a revolt that temporarily seizes the Defense Ministry and the national radio station early in December. Romulo Betancourt is elected President.

1960 (April): Unsuccessful revolt against government of Romulo Betancourt quelled by police and military.

1960 (June): Unsuccessful assassination attempt on President Betancourt leads to condemnation of the Dominican Republic for acts of aggression against Venezuela.

1961: Sporadic street violence is climaxed by unsuccessful military uprising in June. Venezuela blames Communists for disturbances and breaks diplomatic relations with Cuba because of them.

1962 (May): Unsuccessful revolt at Carupano by group of navy and marine officers is put down by forces loyal to Betancourt government.

1962 (June): Unsuccessful revolution at Puerto Cabello, which Venezuelan government blames on Communists, results in death of some 200 persons and injury to more than 300 others.

1962 (October): Wave of sabotage and terror causes government of Venezuela to take strong steps against Cuban insurgents.

1963: Street violence and terror continues in June, climaxed by another assassination attempt against President Betancourt. In spite of Communist efforts to block elections, Raul Leoni is elected President in December.

1964-65: As violence and terror expand, the Organization of American States receives evidence of the smuggling of Communist arms into Venezuela, votes sanctions against Cuba for its attempts to subvert government there. Opposition centers in leftwing organization, called the "Armed Forces of Liberation", which is accused of damaging factories and pipelines, sacking stores, raiding towns, kidnapping opponents, and hijacking a Venezuelan freighter. Unrest continues through 1965 and Communist guerrilla bands expand operations in parts of the Venezuelan countryside.

VIETNAM *(Subject of Chapter IX)*
1945-54: See INDOCHINA.
1956-64: Communist-organized revolution, supported by supplies and

guerrilla forces from North Vietnam, spreads over broad rural areas, terrorizes villages and cities, and, during the year 1964, becomes so successful that the United States and its non-Communist allies are forced to increase both economic and military support for the government of South Vietnam. Action grows into a limited war.

1960 (November): Unsuccessful army coup against regime of President Ngo Dinh Diem is put down by pro-government forces.

1962 (February): Unsuccessful coup by segment of air force. Some bombs are dropped on Presidential Palace, but other military elements fail to rise. Diem government carries out widespread arrests, and coup fails.

1963 (May-October): Growing political-religious opposition to autocratic methods of Diem regime leads to mob violence, led in part by militant Buddhists guided by Thich Tri Quang. Insurgency involves violence and self-immolations by Buddhist monks.

1963 (November): Successful national coup by junta of military leaders of South Vietnam results in death of President Diem, his powerful brothers Ngo Dinh Nhu and Ngo Dinh Can and the coming to power of a twelve-man Military Revolutionary Council of twelve generals headed by Duong Van Minh ("Big Minh").

1964 (January): Successful army coup by General Nguyen Khanh ousts General Duong Van Minh, head of Military Revolutionary Council, and Prime Minister Nguyen Mgoc Tho. General Khanh explains his action on grounds that Military Revolutionary Council had proved ineffective, and that neutral "pro-French" elements were gaining control of the country. He then declares self Chief-of-State and Chairman of reorganized Revolutionary Council.

1964 (August-September): New wave of student demonstrations and mob attacks on radio stations and government buildings joined by Buddhist extremists and Communist agitators, as violence spreads from Saigon to such towns as Hue and Danang. Growing political pressures finally force resignation of General Nguyen Khanh.

1964 (September): Three generals—Minh, Khiem, and Khanh, assume control of state. Conservative groups clash with leftists in bloody street fighting, and, when unrest continues, General Khanh produces letters of support from various groups, including the Buddhists and the Army. A coup by former office-holders fails on September 13, and support for the triumvirate is shown by younger officers, including Air Vice Marshal Nyguyen Cao Ky.

1964: Attempted independence rebellion in autumn by some of tribal Montagnards of the Central Highlands, acting in part with Communist support, is suppressed by troops loyal to Saigon.

1964 (October): Opposition to continued rule of triumvirate of generals headed by General Khanh grows among students, Buddhist extremists, and pro-Communist infiltrators. Bloody riots force government to re-establish martial law.

1964 (December): Unhappy over lack of political, economic, or military progress, a group of younger generals, led by General Nguyen Chanh Thi and Air Vice Marshal Nguyen Cao Ky, purge "Old Guard elements" among the military.

1965 (January): Student and Buddhist riots break out again and continue in spite of moves by military to give civilian Vietnamese a greater voice in running government. Demonstrations assume greater anti-U. S. slant, including sacking of the U. S. Information Office in Hue. Yielding to pressure, Prime Minister Van Huong, who had held office only since October, resigns, but General Khanh continues as strongman. Dr. Phan Huy Quat, a former Foreign Minister, then becomes Prime Minister in a Coalition Cabinet which contains strong Buddhist representation.

1965 (February): Successful army coup by troops under command of Lieutenant Colonel Phan Ngoc Thao leads to transfer of General Nguyen Khanh from Vietnam to be Ambassador to United Nations. He is succeeded as Commander-in-Chief by General Tran Van Minh ("Little Minh"), while Dr. Phan Huy Quat remains as Prime Minister.

1965 (March): Student demonstrations and Buddhist suicides continue, leading many members of government, army leaders, and anti-Communists to conclusion that only possibility of gaining stability is through strong, active, and youthful military leader. Dr. Phan Huy Quat resigns as Prime Minister and is succeeded in June, by Air Vice Marshal Nguyen Cao Ky. He takes steps to contain rioters, and, after some difficult months, gives South Vietnam a government with more stability than any regime since that of Diem.

YEMEN

1948: Successful palace revolution results in death of Imam Yahya. When Prince Ebrahim is chosen to head the government, there is unrest, and Prince Seif el-Islam Ahmed of Hamidudin dynasty marches on San'a, the capital, and seizes the government.

1962-66: Imam Ahmed assassinated in September, 1962, by Republican Forces. Civil war rages over succession in Yemen, with Saudi Arabia supporting the forces of Ahmed's heir, Imam Mohammad al-Badr, while the troops and supplies of the United Arab Republic bolster the government of President Brigadier General Abdullah al-Salal. Efforts at mediation by various Arab leaders and the United Nations produce only temporary results.

YUGOSLAVIA
1948: Political rebellion by President Tito and leaders of Communist Party in Yugoslavia lead to seeking of virtual independence by the Yugoslav Communists from the Soviet Communist Bloc. The result has been a somewhat more moderate regime. "Titoism" is generally used to describe the political orientation of a Communist nation relatively independent of the Soviet Union.

ZAMBIA *(former Northern Rhodesia)*
1964: Following the dissolution of the Federation of Rhodesia and Nyasaland in October, 1964, Northern Rhodesia takes the name of Zambia, and becomes an independent nation. Relations are strained when Southern Rhodesia adopts policy of white supremacy and unilaterally declares itself independent of Great Britain.

After the blowing up of a power station, President Kenneth Kaunda of Zambia calls upon Great Britain for protection against terrorists, who he claims are coming from Southern Rhodesia.

ZANZIBAR—See TANZANIA

1967-1970

Since the first edition of this book, political violence has continued and even increased in frequency. There follows a list of some of the more significant outbreaks between 1967 and 1970.

ADEN
1967-69: Independence rebellion against Britain, complicated by struggle for control between Republican and Royalist groups, keeps crown colony and states of interior in frequent and bloody conflict.

ALBANIA
1967-68: Chinese-type "Cultural Revolution" hits Catholic and other churches. Some provinces later disturbed by agitators seeking political autonomy.

ALGERIA
1967-68: Unsuccessful coup by part of army. President Boumediene later survives unsuccessful assassination attempt.

ANGOLA
1967-69: Continuing anti-Portugese independence rebellion smolders in isolated areas.

ANGUILLA
1967-69: Successful rebellion against inclusion in Federation of St. Kitts and Nevis forces British to land paratroopers and govern island through local council.

ARGENTINA
1969: Bitterness over strict government rule causes riots. Army remains in control.

BOLIVIA
1967-69: Cuban-backed rural guerrilla activity subsides with death of Che Guevera in October, 1967. Violence shifts to cities. Military Junta overthrows civil government in September, 1969 and nationalizes some foreign companies.

BRAZIL
1967-69: Prolonged rioting curbed by army. Urban guerrillas expand activities, including kidnapping of U.S. ambassador.

CENTRAL AFRICAN REPUBLIC
1967: Coup by President Bokassa against leftist government.

CHILE
1967-69: Scattered violence includes uprisings by students, peasants, and workers in copper mines and city industries plus some anti-government guerrilla activity.

CHINA
1967-69: Nationwide violence as clash between Maoist and opponents continues. Widespread casualties caused by conflicts over Proletarian Cultural Revolution. China involved in disputes with British over Hong Kong and with U.S.S.R. concerning border areas.

CONGO, Democratic Republic of
1967: Unsuccessful rebellion by local dissidents, aided by foreign mercenaries in eastern provinces, overcome by troops from Kinshasa.

CONGO, Republic of
1968 (August): Spread of unrest causes army to seize power in Brazzaville. President Debat leaves capital; then reaches agreement with military and returns.

CUBA
1967-69: Growing dissatisfaction with severity of Communist rule and declining economy causes thousands to leave Cuba. Castro-backed guerrillas fail to achieve significant victories in various Latin American countries. Massive Russian aid continues. Epidemic of planes hijacked to Cuba.

CURACAO
1969 (May-June): Rioting by workers causes considerable damage until Dutch Marines restore order.

CYPRUS
1967 (November-December): Long-standing Greek-Turkish feud explodes in worst violence since 1963 until U.S. negotiator Cyrus Vance works out pact.

CZECHOSLOVAKIA
1968-69: Invasion of country by Russian and other Bloc troops produces deep bitterness. Anti-Russian protests by patriots, students and others increase as Moscow tightens its control.

DAHOMEY
1967-69: Army continues as real power carrying out five coups in six years in order to bring "calmness and unity".

ENGLAND
1967-69: Normally peaceful political scene disturbed by outbreaks of racial violence, demonstrations by Chinese Communists, and angry outbursts against U.S. involvement in Vietnam.

ETHIOPIA
1967-69: Growing student unrest continues, sparked by slowness of progress in education and in country as whole.

FRANCE
1968-69: Student unrest grows into nationwide strike as workers, some civil servants and others join anti-DeGaulle movement. Eventually educational system modernized, but DeGaulle resigns.

GERMANY, Federal Republic of
1967-69: Student violence spreads through many universities and schools in protest against rigid educational system, strict organization of society, conservative government and Vietnam war.

GHANA
1968-69: Protesting students close Ghana University. Opposition to regime results in arrest of military Commander-in-Chief.

GREECE
1967-69: Opposition to army regime grows, but attempted coup by King Constantine in December, 1967, fails. Tight government restrictions and widespread arrests.

GUATEMALA
1967-69: Cuban-backed guerrillas active in mountains and cities. Many killed, kidnapped or robbed. U.S. Ambassador John Mein slain.

HAITI
1967-69: Opposition to Duvalier government grows leading to attempts on his life. Unsuccessful infiltration of rebels and small-scale air raids on capital.

HONG KONG
1967-68: Effort by Chinese Communists, principally young Red Guards, to oust British and upset economy fails. Clashes with police lead to many arrests and crackdown by colonial government.

INDIA
1967-69: Economic, racial, religious and political grievances lead to outbreaks of bloody violence.

INDONESIA
1967: Student strikes, anti-Chinese bitterness and scattered guerrilla activity, plus unsuccessful attempt at coup against Suharto, keep country in state of unrest.

IRAQ
1968-69: Successful right-wing coup by General al-Bakr in July, 1968. Kurdish unrest in north continues. Extensive executions on charges of spying for Israel.

IRELAND
1968-69: Violent clashes between Protestant majority and Catholic minority in Belfast, Londondery and other cities checked by presence of British troops.

ISRAEL—See NEAR EAST

ITALY
1967-69: Violence among discontented students, workers, and poor farmers. Street clashes, fires and bombings in many cities.

JAPAN
1967-69: Leftist students carry on massive sit-ins and street battles with some support from workers. Universities closed for weeks.

JORDAN—See NEAR EAST

KENYA
1969: Student activists shut down university. Assassination of Economic Minister, Tom Mboya in July brings rioting and tribal clashes.

KOREA
1967-69: Violent protests against allegedly fraudulent election of President Chung Hee Park (1967) and against college administration and repressive government policies. Infiltrators from North Korea seek to kill President (1968) and continue activities as rural and urban guerrillas.

LEBANON
1968-69: Unsuccessful attempt to kill President Chamoun in June, 1968. Summer of 1969 sees repeated clashes between regular Army and guerrillas supported by units from Syria.

LIBYA
1969 (September): Military Junta ousts aging King Idris I and sets up socialist-oriented Libyan Arab Republic.

MALAYSIA
1967-69: Continued bloody clashes between Malays and "Overseas Chinese". Communists believed active in fomenting troubles.

MALI
1968 (November): Socialist President Modibo Keita deposed in coup by junior Army officers.

MEXICO
1967-69: Peking-backed guerrillas killed or captured. Summer of 1968 brings repeated and bloody clashes of students with police. Army takes over National University.

MOZAMBIQUE
1969: Dr. Eduardo Mondlane, President of Liberation Front, killed by bomb. Five-year-old rebellion against Portugese rule continues in north.

NEAR EAST CRISIS *(including Israel, Jordan, Syria and Egypt)*
1967-69: Fighting between Arabs and Israelis resumes within month of June, 1967 War. Small patrol actions and raids grow into battles. U.S.S.R. rearms Egypt and sends advisors and pilots. In 1968 almost daily fighting along Suez Canal, across Jordan River, on Syrian Golan Heights and, by 1969, in southern Lebanon.

NIGERIA
1967-69: Troops of Federal Government in Lagos expand attacks against secessionist rebellion in Eastern Region. Famine takes high civilian death toll in Biafra.

PAKISTAN
1968-69: Following months of violent protest against his government,

which left hundreds dead, President Ayub Khan resigns in March 1969 leaving power to army.

PANAMA
1967-69: Political unrest and violence stirred up by Communist and urban and rural guerrillas. Bloodless coup by National Guard in October 1968 removes President Arias. New leader, General Torrijos, is deposed briefly, but returns to country.

PERU
1968: President Belaunde Terry ousted in military coup in October. Replaced by Nationalist-oriented General Velasco. Some student unrest.

PHILIPPINES
1967-69: Anti-government movement of Huks revived. Terror widespread in Luzon by late 1968. Guerrillas raid provincial capital and urban terrorists bomb near U.S. Embassy in 1969.

POLAND
1968-69: Warsaw restless at strict Soviet regime in 1968. Bloody confrontations with police as students and workers demonstrate. Workers go on strike until Soviet restrictions enforced.

PUERTO RICO
1967-69: Student rioting and anti-U.S., anti-war and pro-independence demonstrations.

RHODESIA
1967-69: Pro-white security forces battle African Nationalists and infiltrators in August, 1967. Urban terror expands. Federal government uses planes against guerrillas in mid-1969.

SIERRA LEONE
1968: Successful coup by army in April leads to arrest of government leaders and control of country by 14-man committee.

SOMALIA
1969 (October): President Abdurashid Ali Shermarke shot.

SPAIN
1967-69: Winter of 1967-68 sees growing student unrest. Some schools closed. In 1969, riots in Basque provinces over desire for greater autonomy. Nationwide demonstrations against regime.

SUDAN
1967-69: Rebellion of black, largely Christian tribes in 3 southern provinces continues for freedom from Moslem north. In spring and fall of 1969 series of coups by army.

TIBET
1967-69: Arrests and violence in 1967 as Chinese Red Guards, with Tibetan supporters, seek to purify lamassaries. Power struggle renewed in 1969.

U.A.R. (Also see Near East)
1967: Reported plot against Nasser leads to arrests and government purge. Student riots close all universities.

URUGUAY
1968-69: Demonstrations, fires, and bombings as leftist students protest about educational system and government policy. Urban guerrillas attack radio stations, banks, power stations and police.

U.S.A.
1967-69: Summer of 1967 sees racial rioting in more than 40 cities leaving dead, wounded, and extensive property damage. Assassination of Dr. Martin Luther King in 1968 triggers rioting, looting, sniping, and death in cities. Assassination of Senator Robert Kennedy in 1969 adds to deep disturbance. Following anti-Vietnam demonstrations at Pentagon in 1967, student unrest and violence at colleges and universities grows in 1968 and 1969.

U.S.S.R.
1967-69: Increasing resentment among intellectuals against restrictions in many areas. Small demonstrations, some arrests. Two wounded as gunman attacks motorcade carrying astronauts. Clashes with Chinese Communists along eastern borders grow in violence and frequency.

VENEZUELA
1967-69: Widespread guerrilla activity in countryside and cities.

VIETNAM
1967-69: Fighting continues with Saigon believing it is a struggle to free South Vietnam from Communist infiltrators, and Hanoi believing it is involved in continuing battle against European neo-colonialism. Student riots over September 1967 elections. Scattered opposition to government corruption and personalities in 1968. Conflict of ideas in 1969 on how to end war leads to sporadic incidents of political violence.

YEMEN

1967-69: Civil war continues as Nasser and Soviets back Republicans and Saudis support Royalists. Egyptian air raids, substantial military and civilian casualties.

A Word of Thanks
and a Partial List of Sources

Material for this book has been gathered over a good many years. It has come in part from books and research and in part from private or official travels I have made in some sixty countries, including all of the countries dealt with here in separate chapters. This has involved official contacts, talks with foreign friends, and long discussions with American diplomats, businessmen, and journalists overseas. I appreciate the time and interest they have given me.

More specifically, I wish to state my indebtedness to the many persons here in Washington who have helped me with the preparation of this book. Among them are various past and present members of the faculty of the National Interdepartmental Seminar, including Ralph Collins, Donald Coster, James Ludlow, Gordon Mattison, and John Topping. I also express my gratitude to Miss Edna Barr, Ambassador Philip Bonsal, William Duggan, Harold Glidden, James Leonard, Herbert Libesney, and Thomas Thornton of the Department of State for their kindness in reading over the chapters dealing with revolt in specific countries.

I am grateful for valuable suggestions from J.A. Frank, Cary T. Grayson, Jr., and Jan Sue Watkins of Potomac Books; for comments from Gordon Arneson, Milton Crane, John C. Kimball and Burke Wilkinson; for research by Frederick Merrill, Jr. and for the maps by Roy Bruce.

I give special thanks to my wife for her careful and detailed review of the copy and for her help throughout the writing of the book.

To the various secretaries who worked long hours, often on weekends and holidays, I am deeply obliged. These include Mrs. Joyce A. Atkins, Mrs. Constance McGregor, Miss Janet Rice, Mrs. Shirley Sullivan, and particularly Mrs. Edith Sagal.

In regard to written sources, I wish to mention a few, but by no means all, of the books I found stimulating and useful.

GENERAL REFERENCES

Adams, R.N. and others, *Social Change in Latin America Today: Its Implications for United States Policy.* Harper & Row, New York, 1960.

Black, C.E., *The Dynamics of Modernization: A Study in Comparative History.* Harper & Row, New York, 1966.

Black, C. E. and Thornton, T.P., eds., *Communism and Revolution: The Strategic Uses of Political Violence.* Princeton University Press, Princeton, New Jersey, 1964.

Daniels, R.V., *The Nature of Communism.* Random House, New York, 1962.

Friedrich, C.J. and Zbigniew, B.K., *Totalitarian Dictatorship and Autocracy.* Praeger, New York, 1966.

Hagen, E.E., *On the Theory of Social Change.* The Dorsey Press, Homewood, Illinois, 1962.

Halpern, Manfred, *The Politics of Social Change in the Middle East and North Africa.* Princeton University Press, Princeton, New Jersey, 1963.

McNeill, W.H., *The Rise of the West: A History of the Human Community,* University of Chicago Press, Chicago, 1963.

Polk, W.R., *The Developmental Revolution: North Africa, Middle East, and South Asia.* The Middle East Institute, Washington, D.C., 1963.

Toynbee, Arnold, *The World and the West.* Oxford University Press, New York, 1953.

Ward, Barbara, *The Rich Nations and the Poor Nations.* W.W. Norton, New York, 1962.

SOCIETAL REVOLUTIONS

Crozier, Brian, *The Rebels: A Study of Post-War Insurrections,* Beacon Press, Boston, 1960.

Draper, Theodore, *Castro's Revolution.* Praeger, New York, 1962.

Fairbank, J.K., Reischauer, E.O., and Craig, A.M., *East Asia: The Modern Transformation.* Houghton Mifflin, Boston, 1965.

Kennan, George, *Russia and the West Under Lenin and Stalin.* Little, Brown, Boston, 1961.

Mao Tse-tung, *Mao Tse-tung: An Anthology of his Writings.* Anne Fremantle, ed. The New American Library, New York, 1962.

Nasser, Gamal, *The Philosophy of the Revolution,* Dar Al-Maaref, Cairo, 1952.

Trotsky, Leon, *The Triumph of the Soviets,* University of Michigan Press, Ann Arbor, 1957.

Wolfe, Bertram D., *Three Who Made a Revolution,* Dial Press, New York, 1964.

INDEPENDENCE REBELLIONS

Fall, Bernard, *The Two Vietnams: A Political and Military History*. Praeger, New York, 1963.

Fischer, Louis, *Gandhi: His Life and Message for the World*, The New American Library, New York, 1954.

Gokhale, B.G., *The Making of the Indian Nation*, Asia Publishing House, New York, 1960.

Hammer, Ellen J., *The Struggle for Indochina*, Stanford University Press, Stanford, California, 1954.

Vo Nguyen Giap, *People's War, People's Army*, Praeger, New York, 1962.

COLD WAR CONFLICTS

Browne, Malcolm W., *The New Face of War*. Bobbs-Merrill, Indianapolis, Indiana, 1965.

Carter, Gwendolen M., *Independence for Africa*. Praeger, New York, 1960.

Hayden, Joseph R., *The Philippines: A Study in National Development*. Macmillan, New York, 1942.

Hennessy, Maurice N., *The Congo*. Praeger, New York, 1962.

Higgins, Marguerite, *Our Vietnam Nightmare*. Harper & Row, New York, 1965.

Lacoutre, Jean, *Vietnam: Between Two Truces*. Random House, New York, 1966.

Lefever, Ernest, *Crisis in the Congo: A United Nations Force in Action*, The Brookings Institute, Washington, D. C., 1965.

Lemarchard, Rene, *Political Awakening in the Congo*. University of California Press, Los Angeles, 1964.

Scaff, Alvin H., *The Philippine Answer to Communism*, Stanford University Press, Stanford, California, 1955.

Schurmann, Franz, *The Politics of Escalation in Vietnam*. Fawcett Publications, Greenwich, Conn., 1966.

Scigliano, Robert, *South Vietnam: Nation Under Stress*. Houghton Mifflin, Boston, 1963.

Warner, Denis, *The Last Confucian*, Macmillan, New York, 1963.

Glossary

Because limited war, internal defense, and insurgency are relatively new areas of study, I have included a glossary to give readers a clearer understanding of the terms used in this book. They correspond in general, but not always, with definitions used by other writers.

Bourgeois, national. A term applied by the Communists to wealthier elements in the population whose holdings are of such size as to have an impact on the national economy.

Bourgeois, petit. Small property owners and traders who are the least influential and affluent of the middle class.

Cold war conflicts. Power struggles in which communist and non-communist nations clash to determine the socio-political course of a country. Theoretically a cold war conflict is bloodless, but often, as in the case of the Korean conflict, this is far from the case.

Coup d'etat. A sudden exercise of force leading to change in government. It is not necessarily based on popular support, and may frequently be staged by a "strongman" for reasons of personal ambition.

Coup, army. A quick seizure of power by army officers to protect the military establishment and their own positions.

Coup, national. A coup carried out, usually by high army officers, to "save" the nation from what they feel to be objectionable leaders or unwise policies.

Coup, personal. The seizure of power by an individual, frequently with little or no political, social, or economic justification, but merely a power play of the "one colonel out, one colonel in and they both went to the same school" type.

Front organization. A group, association, or other form of organized activity which professes one goal, but is controlled or manipulated behind the scenes by the Communists for their own purposes, which are usually quite different.

Guerrilla warfare. Military actions, usually carried out in the rear of an enemy by irregular forces, with the object of harassing, interrupting lines of communication, and destroying supplies.

Guerrilla, counter-. A phrase used to designate the military aspect of the struggle against guerrilla forces.

Insurgency. As used in this book, the term insurgency is an overall expression referring to revolts in general. These include revolutions, rebellions, insurrections, coups, or violent protests in which the goal is to bring about basic political, economic, or social change by violence or unconstitutional means. It may or may not have outside assistance, although the number of cases in which there is outside assistance are increasing; and it may last a day, a month, a year, or a decade.

War, banditry, pure religious strife, inter-racial conflicts, and family or clan bloodfeuds, which do not involve political changes of government or the area or policies of the state, are not insurgency as here defined.

Insurgency, counter-. A phrase now being used frequently to designate the political, economic, social, and psychological phases of non-military actions against insurgents, including work in the fields of civil affairs and civic action.

Insurrection. An internal revolt to force a government to change its policies.

Internal defense. A term coming into more general use with reference to strengthening a country against communist subversion. It involves all forms of aid, political, military, economic, etc., and is calculated to "help a country under attack help itself". It may include both counter-guerrilla military operations as well as peaceful counter-insurgency involving civil affairs and civic action.

Limited war. A conflict which is more extensive than guerrilla fighting, but not of the proportions of regular or nuclear warfare.

Neo-colonialism. A term used to describe the situation in a colony which has obtained independence from its metropole, but in which most of the direction is still supplied by the citizens of the former colonial power, or some other nation.

Phases of revolt. This rather arbitrary and frequently overworked categorization of stages of violence, developed by Mao Tse-tung, divides insurgency into the following phases:

Phase I—A period of organization and consolidation by insurgents which includes the development of secure bases for training, propaganda, etc.

Phase II—In this period, the insurgents shift to small-scale action by terrorists and guerrillas. An important purpose of these attacks is the obtaining of arms, munitions, medical supplies, etc. In these operations, the regular guerrillas are assisted by a newly-organized "People's Militia" who serve as vigilantes, intelligence procurers, fund-raisers, and "liquidators of the enemies of the people".

Phase III—This involves expansion of the rebel forces, their regroupment into larger units including battalions, regiments, and even divisions; the expansion of the rebel-held territory; and insurgent attacks on the main forces of the enemy.

Negotiations and even the apparent ending of hostilities are related to this strategy. Depending upon the exigencies of the moment, communist leaders might move upward or downward if necessary through these phases.

Protracted conflict. A term often used by the Communists to describe a "war of national liberation" which they cannot win rapidly and which therefore is purposely prolonged in order that their opponents may become war-weary and seek peace on communist terms.

Rebellion. An effort to obtain independence for a part of a state through violence or unconstitutional means.

Returned Students. A phrase used to designate the Chinese revolutionaries who went to Moscow for training. They returned to their homeland in 1930 in order to dominate the central committee of the Communist Party and to work for revolution in the Russian pattern, largely through the workers.

Revolt. A catchall or "umbrella" term used in this book as a synonym for insurgency in general, and sometimes for specific types of violence such as revolutions, rebellions, insurrections, coups, or violent protests.

Revolt, wave of. A phrase used by the author to designate some seven groups or related series of violence which have occurred over approximately the last 300 years. The first six were located largely in Europe, North America, or else were brought about by western European-oriented modernizers. The seventh and current wave since 1945 is worldwide, but is centered in the developing nations of Latin America, Africa south of the Sahara, North Africa, the Near and Middle East, and Southeast Asia.

Revolution. An effort to overthrow a legitimate government or ruler by violence or unconstitutional means.

Revolution betrayed. This involves the coming to power of a party of revolt through its support of one or more grievances which are genuine and widely felt throughout the country. Then, once the party of revolt, capitalizing on support for these desirable goals, has taken over the country and secured its power base, it strips off its democratic mask and discloses its communist philosophy.

Revolution, continuing. Such a situation occurs when the balance of power (for example, between conservative and progressive forces) is so close that neither side can dominate the country and carry out its programs for long. This may lead to a series of revolutions, counter-revolutions, etc., continuing over many years until a final balance has been achieved.

Revolution, interrupted. If an insurgency is put down by violence and the *status quo* elements do not take steps to correct the grievances of the people, it is likely that the insurgency will break out again when conditions make this possible.

Revolution, multi-step. Sometimes a party of revolt has a whole series of objectives but knows it is not strong enough to achieve them all through a single coup or quick revolution. The insurgents therefore strike against their targets one at a time. There may be a certain amount of violence in the achievement of each step, but without risking open revolution or strong counterblows by the government in power.

Safe haven. Originally a communist term, but now generally used to describe a secure base for guerrillas and other insurgents, most frequently in a neighboring land.

Societal revolution. A term used by the author to describe a change in a national power structure. This usually involves moving control of the state from one class to another.

Strategic hamlet. A fortified village in which persons from a series of isolated homes or hamlets have been collected. It is a term which was widely employed in Malaya and is now used in the Vietnam conflict.

Violent protest. An effort to change government policy by mob action or terror.

War of national liberation. A phrase adopted by the Communists to describe the "liberation" of a country, or part of one, from some government, group, race, or class. Tactics include assisting a colony in gaining independence from its metropole, helping part of a country break away from a central government, or encouraging groups or classes, such as peasants and workers, to free themselves from the control of "capitalists and landlords".

INDEX

Italics indicate terms in Glossary.

Abako Party, 115, 116
"actions", 20, 114
Aden, 175
Adoula, Cyrille, 180
Africa, 41, 43, 107-125, 221
Aguinaldo, Emilio, 127
Albania, 175
Alejandrino, Casto, 130
Algeria, 12, 15, 24, 115, 121, 175, 184, 208
Ali, Mohammed, 3, 45
Allen, James, 129
All-India Congress Party, 94, 98, 101
Alvarez, Dr. E.R., 68
al-Zaim, Husni, 22, 204
American Revolution, 2, 3, 10, 83
Amritsar Massacre, 96-97
Angola, 107, 176
Annam, 78, 79, 84-85
"apartheid", 107, 203
Arabi, Colonel Ahmed, 45-46
Arayat, Mount, 130, 131, 135
Argentina, 176, 200
assassinations, 24, 52, 62, 152, 162, 176, 179, 180, 182, 185, 187, 189, 191, 192, 194, 198, 199, 203, 209, 210, 211, 212
Aswan Dam, 46, 54, 55
Ataturk, Mustapha Kemal, 10
Atlee, Clement, 102
Australia, 167
Austria, 208
Autumn Crop Uprising, 34

Ayub Khan, General, 10, 199
Azad, Maulana, 94

Bagdad Pact, 191
Bajaj, Seth, 94
Balaguer, Joachim, 182, 183
Bao Dai, 79, 81, 84, 143, 144
Batista, Fulgencio, 10, 59-68, 181, 182
Baudoin I, King of Belgium, 117
Bay of Pigs, 182
"Beatrice", 88
Belgian Congo, *see* Congo, Democratic Republic of
Ben Bella, Ahmed, 175
Besant, Mrs. Annie, 94
Betancourt, Romulo, 210
Bhave, Vinoba, 94
Bhutan, 176
Bihar district, 95
Binh Xuyen, 144
Birla, G.D., 94
Blouin, Madame Andree, 121-122
"Bogotazo", 59
Bolikango, Jean, 124
Bolivia, 176-177
Bolsheviks, 24, 29, 30, 31
Borodin, Michael, 33-34, 80
Bosch, Juan, 183
Boun Oum, Prince, 194
Bouras, Elie, 121

bourgeois
  national, 40, 41, 45, 73, 80, 219
  petit, 40, 41, 219
Brazil, 177
Brazzaville, 113, 120, 180
British East Africa, 75, 107
British Guiana, *see* Guyana
British North Borneo, *see* Brunei; Sabah; Sarawak
British Revolution, 2
British Salt Act, 17, 100
Brunei, 177
Buddhist-Catholic strife, 22, 159-161, 211, 212
Buganda, 209
Bulgaria, 177
Burma, 177
Burundi, 177-178, 202

Cambodia, 78, 87, 178, 188, 206
Cameroon, 178
Can, Ngo Dinh, 211
Canada, 143, 178
Cao Dai, 144, 159
Capadocia, Guillermo, 129, 130
de Castillo, Mateo, 130
Castro, Fidel, 9, 10, 57-73, 181-2
Castro, Raul, 63, 66, 67
Catholic-Buddhist strife, 22, 159-161, 211, 212
Central African Republic, 178
Ceylon, 46, 178-179
Cheng Feng, 38
Chiang Kai-shek, 33-40, 80, 82, 179
Chile, 179
China, ancient, 77-78
China, Nationalist, *see* Formosa
China, People's Republic of, 1, 4, 5, 15, 27, 31-42, 43, 56, 70, 81, 82, 86, 145, 146, 167, 179, 194; map, 32
Chinese Communist Party, 37-42, 130
Chinese Revolution, 27, 37
Chou En-lai, 33
Cienfuegos, Camilo, 65
civil rights, in U.S., 18, 104, 209
Cochin China, 78, 79, 81, 83, 84, 143

cold war, 2, 35, 37
cold war conflict, 9, 24, 27, 125, 141, 171-172, 219
Colombia, 59, 179
colonialism
  Belgian, 107-125, 179-181
  British, 45-47, 75, 91-104, 177, 186, 192, 196, 199, 206
  Dutch, 188
  European, 1, 5, 75, 107
  French, 77-89, 107, 113, 175, 178, 188, 195, 196, 203, 208
  Portuguese, 176, 187, 195, 196, 201
  Spanish, 57, 127
  United States, 127-128
"Colons", 24
Communists, 6-7, 13-15, 29-42, 47, 51, 72-73, 79-89, 121-125, 129-132, 134-136, 145-155, 159-161, 163-169, 171, 172, 175, 177, 178, 179, 180, 182, 183, 184, 185, 187, 188, 189, 190, 191, 192, 193, 194, 195, 196, 197, 199, 200, 201, 202, 206, 207, 210, 212, 213, 219, 220, 221, 222
"complaints committees", 139
"compradores", 31
conflict, cold war, *see* cold war conflict
conflict, protracted, 77, 168, 221
Congo, Democratic Republic of, 1, 5, 10, 15, 24, 107-125, 179-181, 202; map, 106
Congo Free State, 111
Congo, Republic of, Brazzaville, 181
Constantine, King of Greece, 185
corruption, 38, 39, 59, 66, 133, 139, 157
Costa Rica, 64, 181, 197
coup
  army, 21-22, 60, 141, 157, 176, 177, 178, 180, 181, 182, 183, 184, 186, 187, 190, 191, 193, 197, 199, 200, 203, 204, 205, 206, 207, 209, 211, 212, 219
  counter-, 34, 62, 116
  d'etat, 15, 21-23, 136, 162, 171, 181, 219
  national, 22, 53, 59, 141, 178, 211, 219
  personal, 22, 219
Cripps, Sir Stafford, 102

INDEX

Cuba, 1, 15, 27, 57-73, 181-182, 183, 200, 210; map, 58
Cyprus, 182
Czechoslovakia, 15, 54, 67, 182

Dahomey, 182
Dalai Lama, 206-207
Das, D.C.R., 94
Dayal, Rajeshwar, 123
De Gaulle, General Charles, 83, 113, 115, 184
De Schrijver, 115, 116
"defense corps", 131, 150, 153
"delegations", 16, 50
Delhi Pact, 101
Democratic Republic of Vietnam, see Vietnam, North
demonstrations, 17, 19, 25, 47, 50, 52, 62, 80, 114, 119, 157, 161, 178, 183, 185, 186, 189, 192; 193, 197, 198, 208, 209, 212
Diem, Ngo Dinh, 22, 81, 143, 145, 150, 156-168, 211
Dienbienphu, 88-89, 141, 186; see also "Beatrice"; "Gabrielle"
Directorio Revolucionario, 64
Dominican Republic, 59, 182-183, 186, 210
Duvalier, Dr. Francois, 186
Dyer, General Reginald E.H., 96-97

East Germany, see German Democratic Republic
Economic Development Corps, 139
Ecuador, 183
EDCOR, 139
Egypt, 1, 3, 10, 11, 12, 27, 43-56, 183-184, 190, 203, 204; map, 44
Eighth Route Army, 37, 130
Eisenhower, Dwight D., 122, 163
El Salvador, 184
Elengesa, Pierre, 121
Elizabethville, 109, 124
England, see Great Britain

Ethiopia, 184, 203
Evangelista, Crisanto, 129, 130

Faisal, King of Saudi Arabia, 202
Farouk, King of Egypt, 47, 48, 50-54, 183
Federation of Rhodesia and Nyasaland, see Malawi; Rhodesia; Zambia
"fellahin", 48
Force Publique, 109, 112, 114, 118, 124, 180
Formosa, 40, 179
"Fourteen Points", 46, 79
France, 24, 27, 58, 75, 141-143, 184; see also colonialism, French
Free Officers Society, 50-51, 53-55, 183
French Congo, see Congo, Republic of, Brazzaville
French Foreign Legion, 85, 87
French Revolution, 2, 3, 11, 27
French West Africa, 107
"front" organization, 6, 14, 19, 80, 86, 153, 219
Fuad I, King of Egypt, 47

Gabon, 184
"Gabrielle", 88-89
Gaitan, Jorde Eliecer, 59
Gandhi, Mahatma, 9, 10, 17, 47, 56, 75, 91-104, 187
Gbenye, Christophe, 180, 181
Geneva Agreements, 143, 144, 151, 168
German Democratic Republic, 184
Ghana, 114, 122, 123, 184-185
Giap, General Vo Nguyen, 82, 83, 85, 88, 151, 154, 165
Gizenga, Antoine, 117, 121, 180
Goa, 187
Gomulka, Wladyslaw, 201
Government of India Act of 1935, 101-102
graft, 38, 39, 133, 157
"Granma", 63

Great Britain, 27, 45, 47, 49, 69, 75, 190, 213; *see also* colonialism, British
Greece, 15, 185
Groupe Mobile 100, 87-88
Guatemala, 185-186
guerrillas, 3, 7, 10, 25, 35, 36, 37, 38, 39, 40, 62, 63, 65, 67, 71, 77, 84, 86, 87, 88, 127, 129-139, 151, 152, 155, 162, 164, 165, 166, 178, 179, 180, 182, 185, 186, 194, 196, 198, 201, 203, 206, 211, 212, 219-220
guerrillas, counter-, 137, 150, 151, 152, 162, 192, 196, 201, 220
Guevara, Che, 10, 65, 67
Guinea, 123
Guinea, Portuguese, 201
Guyana, 186

Haiti, 186
Hammarskjold, Dag, 123
"harijans", *see* "untouchables"
"hartal", 96
Havana, University of, 59, 60
Higgins, Marguerite, 160
Hindu-Moslem disputes, 95, 102, 103, 104, 199
Hitler, Adolph, 9, 10
Hoa Hao, 144, 159
Ho Chi Minh, 79-85, 141, 144-148, 152, 159, 165
Ho Chi Minh Trail, 57, 154, 165
Honduras, 185, 186-187, 198
Hoxha, Enver, 175
Hukbalahap guerrillas (Huks), 129-140, 155
Hungary, 187
Hussein I, King of Jordan, 191-192

Ileo, Joseph, 124
immolation, 160, 161
independence rebellion, 3, 9, 15, 27, 75, 77, 89, 141, 171, 175, 176, 178, 180, 184, 188, 190, 192, 193, 195, 196, 197, 199, 201, 203, 204, 207, 208, 209, 221
India, 1, 10, 17, 18, 56, 75, 91-104, 118, 143, 187-188, 192, 199, 207; map, 90
Indochina, 77-89, 153, 188, 193; map, 76
Indochinese Communist Party, 80, 83, 86, 145
Indonesia, 43, 56, 177, 188, 196
insurgency, 18, 21, 57, 125, 141, 150-151, 171-172, 220; *see also* assassinations; cold war conflict; coup; demonstrations; independence rebellion; revolt; revolution; societal revolution; violent protest
insurgency, counter-, 220
insurrection, 171, 220
internal defense, 220
interrupted revolution, *see* revolution, interrupted
Iran, 188-189
Iraq, 189-190
Ireland, Northern, 190
Islam in Egypt, 43-45, 48, 56
Israel, 49, 190-191
Italy, 208
Ivory Coast, 191

Jallianwalla Bagh, 96
Jansen, General, 118
Japan, 3, 37, 39, 40, 79, 82, 83, 128, 130, 134, 136, 137, 141, 179, 193
Jefferson, Thomas, 10
Jinnah, Mohammed Ali, 97, 102
Johnson, Lyndon B., 164, 167, 183, 200
Jordan, 191-192
July 26 Movement, 61, 62, 64, 66, 67, 72

Kalonji, Albert, 123
Kasai tribal area, 123
Kasavubu, Joseph, 115, 118, 119, 121, 124, 180-181
Kashamura, Anicot, 116, 120, 121

INDEX

Kashmir, 192, 199
Kassem, General Abdul Karim, 10, 189-190
Kasturbai, 92
Katanga Province, 111, 117, 122, 123, 124, 125, 180
Kennedy, John F., 6, 143, 162, 164, 209
Kenya, 11, 192-193, 203
Kenyatta, Jomo, 192
Kerensky, Alexander, 29, 30
Khanh, General Nguyen, 211-212
Kikuyu tribe, 11, 192
"Kimbanguist", 119
KMT, see Kuomintang
Korea
  North, 193
  South, 7, 167, 193
Korean War, 1, 193, 219
Khrushchev, Nikita, 6, 7, 56
Kuomintang, 33-35, 37, 38, 80
Kwilu Province, 117, 119, 180
Ky, Nguyen Cao, 163, 211-212

landlords, 35, 40, 51, 127, 130, 138, 146, 147, 148, 149, 154
Laos, 188, 193-194, 206
Latin America, 2, 22, 27, 57, 59, 60, 70, 71, 221
Laurel, Jose, 133
Lava, Jesus, 130, 134
Lebanon, 190, 194-195
Lenin, Nicolai, 4, 24, 27, 30, 72, 129
Leningrad, see Petrograd
Leopoldville, 108, 110, 111, 114, 122, 123, 124, 180-181
Liberia, 107
"liberty wells", 140
limited war, 77, 105, 141, 163-169, 172, 193, 211, 220
Lodge, Henry Cabot, 161
Lucknow Pact, 95
Luluabourg, 110, 115, 120
Lumbala, Jacques, 121
Lumumba, Patrice, 9, 10, 114-124, 180
Luzon, 127, 128, 130, 131, 132, 134, 135, 136, 201

Macao, 81, 195
MacArthur, General Douglas, 129, 131, 132
Machado, Gerardo, 57-59
Madagascar, see Malagasy
Magsaysay, Ramon, 136-140, 155, 163, 201
Maher, Ahmad Ali, 52, 53
Malagasy, 195
Malaka, Tan, 129
Malawi, 195, 202
Malaya, Federation of, 79, 153, 195-196, 222
Malaysia, Federation of, 196
Mao Tse-tung, 4, 10, 25, 34-42, 56, 82, 86, 146, 179
march
  cross-country, 17, 93
  Dharsana Saltworks, 100-101
  Long, 36
Marshall, General George, 39
Marx, Karl, 80, 129
Matthews, Herbert, 63-64
Mau Mau, 11, 192
McDonald, Ramsey, 101
McNamara, Robert S., 167
Mekong River Delta, 78, 153, 165, 167
metropole, 3, 220, 222
Mexico, 62, 63
Michel, Serge, 121
Middle East, 3, 22, 27, 41, 221
Milner, Lord, 45, 47
Mindinao, 139
Minh, Doung Van, 163, 211
Minh, Tran Van, 212
"minutemen", 19, 20
Miro, Jose, 66
MNC, see Movement National Congolais
mobs, 19, 20, 50, 114, 176, 179, 188, 189, 191, 210
Mobutu, Joseph, 124, 125, 181
Montagu, Sir Edwin, 95
Montagu-Chelmsford Reforms, 97
Morocco, 196
Moslem Brotherhood, 48, 49, 50, 51, 52, 205
Moslem-Hindu disputes, 95, 102, 103, 104, 199

Mountbatten, Lord Louis, 102, 103
Movement National Congolais, 115, 116, 117
Mozambique, 107, 196
Mulele, Pierre, 117, 121, 180
Muscat and Oman, 197

Oman, Muscat and, 197
Ong Kiet, General, 130
Organization of American States, 181, 183, 198, 210
Ortodoxo Party, 60
Osmena, Sergio, 132
OTRACO, 109

Naguib, General Mohammed, 47, 50-51, 53-56, 183
Naidu, Sarojini, 94
Nasser, Gamal, 10, 45, 50-51, 53-54, 56, 183, 204-205
National Liberation Front, 154
national liberation, war of, 6, 7, 42, 178, 193, 222
Near East, 22, 27, 48
Nehru, Jawaharlal, 91, 94, 98, 102, 103
Nehru, Pandit Metilal, 93-94
neo-colonialism, 50-51, 135, 171, 220
Nepal, 95, 197
New York Times, 63-64, 71
New Zealand, 167
Ngo Dinh Can, see Can, Ngo Dinh
Ngo Dinh Diem, see Diem, Ngo Dinh
Ngo Dinh Nhu, see Nhu, Ngo Dinh
Nguvulu, Alphonse, 121
Nguyen Ai Quoc, see Ho Chi Minh
Nguyen Cao Ky, see Ky, Nguyen Cao
Nhu, Madame Ngo Dinh, 156, 158, 161, 162
Nhu, Ngo Dinh, 157, 158, 162, 211
Nicaragua, 181, 187, 197-198
Niger, 198
Nigeria, 75, 107, 110, 198-199
Nixon, Richard M., 163
Nkrumah, Kwame, 184-185
"non-violence", 17-18, 75, 95, 98, 103, 187
North Borneo, see Brunei; Sabah; Sarawak
Nyasaland, see Malawi
Nyerere, Julius, 205-206

OAS, see Organization of American States

Paine, Thomas, 10
Pakistan, 1, 43, 103, 187, 192, 199
Palestine, see Israel
Palestinian War, 51, 52, 53
Panama, 199-200
Panama Canal Zone, 199, 200
Panchen Lama, 207
Papandreou, George, 185
Paraguay, 200
Paria, Le, 79
passive resistance, 17, 18, 47
Patel, Vallabhbhai, 94-95
Pathet Lao, 193-194
People's Militia, 30, 39, 41, 67, 85, 86, 155, 220
Peron, Juan, 10, 176
Perry, Commodore M.C., 3
Peru, 200-201
Peter the Great, 1, 36
Petrograd (Leningrad), 23, 29, 30
Philippine Communist Party, 129, 135
Philippines, Republic of the, 1, 15, 43, 105, 127-140, 155, 163, 201; map, 126
Platt Amendment, 57, 60
Poland, 143, 201
political party, communist-backed, 129, 132, 138
Portuguese Guinea, 201
Prasad, Dr. Rajendra, 94

Quang, Thich Tri, 159-161, 211
Quezon, Mrs. Manuel, 135-136
Quirino, Elpideo, 133-134, 135, 136, 138

INSURGENT ERA 235

Taft, William H., 128
Tagore, Rabindranath, 94, 101
Taiping Rebellion, 3
Tanganyika, see Tanzania
Tanzania, 196, 202
Taruc, Luis, 130, 134
Taylor, General Maxwell, 164
terror
  counter-, 25
  government, 62
  material, 23-24, 147, 155
  personal, 24, 25, 62, 134, 147, 155
  total, 24, 68
Thailand, 79, 167, 206
Thich Quang Duc, 160
Tibet, 206-207
Tilak, Bal Gangadhar, 94, 97
Tito, Josip Broz, 56, 175, 185, 213
Togo, 207
Tonkin, 78, 81, 82, 84, 88
Tonkin, Gulf of, 78
Transjordan, 190
Trotsky, Leon, 10, 23, 30, 31
Trujillo, General Rafael, 59, 60, 182
Truman, Harry S, 209
Tshombe, Moise, 117, 122, 181
Tunisia, 122, 208
Turkey, 45, 46, 208
Twenty-sixth of July Movement, 61, 62, 64, 66, 67, 72
Tyrol, 208-209

Uganda, 202, 209
"Ulema", 45
Union Miniere, 122
United Arab Republic, 191, 195, 204, 212; see also Egypt; map, 44
United Nations, 19, 71, 75, 103, 119, 121-123, 125, 160, 164, 180, 182, 192, 193, 199, 201, 202, 207, 208, 209, 212
United Nations Security Council, 122, 123
United States, 18, 38, 39, 49, 56, 57, 60, 61, 62, 65, 69-70, 71, 72, 122, 123, 125, 127, 128, 130, 132, 133, 135, 143, 144, 151, 161, 162, 163-169, 171, 172, 182, 183, 185, 188, 191, 192, 195, 199, 200, 206, 209, 211, 212
UNRRA, 133
"untouchables", 101
Upper Volta, 209
Urundi, see Burundi
U.S.S.R., see Russia

Van Hemelrijck, 115
Venezuela, 209-210
Viet, Kingdom of, 77
Vietcong, 143, 145, 150-155, 162-167
Viet Minh, 82-88, 143
Vietnam, 1, 18, 24, 27, 42, 78, 81-83, 85, 86, 105, 141-169, 211-212, 222; map, 142
  North, 78, 80, 82, 84, 141, 145-150, 155, 164, 165-167, 188, 193, 211
  South, 22, 78, 87, 88, 141-145, 150-169, 188, 211-212
Vietnam Nationalist Party, 80
Vietnam Revolutionary League, 82
Vietnamese Labor Party, 146
Vietnamese Revolutionary Youth Association, 80
violent protest, 176, 177, 179, 184, 185, 191, 193, 194, 198, 199, 210, 222
Vo Nguyen Giap, see Giap, General Vo Nguyen

Wafd Party, 47, 48-49, 50, 51, 52
war, limited, see limited war
war of national liberation, 6, 7, 42, 178, 193, 222
Warner, Denis, 153
Warren Commission Report, 209
Wavell, Lord, 102
Whampoa Military Academy, 33, 34
Wilson, Woodrow, 46, 79
Xa Loi Pagoda, 159-161
Xuan, General Nguyen Van, 86

Yemen, 212
Yuan Shih-k'ai, 33
Yugoslavia, 56, 185, 213
Zaghlul, Sa'd, 46-47
Zambia, 202, 213
Zanzibar, 13, 111, 206; see also Tanzania